Practical Unit Testing with TestNG and Mockito

Tomek Kaczanowski

D1484697

Practical Unit Testing with TestNG and Mockito

Tomek Kaczanowski

Visit us on the web: http://practicalunittesting.com

Published by kaczanowscy.pl Tomasz Kaczanowski, printed by CreateSpace createspace.com

Cover design by Agata Wajer-Gadecka, http://poleznaku.pl

ISBN: 978-83-934893-0-5

First printing, March 2012

Version print_20120414_2307

Dedication

To my wife, Agnieszka, for all her support, and for having faith that I would eventually finish the book.

Table of Contents

List of Figures

List of Tables

About the Author

Tomek Kaczanowski is a technical team leader from Krakow, Poland. He has a strong interest in code quality, testing and automation - preferably all three together. Combining technical with soft skills, he also ventures into the realms of mentoring, teaching, lecturing and article writing, not to mention preaching sermons to the unconverted in the hope of redeeming them (or at least their code)! He hates doing things manually, and is allergic to empty `src/test/java` directories.

Tomek believes that by working with legacy code, and improving it, he can make the world a better place. To his disappointment, the world does not seem to care all that much about his efforts.

Apart from all this weirdness, he is a pretty normal person – a husband, father of two, and cat owner.

Acknowledgments

In various different ways a number of people have helped me with writing this book –
some by giving feedback, others by comforting me in times of doubt.

Marcin Stachniuk was the first person to offer to review the book in the early stages of
its being written, and at the same time the most persistent of my reviewers. He read every
part of the book and gallantly overcame the obstacles I frequently put in his way: frequent
releases, constant juggling of the contents, minor piecemeal adjustments, etc.
Piotr Przybylak helped a lot by introducing me to the concept of "personas".
Michal Margiel read the whole book and sent me a long list of defects he had identified.
Some of his remarks regarding code style were very pertinent, and after I had introduced
them the book seemed far better than before!
Pawel Lipinski, Marcin Zajaczkowski, Pawel Wesolowski, Rafal Janik, Daniel Longosz
and Krzysztof Jelski also contributed by verifying several sections of the book.
Szczepan Faber, Mockito's author, has given me a good bashing, unearthing several
weaknesses in the book as it went along, but at the same time has appreciated my work
and encouraged me to go on with it.
I have also received a great deal of encouragement from Java community members on
social networks. Thanks to all of you!

This book would never have happened if it had not been for the (unwitting) help of
thousands of bloggers and mailing group debaters. I have learned a lot from, and have been
inspired by, numerous Java, PHP, Ruby and .Net articles, blog posts and discussions. It is
amazing to find out that despite the differences in tools and approaches, so many of us share
the same ideals of clean, perfect code, and that we also rack our brains about similar issues.

I have also learned a considerable amount from the participants in training sessions that I
myself have conducted. By sharing their doubts and comments with me, they have helped
me to rethink my stances and look for even better solutions, approaches or tools.
My colleagues at work have given me much food for thought, just by doing things
differently from how I would, while insisting that *their* way is better! :) This has also helped
me go forwards, even if I've sometimes had to take a few steps backwards first!

Carl Humphries has done a splendid job by translating this book from my version of English
into a standard one. You would not enjoy reading this book at all, were it not for his hard
work!

My gratitude also goes out to the authors, contributors and community members of all of the numerous fantastic free tools, libraries and applications I have made use of while writing it. My deepest respect goes to everyone who contributed even a single line of code to the following projects: AsciiDoc, Docbook, vim, Apache FOP, xlstproc, Subversion, IntelliJ IDEA, Inkscape, Gimp, ImageMagick, LibreOffice, PCLinux OS, various bash tools (grep, diff, tree, etc.), xmind.net, toodledo.com, clker.com, wikipedia.org, stackoverflow.com, xp-dev.com and github.com. I would also like to thank all the people on the AsciiDoc and Docbook mailing lists for bearing with me, even when my questions seemed foolish.

 Even though many people have contributed to this book and have carried out reviews, **all bugs still belong to me!**

My family has also made an immense contribution. Agnieszka, my wife, has supported my work from the very beginning, repeatedly reminding me about the need to focus on getting things finished, and giving up some of her so-called "free-time" so that I could have more time to spend on it. Without her help, I would simply have never finished the book!
My daughters - Zosia and Helenka - gave me reasons to smile every day; something I needed very much, being tired and depressed with the amount of work still lying before me. Our cat - Boni - has played a double game. Some evenings she helped me to calm down by sitting on my lap, purring softly, while sometimes she deprived me of sleep by making an awful racket at night! :)

Preface

> Times are bad. Children no longer obey their parents, and everyone is writing a book.
>
> — Cicero

Why Another Testing Book?

There are already a few really good books devoted to developers' tests in bookstores, so why write another one? Here are several reasons for doing so:

The world keeps on moving forward.   Progress never stops. There are still ideas emerging in the testing area. New frameworks. New approaches. New tools. Old techniques are being forgotten, rediscovered and mixed with newly invented ones. New concepts force us to rethink existing paradigms and come up with solutions that are better suited to the constantly changing IT environment.

Lack of knowledge.   In spite of all the books, seminars, JUG meetings, conferences, podcasts, articles, blog entries and forum discussions I deal with, I still meet many developers who have only a very vague idea of what developers' testing is and how to do it. There is definitely still room for improvement in this area.

People are different.   Despite the number of available sources on the subject of testing, some developers still seem oblivious to its importance and to the techniques it involves. Maybe the approach taken in this book will help them (you?) to absorb this knowledge and acquire some testing skills.

Last but not least, let me say that writing a book feels like the natural next step for me. After hours spent honing my testing skills, blogging about this and sharing my knowledge at JUG meetings and conferences, I feel it is time to make this step. I hope you enjoy the results.

Who Is This Book For?

This book is aimed at developers who want to produce high-quality, maintainable unit tests. It is intended especially for those who would like to start unit testing their code, but are unsure about how to get started and what to focus on.

If you are already an experienced developer with some skills in testing, then you might gain various things from reading it. You can expect a good recap of unit testing issues and best practices, along with code examples which might remind you about some rules and best practices you have forgotten. I am also sure that you will find a lot of new things here – some, even, which will make you rethink your current practices.

What I Expect From You

In fact there is very little I expect from you, except that you are willing to learn, and ready not just to rethink your current ways of writing code but also to rethink (and maybe even reject!) things you learn from this book. Stay sharp! Question what you know and what you learn! Authors of books are sometimes wrong too!

Apart from having this attitude, you need to know at least the basics of Java (equivalent, let's say, to a Junior Java Developer).

How To Read This Book

Successive chapters make use of the information given in their predecessors, so it would make sense to read it chapter by chapter. This is certainly true for Part I, *"Developers' Tests"*, and Part II, *"Writing Unit Tests"*. The first introduces developers' tests in general terms and provides some theoretical information about unit tests, and the second gives practical advice about the creation of unit tests. However, Parts III, IV and V, which go more deeply into the realm of unit tests and contain various topics, can largely be read in isolation from the previous parts.

 …and if you really cannot wait to see some code (impatient, aren't we?), go straight to Chapter 3, *Unit Tests with no Collaborators* in the second part of the book. I hope that at some point you will also read Part I, as this may prove necessary for understanding Part II as a whole.

There are also four appendices. If you are new to the idea of automated tests, then you should definitely read the first of these: *"Automated Tests"*. It explains their advantages over manual testing, and provides information about the organizing of the execution of tests. The second appendix, *"Running Tests"*, shows how to use an IDE and build tools to execute unit tests and debug them. The third, *"Test Spy vs. Mock"*, discusses the differences between these two types of test double in detail. The last one, *"Where Should I Go Now?"*, is aimed at the sort of person who is so hungry for knowledge that they want to know more, and more, and more! If you are such a person, then hopefully the pointers you'll find in this appendix will be just what you need!

Vocabulary

I have tried to follow the naming conventions introduced by [meszaros2007]. As far as I know, the terms he introduced (or gave definitions for) have "caught on" within the developer community, and are currently in use by most developers

Exercises

> Tell me and I forget. Teach me and I remember. Involve me and I learn.
> — Benjamin Franklin

Most sections of the book contain some exercises. Remember, they are there to be done, not to be read! No excuses! ;)

Notes On Code Examples

Throughout the book there are many code examples. A few notes about them:

- For the sake of brevity, in many code examples some language constructs - like the use of "private final" variable modifiers – have been omitted. But in general I have tried to write the code adhering to all possible good practices and standards.

- Likewise, auto-generated IDE comments have been removed.

- Not all method names follow the naming pattern suggested in Section 9.3. This is due to the fact, that some of them are here to illustrate some specific case, and their name informs about their purpose.

- Some method names have had to be shortened as otherwise they would not have been correctly wrapped in the PDF version of the book. This is a shame, as I was really attached to them. :)

Icons

The following icons appear within the text:

A helpful tip.

 An additional note.

 Warning, danger ahead!

All three icons were designed by Webdesigner Depot (http://www.webdesignerdepot.com/).

Book Site

The official book site is on http://practicalunittesting.com. Please visit it for news and information on downloadable extras etc.

Code Download

All examples from the book (including exercises) are available online. Please visit http://practicalunittesting.com for detailed information on how to acquire them.

Piracy

I guess the book is already out there.... Well, I take that as a compliment: apparently it must be worth stealing. But of course, you won't be left with that nasty taste in your mouth if you buy it rather than stealing it!

Part I. Developers' Tests

Code without tests is bad code. It doesn't matter how well written it is; it doesn't matter how pretty or object-oriented or well-encapsulated it is. With tests, we can change the behavior of our code quickly and verifiably. Without them, we really don't know if our code is getting better or worse.
— Michael Feathers *Working Effectively With Legacy Code (2004)*

Never in the field of software engineering has so much been owed by so many to so few lines of code.

— Martin Fowler (about JUnit)

Chapter 1. On Tests and Tools

This introductory chapter presents the main categories of test. It will enable us to understand the role of each of them, and also to see the place and purpose of unit tests.

Naming Chaos

If you start digging into the topic of tests, you will be amazed at how many names show up. Unit tests, integration tests, smoke tests, stress tests, end-to-end tests, exploratory tests, system tests, performance tests, user tests, automated tests, acceptance tests, etc. You may well feel perplexed by the sheer number of them, and by the variety of existing classifications. You will get even more perplexed if you start looking for a definition for each of them. Soon you will come across a good few definitions of the same term that differ substantially[1]. This terminological chaos makes testing subjects much harder to follow than they should be.

In this book I follow what I regard as being the most widely used set of test-related terms. I think, that the chosen names describe their purpose well. I can only hope that they do so for you too.

1.1. An Object-Oriented System

We will right away discuss three kinds of tests that are essential for developers: **unit tests** (which are the main topic of this book), **integration tests** and **end-to-end tests**. Because the object-oriented (OO) programming paradigm[2] is dominant in the Java world, we will learn what role each of these tests plays in the testing of an OO system. Figure 1.1 presents a very simple abstraction of such a system. (We will get on to the meaning of "workers" and "managers" very soon.)

---

[1] Alas, even though some terms seem to have a well-established meaning, they still often get to be misused.
[2] See http://en.wikipedia.org/wiki/Object-oriented_programming for more information.

Figure 1.1. An OO system abstraction

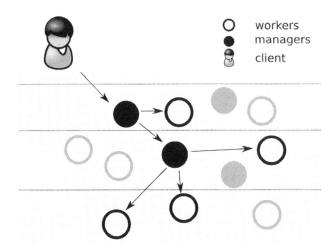

Yes, that is it! A bunch of circles and arrows. Circles are objects, arrows are messages being passed between them. As you can see, we also have a client in this picture, and his action (his request) has initiated a great deal of activity in our OO system. Why so many objects, and so many messages, out there? Why couldn't one smart object deal with the client's request? Well, the inhabitants of an OO world have very limited knowledge, and only a small set of abilities. Each of them has very constrained functionality or, to put it another way, each of them cannot do much on its own. Thus they are forced to cooperate in order to achieve anything useful (from the user's point of view). This results in the following way of acting:

> I am only a simple web controller, so I cannot fetch the data from the database for you. But I know a guy – call him UserDAO – that might help. So I will pass your request on to him. Ah! I have just remembered that UserDAO does not understand what an HTTP request is. I will extract the information he needs and pass it on to him. Let us wait now for his answer.
> — Anonymous Web Controller *Anonymous Web Application (circa 2003)*

That is how it works. In fact, a lot of classes do nothing more than pass on messages, and maybe also transform them in some manner.

If you think about it, there are not many **workers** (that is classes that do a real job) out there. At least, not many workers written by you. Object-relational mapping framework

(ORM[3])? You surely will not have written one. After all, why should you, when there are so many robust solutions around? Dependency-Injection container (DI[4])? Not likely. Logging framework? No. If you think about the amount of real business logic in your application you might be surprised how little there is. Of course, you do have some business logic. That is why your customer placed an order for a new application. But you probably used a lot of ready-to-be-used elements that do a lot of work for you. And that is fine, because code reuse is a fantastic way to build applications fast, allowing you to concentrate exclusively on the custom-designed elements. But if so, then quite probably many of your classes are only tying things together by passing appropriate messages to appropriate collaborators. They coordinate the work of others. We will call such classes **managers**. Their work is substantially different from what workers do.

As you will soon see, this difference has a serious impact on testing.

1.2. Types of Developers' Tests

Having the picture of an OO system in mind, we can try to visualize the parts of the system affected by each type of test. This will help us to understand the scope and purpose of each kind of developers' test.

But before we proceed, let me introduce two important terms that will be used throughout the book: **SUT** and **DOC**. Both were popularized by [meszaros2007] and are used frequently when discussing testing issues.

By **SUT**, or System Under Test, we understand the part of the system being tested. Depending on the type of test, SUT may be of very different granularity – from a single class to a whole application. A **DOC**, or Depended On Component, is any entity that is required by an SUT to fulfill its duties. Usually a DOC is of the same granularity as the SUT, e.g. if the SUT is a class, then it uses other classes, if it is a module, then it collaborates with other modules.

 I will be using the terms "DOCs" and "collaborators" interchangeably.

---

[3]See http://en.wikipedia.org/wiki/Object-relational_mapping
[4]See http://en.wikipedia.org/wiki/Dependency_injection

The following sections will introduce very briefly the various kinds of test. Much more could be said about each of them, but right now let us stick to the picture of the OO system and just try to see which part of it is covered by each kind of test.

1.2.1. Unit Tests

Unit tests focus on single classes. They exist to make sure that **your code** works. They control all aspects of the context in which the class to be tested is executed, by replacing real collaborators with test doubles[5]. They know nothing about the users of the system they put to the test, and are unaware of layers, external systems and resources. They run incredibly quickly, and are executed frequently.

This is shown in Figure 1.2, where only one object is clearly visible and all other elements of the system are greyed out. The single visible element is an SUT - the object to be tested. The greyed out elements symbolize those parts of the system not touched fully by the test, or replaced by various test doubles. Horizontal lines represent borders of layers (e.g. view, services, DAO layers). As the picture shows, a unit test is located inside one layer.

Figure 1.2. Scope of a unit test

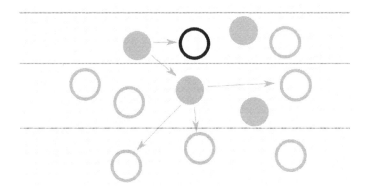

 Not every test run with a unit testing framework is a unit test! Make sure that your unit tests conform to the definition presented in Section 2.1!

---

[5]Test doubles are fake replacements of real parts of the system (e.g. classes or modules). This topic will be discussed in detail in Chapter 5, *Mocks, Stubs, Test Spies*.

1.2.2. Integration Tests

Integration tests focus on the proper integration of different modules of your code, including - and this is especially valuable - with code over which you have no control. An example might be a connection between your business classes and an OSGi container, ORM framework or with a web services framework. Even though the integration tests cover a much wider area of code than unit tests, they still test code as it looks from the developer's standpoint.

Integration tests run much more slowly than unit tests. They usually require some resources (e.g. an application context) to be set up before they can be executed, and their execution involves calling some entities that tend to respond slowly (e.g. databases, file system or web services). In order to verify the results of integration tests, it is often necessary to look into external resources (e.g. issue an SQL query).

Figure 1.3. Scope of an integration test

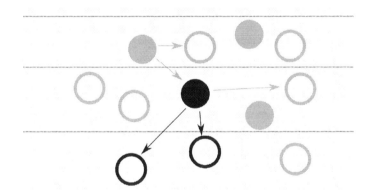

As Figure 1.3 shows, integration tests usually extend across a few layers (e.g. when testing whether your services work correctly with a DAO layer). They execute code written by your team, but also code from third-party libraries used by the tested application. As with unit tests, vast areas of the system are either not touched by integration tests or are replaced by test doubles. Integration tests usually do not touch the user interface (the GUI). Because of this, the client (user of the system) is not shown in the picture.

1.2.3. End-to-End Tests

End-to-end tests exist to verify that your code works from the client's point of view. They put the system as a whole to the test, mimicking the way the user would use it. As such they extend across all layers. Test doubles are rarely used in end-to-end tests – the point is to test the real system. End-to-end tests usually require a significant amount of time to execute themselves.

Figure 1.4. Scope of an end-to-end test

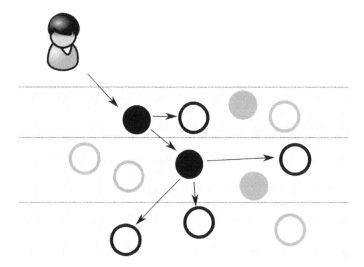

Figure 1.4 shows an end-to-end test that puts to the test elements from all layers - from the front end (GUI, web services layer or any other external API of the tested system) to the storage layers (e.g. database storage). End-to-end tests are initiated through a request identical to those issued by real users of the system (e.g. clicks on GUI elements).

1.2.4. Examples

Table 1.1 gives examples of each type of tests.

Table 1.1. Types of test example

type of test	test examples
unit test	<ul><li>An object of the class `FootballPlayer` should change its status to `fired` after receiving a second yellow card.</li><li>A constructor of the class `Product` should throw an `IllegalArgumentException` (with meaningful message) if the `price` argument is less than 0.</li></ul>
integration test	<ul><li>An invocation of `deleteAccount()` method of the class `UserService` with an argument `ID` of value 1 should result in removal of the account with this `ID` from the database.</li><li>When asked for an item with ID = 5 for a second time, the `ItemDAO` class should not touch the real database, but fetch the requested item from the cache instead.</li><li>`ParcelService` should communicate with some web service, in order to find the parcel's details, and send an email with the appropriate error information (using `EmailService`), if the parcel is not found.</li></ul>
end-to-end test	<ul><li>A logged on user can add comments to any public picture by clicking on the "add comment" button next to it. Guest users (users not logged on) can see this comment after it is published, but cannot post their own comments.</li><li>When a shop owner adds a new product to his shop using an `Add Product` form, it will be possible to locate this product using a `Search Form` by entering its name in the search field.</li><li>When a user sends his/her geo-location data using a `whatCityIsThis` web service, the system should respond with a city name.</li></ul>

Table 1.2 presents examples of SUTs and DOCs for each type of test. It shows how SUTs and DOCs "grow" when moving from unit tests (smaller), via integration tests (medium), to end-to-end tests (large). The difference in granularity is clearly visible. In the case of unit tests, the SUTs and DOCs are simply classes. Integration tests act at the level of modules or layers. In the case of end-to-end tests, it is the whole application that is tested (making the application itself into an SUT), and other applications are collaborators (DOCs).

Table 1.2. Examples of SUT and DOC

type of test	SUT example	DOC example
unit test	`UserService`	`UserDAO`
	`Invoice`	`Product`
	`Client`	`Account`
integration test	DAO layer (ORM based)	Hibernate
	DAO layer (JDBC based)	MySQL 5
	FullTextIndexer module	FileStorage module
end-to-end test	Whole application	External web service(s)
		LDAP repository

1.2.5. Conclusions

All of the types of test presented in the preceding sections are important. From the point of view of a development team, each of them will have its own value. Unit tests help to ensure high-quality code, integration tests verify that different modules are cooperating effectively, while end-to-end tests put the system through its paces in ways that reflect the standpoint of users. Depending on the type of application you are implementing, some of them may be more suitable than others.

Another way to think about the various types of test is to place them on an scale. At one end of this scale are unit tests, whose role is just to check whether we are **implementing a given system correctly**. At the other are end-to-end tests, whose main purpose is to verify that we are **implementing the right system**. Integration tests lie somewhere between.

This book concentrates on unit tests, only to a very limited extent touching on other kinds of test. However, it is very important to be aware of their existence, and **not** to rely solely on unit tests. Unit tests are the foundation of developers' tests, but rarely are they sufficient in themselves. Please bear this in mind as you learn about unit tests.

 So which tests should you write for your application? Alas, there is no easy answer to this question. No golden rule exists, which would describe the right proportion of tests of different kinds. It depends to a very high degree on the type of application you are writing.

1.3. Verification and Design

The continuum of testing approaches falls between two opposing beliefs. I will introduce both extremities to make the distinction clear.

Some people (I will call them **verifiers** for convenience) want to check that their code works. That is their goal – to make sure it does what it should do. In the case of code that is hard to test, they will resort to any available techniques to be able to test it. They will sacrifice some OO rules if they believe that is what they need to do to achieve their Holy Grail of testability. They will modify method visibility using reflection or use classloading hacks to deal with final classes. In this way they are able to test just about anything, including tons of nightmarish legacy[6] code. When accused of using "dirty hacks", they shrug their shoulders, and reply that they *"don't feel dirty if they are already swimming in mud"*.

The other group – let us call them **designers** – believe that following OO rules is the most important thing, and that it leads to easily testable code. They treat tests as an indicator of code health. Easy-to-write tests denote sound code. Difficulties encountered during test-writing indicate problems in the code, and are treated as a clear sign that the code should be reworked. They tend to write tests using the same techniques as they use for production code, and renounce the use of reflection or classloading hacks. Designers particularly like the TDD approach, which guarantees a certain level of code quality. In the case of legacy code they will tend to refactor (or rather rewrite) it in order to make it more testable.

As you can see, the conflict between these two approaches could never be resolved. The proponents hold different views, have different needs and value different things. Both also have some good examples to "prove" their superiority. The following paraphrase of a discussion on StackOverflow[7] shows the difference between these two worlds:

    - Reflection is the best way to test private methods.
    - Yes, you should reflect on your design!

---

[6]By **legacy code** I mean any code without tests (i.e. unit tests).
[7]http://stackoverflow.com

— Stack Overflow discussion (paraphrased)

This distinction is also visible if you examine the features offered by different testing tools that are available. Some of them (e.g. JMockit and Powermock) are there to test the untestable, by giving you the power to mock static classes, final classes and constructors, or to call private methods. Others avoid using any such hacks. For example JUnit has never introduced any feature that would make testing of private methods easier, even though many have requested such a thing since JUnit's early days.

 The terms **designer** and **verificator** have been introduced to stress a significant difference in how one may approach testing. However, I know no one who would be 100% a designer or 100% a verificator. We all fall somewhere in between.

I'm inclined to position myself closer to **designers** – I share their concern for good design. This has an obvious impact on the tools and testing techniques I use.

1.4. But Should Developers Test Their Own Code?!

Probably you have heard, many times over, that **you (a developer) should not test your own code**. Many reasons are given in support of this claim, but two of them seem to stand out as being the strongest and most commonly used:

- developers lack testing skills,

- you should not be your own judge.

Let us be clear about this. Both of them are well-reasoned and, without a doubt, both emerged on the basis of the real – and no doubt sad – experiences of many development teams. They should not be dismissed too easily. Yet I am convinced that this "common knowledge" about testing reflects a kind of misunderstanding – or maybe, rather, a general failure to appreciate the multifariousness of the characteristics and purposes of testing.

If we are talking about final tests before shipping software to customers, then I believe that in general such tests should be executed by professional testers. I would agree that no developer can click through the GUI and be as aggressive and inquisitive as an experienced tester. But those are not the only tests out there! There are many valuable tests that can, and should, be performed by developers themselves.

 What is more, some software is not easily testable by anyone other than developers themselves! Think about all those back-end solutions. No GUI, no decent entry points, a (sometimes) strong relation to architectural (hardware) aspects of the environment, etc.

Checking software from the customer's point of view is crucial, but this is only a single piece of a larger puzzle. Before you can do that, a development team must provide you with software. And if they do not perform their own tests – developers' tests – they will probably furnish you with something of low quality. Developers' tests increase the quality of the product delivered to the customer, but also that of the codebase, which means a great deal for any development team. This is not something to be disdained. The more trust a development team has (and the more pride it takes!) in its code, the better the results it will achieve. Developers' tests help a team to gain confidence and proceed further without being hampered by too much self-doubt.

Also, catching bugs early on (greatly) reduces cost, and shortens the time of repair. The more bugs you find early on, the less they will cost you. This well-known time-to-cost ratio is shown in Figure 1.5.

Figure 1.5. The cost of bug fixing

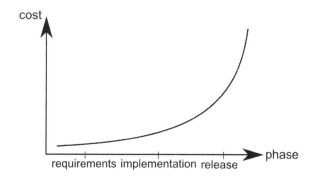

Developers' tests are the first line of defense against bugs. They kill them as soon as they appear. Of course, for the reasons mentioned at the beginning of this section, some bugs will probably make it through. Well, yes, it might just happen! That is why other lines of defense have to be in place, too: i.e. highly skilled, specialized testers. Hopefully they will hunt down all the remaining bugs[8].

 In fact, many companies rely (almost) solely on developers' tests. Big names – like Facebook or WordPress – adopt a **continuous deployment** approach, which can be summarized as *"if it has passed the automatic tests it goes into production"*. No human testing involved! So it is possible after all, isn't it?

So, should developers tests their own code? Oh yes, they should!

…and if you disagree, please stop reading now.

1.5. Tools Introduction

> Use the right tool for the job.
> — Andrew Hunt and David Thomas *The Pragmatic Programmer: From Journeyman to Master (1999)*

This section introduces the tools that I will be using for the writing and execution of tests. It relates to our recent discussion about the different approaches to testing (see Section 1.3). These different approaches are responsible for the existence of many tools covering (almost) identical problem areas. Take, for example, mocking frameworks. Do we really need so many of them? The answer is "yes", and the reason is that each mocking framework is slightly different, and facilitates a slightly different approach to writing test doubles. This is also true for other groups of tools – from test frameworks to IDEs.

In general, tools for testing are very simple to use. That is good news, isn't it? But be warned – there is a catch! This deceptive ease of use leads many developers to assume that they know how to test, just because they can use testing tools – i.e. they are able to write a few lines of JUnit code. This is plainly wrong. Tools can be used mindlessly, or they can be used by a skilled hand. They can dominate you or they can become your obedient servants. The point is to grasp the 'why' and the 'what for', so that you know when to use (or not use) them.

Throughout this book I will be stressing the importance of the ideas embodied in certain tools. If you get a good grasp of those ideas, you will be able to follow them with almost

---

[8]We will discuss this topic some more in Section A.1.

any tool. If you concentrate on tools, you will soon need to relearn all that was dear to you. Ideas are everlasting[9], but tools are there only for a short period of time.

Let me introduce my friends now. There are a few of them, but we will mostly use just two: **TestNG** and **Mockito**. The remainder will only play a secondary role.

 And what if your choices are different, and you use different tools? It is not a problem. Nowadays tools are very similar. They have evolved along different paths, but have also influenced one another, and have often ended up in the proximity of their competitors, with similar sets of features. Using any modern tools you can achieve similar results and still utilize the techniques presented in this book. The ones I have selected are my personal favourites, and have been chosen with great deliberation. I suspect that some of the techniques presented in the book may be easier to master using them than they would be using any other tools. The only risk for you is that you, too, may end up convinced of their superiority, so that you then add some new toys to your toolbox. This doesn't sound so bad, does it?

Testing Framework: TestNG

TestNG (http://testng.org) is an open-source testing framework created by Cédric Beust and was born *"out of frustration for some JUnit deficiencies"*[10]. It covers *"all categories of tests: unit, functional, end-to-end, integration, etc..."*. It is supported by major IDEs (Eclipse, IntelliJ IDEA) and build tools (Ant, Maven, Gradle). TestNG relies on annotations, and requires JDK 5 or higher. It can also be used with Groovy.

I used version 6.4 of TestNG when writing this book.

Mock Library: Mockito

Mockito (http://mockito.org) is a relatively new mocking framework (or rather test-spy framework). It was born in Q4 2007 (Szczepan Faber being the proud father) and has quickly matured into a top-quality product. It offers complete control over the mocking process, and *"lets you write beautiful tests with clean & simple API"*. Originally, Mockito was derived from Easymock, but has evolved substantially, and now differs in many respects from its predecessor. It is very easy to use Mockito in combination with TestNG.

---

[9]Or rather, they live as long as the paradigm they belong to does.
[10]All citations in this section come from the TestNG website and Cédric's blog.

I used version 1.9.0 of Mockito when writing this book.

Other Tools

It would be simplistic to say that everything other than the testing framework and mock library plays a secondary role. If you master writing unit tests, you will find good uses for many more tools. Here are my choices.

Matcher Libraries: FEST And Hamcrest

In order to make tests more readable and easier to maintain, in some parts of the book I have used the following matcher libraries: FEST Fluent Assertions (http://code.google.com/p/fest/) and Hamcrest (http://code.google.com/p/hamcrest/).

I used version 1.4 of FEST and version 1.3.0RC2 of Hamcrest when writing this book.

Code Coverage: Cobertura

Among code coverage tools there are a few interesting ones, my personal choice being Cobertura (http://cobertura.sourceforge.net). It works well with all build tools, IDEs, and continuous integration servers.

I used version 1.9.4.1 of Cobertura when writing this book.

Mock Libraries: PowerMock and EasyMock

Even though Mockito is **the** mocking framework used within the book, in some situations it might be worthwhile to take a look at the other options. Powermock (http://code.google.com/p/powermock/) offers some powerful features (e.g. mocking of final classes and static methods), which we will use once, just in order to be able to demonstrate and discuss an alternative approach to testing. EasyMock (http://easymock.org) will be used to demonstrate the difference between mock-based testing and spy-based testing.

I used version 1.4.10 of PowerMock, and version 3.1 of EasyMock, when writing this book.

Mutation Testing: PIT

PIT Mutation Testing (http://pitest.org) is *"a fast bytecode based mutation testing system for Java that makes it possible to test the effectiveness of your unit tests."* It works with Java 5, JUnit 4.6, and TestNG 6.1 (and above).

I used version 0.25 of PIT when writing this book.

Utilities: catch-exception and Unitils

The catch-exception library (http://code.google.com/p/catch-exception/) helps to write tests that verify whether appropriate exceptions have been thrown by production code. It requires Java 1.6.

Unitils (http://www.unitils.org) is an *"open source library aimed at making unit and integration testing easy and maintainable"*. We will use only a small subset of its features, namely the "Reflection asserts" module.

I used version 1.0.3 of catch-exception, and version 3.3 of Unitils when writing this book.

Build Tools: Gradle and Maven

Unit tests are usually included within the build process, which means they are run by a build tool. In this book I present how to run tests using Maven (http://maven.org) and Gradle (http://gradle.org).

I used version 1.0-milestone-7 of Gradle, and version 3.04 of Maven, when writing this book.

IDEs: IntelliJ IDEA and Eclipse

Even though IDE is **THE** tool in your toolbox, we will not devote a lot of time to it. All we need to know is how to use an IDE to execute unit tests. I decided to discuss it with reference to two very popular IDEs: Eclipse (http://eclipse.org) and IntelliJ IDEA (http://www.jetbrains.com/idea).

I used version 3.7.1 of Eclipse, and version 11 (Community Edition) of IntelliJ IDEA, when writing this book.

Operating System: Linux

Linux is my preferred development platform. It is robust, stable, offers a great shell and total control over the programming environment. But frankly, I will not use many Linux-specific features (if any). All of the tools previously listed in this section also work with Windows, so if you are a Windows user you need not worry.

Chapter 2. Unit Tests

After the introductory sections devoted to developers' testing in general we now move on to the central topic of the book: unit testing.

2.1. What is a Unit Test?

The idea behind unit tests is simple: it is to **make sure the class you are working on right now works correctly** – to make sure it does its job. This concerns whether, given certain input data, it will respond with a certain expected output, or whether, fed with nonsense data, it will throw an appropriate exception, and so on. The idea, then, is to write tests that will verify this expected behaviour.

But that is not enough. You should test your classes **in isolation**, and test them to verify that they work in any environment. When writing unit tests it is important to test a single class and nothing more. Forget about databases, Spring configuration files, and external web services. You do not want to include them in your unit tests. Concentrate on the logic of your class. Once you are sure your code works fine, then test its integration with other components! But first conduct unit tests!

 Unfortunately, even now many confuse unit tests with other kinds of test (e.g. you can read about "unit testing of your database"), or use this term to describe just any kind of test developers write. Many people claim that every test they write is of the "unit" variety, just on the basis that it is executed by some unit testing framework! Others claim that they are doing "unit testing" and have chosen three layers of software as the unit they are going to test… This is, of course, wrong: it sows confusion and makes discussion difficult. Do not do that! You know what unit tests really are.

Unit tests have some properties which distinguish them from other developers' tests. As discussed in Section 1.2, they are focused on single classes and they strictly control the context in which an SUT is executed. They also run extremely fast and are able to pinpoint bugs with great accuracy, often leading the developer straight to the guilty method, if not to the guilty line of code itself! By giving such precise and immediate feedback on the quality of our work they help us to fix the bugs quickly before they spread through the whole system (see Section 1.4).

The existence of a comprehensive and rigorous set of unit tests allows us to refactor code without any fear of breaking something: once all your classes are covered by unit tests, there are no areas of code left that *"no one dares to touch"*!

Another benefit of writing unit tests is that they serve as a live (that is, always up-to-date) documentation of our code. They are much more reliable than Javadocs or any other kind of textual description that might be developed in parallel to the creation of the code itself.

Last but not least, a skillful developer can turn the process of creating unit tests into a design activity. This, quite surprisingly, might be the most important of all the benefits conferred by unit tests!

 And remember one more thing: unit tests have been brought into this world by developers, and they are our responsibility, our tool and something we take pride in – or, if not done properly, something for us to be ashamed of.

2.2. Interactions in Unit Tests

To understand what should be tested by unit tests, and how, we need to take a closer look at the interactions between:

- the test class and the SUT,

- the SUT and its DOCs[1].

First, some theory in the form of a diagram. Figure 2.1 shows possible interactions between an SUT and other entities.

Figure 2.1. Types of collaboration with an SUT

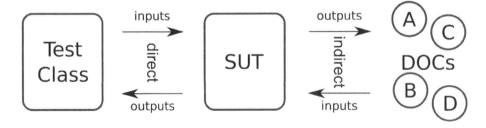

---

[1]An SUT is a thing being tested; DOCs are its collaborators. Both terms are introduced in Section 1.2.

Two interactions are **direct**, and involve the SUT and its client (a test class, in this case). These two are very easy to act upon - they are directly "available" from within the test code. Two other interactions are **indirect**: they involve the SUT and DOCs. In this case, the client (a test class) has no way of directly controlling the interactions.

Another possible classification divides up interactions into **inputs** (the SUT receiving some message) and **outputs** (the SUT sending a message). When testing, we will use direct and indirect **inputs** to set the SUT in a required state and to invoke its methods. The direct and indirect **outputs** of the SUT are expressions of the SUT's behaviour; this means we shall use them to verify whether the SUT is working properly.

Table 2.1 summarizes the types of possible collaboration between an SUT and DOCs. The first column – "type of interaction" – describes the type of collaboration from the SUT's point of view. A test class acts as a client (someone who uses the SUT); hence its appearance in the "involved parties" column.

Table 2.1. Types of collaboration with an SUT within test code

type of interaction	involved parties	description
direct input	Test class & SUT	Calls to the methods of the SUT's API.
direct output	Test class & SUT	Values returned by the SUT to the test class after calling some SUT method.
indirect input	SUT & DOCs	Values returned (or an exception thrown) to the SUT by collaborators, after it called some of their methods
indirect output	SUT & DOCs	Arguments passed by the SUT to the methods of its collaborators.

A code example will make all of this clear. Let's imagine some financial service (`FinancialService` class) which, based on the last client payment and its type (whatever that would be), calculates some "bonus".

Listing 2.1. Example class to present various types of interaction in unit tests

```
public class FinancialService {

    .... // definition of fields and other methods omitted

    public BigDecimal calculateBonus(long clientId, BigDecimal payment) {
        Short clientType = clientDAO.getClientType(clientId);
        BigDecimal bonus = calculator.calculateBonus(clientType, payment);
        clientDAO.saveBonusHistory(clientId, bonus);
        return bonus;
    }
}
```

As you can see the SUT's `calculateBonus()` method takes two parameters (`clientId` and `payment`) and interacts with two collaborators (`clientDAO` and `calculator`). In order to test the `calculateBonus()` method thoroughly, we need to control both the input parameters (direct inputs) and the messages exchanged with its collaborators (indirect inputs). Then we will be able to see if returned value (direct output) is correct.

Table 2.2 summarizes the types of interaction that happen within the `calculateBonus()` method, and that are important from the test point of view.

Table 2.2. Collaborations within the calculateBonus() method

type of interaction	involved parties	description
direct input	Test class & SUT	Direct call of the `calculateBonus()` method of the SUT with `clientId` and `payment` arguments
direct output	Test class & SUT	`bonus` value returned by the SUT to the test class after it called the `calculateBonus()` method
indirect input	SUT & collaborators	`clientType` returned by `clientDAO`, and `bonus` returned by `calculator` to the SUT
indirect output	SUT & collaborators	• `clientId` and `bonus` passed by the SUT to the `saveBonusHistory()` method of `clientDAO` • `clientType` and `payment` passed by the SUT to the `calculateBonus()` method of `calculator`

2.2.1. State vs. Interaction Testing

Let us now recall the simple abstraction of an OO system shown in Figure 1.1. It shows how two kinds of classes - **workers** and **managers** - cooperate together in order to fulfill a request issued by a client. The book describes unit testing of both kind of classes. First we shall dive into the world of **workers**, because we want want to make sure that the computations they do, and the values they return, are correct. This part of unit testing – called **state testing** – is really simple, and has been fully recognized for many years. This kind of test uses **direct inputs and outputs**. We will discuss state testing in Chapter 3, *Unit Tests with no Collaborators*.

Then we will move into the more demanding topics connected with **interactions testing**. We will concentrate on the work of **managers**, and we will concentrate on how messages are passed between collaborators. This is a far trickier and less intuitive kind of testing. Every so often, new ideas and tools emerge, and there are still lively discussions going on about how to properly test interactions. What is really scary is that interaction tests can sometimes do more harm than good, so we will concentrate not only on **how** but also on **whether** questions. This kind of test concentrates on **indirect outputs**. We will discuss interactions testing in Chapter 5, *Mocks, Stubs, Test Spies*.

 Testing of direct outputs is also called "state verification", while testing of indirect outputs is called "behaviour verification" (see [fowler2007]).

2.2.2. Why Worry about Indirect Interactions?

An object-oriented zealot could, at this point, start yelling at me: *"Ever heard of encapsulation and information hiding? So why on earth should we worry about what methods were called by the SUT on its collaborators? Why not leave it as an implementation detail of the SUT? If this is a private part of the SUT implementation, then we should not touch it at all."*

This sounds reasonable, doesn't it? If only we could test our classes thoroughly, just using their API! Unfortunately, this is not possible.

Consider a simple example of retrieving objects from a cache.

Let us remember what the general idea of a cache is. There are two storage locations, the "real one", with vast capacity and average access time, and the "cache", which has much smaller capacity but much faster access time[2]. Let us now define a few requirements for a system with a cache. This will not be a fully-fledged cache mechanism, but will be sufficient to illustrate the problem we encounter.

When asked for an object with key x, our system with its cache should act according to the following simple rules:

1. if the object with key x is not in any storage location, the system will return `null`,

2. if the object with key x exists in any storage location, it will be returned,

    a. if it exists in the cache storage, it will be returned from this storage location,

    b. the main storage location will be searched only if the object with key x does not exist in the cache storage[3].

The point is, of course, to have a smart caching strategy that will increase the cache hit ratio[4] – but this is not really relevant to our discussion. What we are concerned with are the outputs (returned values) and the interactions between the SUT and its collaborators.

If you consider the requirements listed above, you will notice that with state testing we can only test two of them - **1** and **2**. This is because state testing respects objects' privacy. It does not allow one to see what the object is doing internally – something which, in our case, means that it cannot verify from which storage area the requested object has been retrieved. Thus, requirements **2a** and **2b** cannot be verified using state testing.

This is illustrated in the picture below. Our SUT, which consists of two storage locations (a fast **cache** storage and a slower **real** storage), is accessible via a single `get()` method. The client, who sends requests to the SUT, knows nothing about its internal complexity.

---

[2]In fact, it would be more correct to say that access to one storage area is cheaper than to the other one. Usually, the unit of cost is time-relative, so we will make such a simplification here.

[3]Requirements **2a** and **2b** could also be expressed as follows: *"first search in the cache storage, then in the main storage"*.

[4]Which basically means that most of the items will be in the cache when requested, and the number of queries to the real storage will be minimalized.

Figure 2.2. Is this storage working correctly or not?

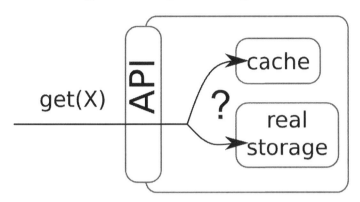

Ideally, when a request comes first the cache storage is searched and then, in case the cache storage does not have an entry with the given key (x in this example), the main storage is searched. However, if the SUT is not implemented correctly then it can first look into the main storage without checking the faster storage first. The client who waits for an object with the given key can not distinguish between these two situations. All he knows is that he requested an object with key x and that he got it.

In order to really verify whether our system is working as it is supposed to or not, interaction testing must by applied. The order of calls to collaborators – cache and real storage – must be checked. Without this, we cannot say whether the system is working or not.

This simple example proves that verification of the observable behaviour of the SUT (its direct outputs) is not enough. Similar issues arise when testing **managers** (see Section 1.1), which coordinate the the efforts of others. As mentioned previously, such coordinating classes are quite popular in OO systems. This is why we will be spending a great deal of time discussing techniques, tools and issues related to indirect outputs testing.

But to begin with let's concentrate on the simpler case. In the next section we will learn how to test simple objects that do not have any collaborators.

Part II. Writing Unit Tests

Chuck Norris doesn't need unit tests because his code always works. ALWAYS.

— Wisdom of the Internet *;)*

If there is a technique at the heart of extreme programming (XP), it is unit testing.

— Kent Beck *Extreme Programming Explained: Embrace Change (1999)*

In a way, the phrase "unit test" is kind of misleading – it's really more akin to forcing yourself to use your own code like another developer or user would… and taking off those developer blinders for a moment.

— Jeff Atwood

A test is not a unit test if:

- It talks to the database
- It communicates across the network
- It touches the file system
- It can't run at the same time as any of your other unit tests
- You have to do special things to your environment (such as editing config files) to run it.

— Michael Feathers *A Set Of Unit Testing Rules (2005)*

Chapter 3. Unit Tests with no Collaborators

It is really fun to understand the types of interaction and parts of unit tests, but since *"practice makes perfect"* it is high time to put this knowledge to use. Just for now, we will be concentrating on a subset of testing issues, assuming as we shall that our **SUT does not need any collaborators**. This assumption – even if it does not hold for the majority of real-life classes – will permit us to demonstrate some important concepts, ideas and techniques. They will be much easier to explain under such conditions, even though their use is by no means limited to a no-collaborators environment. In fact some of them – e.g. the TDD approach – are not even confined to unit testing itself.

In later sections (starting with Chapter 5, *Mocks, Stubs, Test Spies*) we drop this unrealistic assumption and discuss techniques for testing an **SUT which cooperates with collaborators** in various ways. But for now, let us pretend that our SUT is all alone.

After reading the tools introduction you will already know that TestNG is a top-notch Java testing framework. It is not limited to unit tests, and can be used for writing and executing all kinds of test. In this section we will learn to write and execute TestNG tests, and also learn some TestNG features that will be reused throughout the book. Some of them will only be briefly mentioned here, prior to being discussed in more detail in subsequent chapters.

 This book is not an all-embracing TestNG tutorial, even though it contains everything you should know if you want to write high-quality unit tests. TestNG offers more than is described here, including some features useful for integration and end-to end tests. To truly master this tool, you should refer to other resources, i.e. TestNG documentation.

3.1. Project Structure and Naming Conventions

Java developers tend to use similar layout for their projects these days. All sources of production code commonly reside in the `src/main/java` directory, while all test source files are kept at `src/test/java`.

Below, you can see an example of a typical project layout:

Listing 3.1. Typical project layout

```
`-- src
    |-- main
    |   `-- java ❶
    |       `-- com
    |           `-- practicalunittesting
    |               `-- Money.java ❷
    `-- test
        `-- java ❸
            `-- com
                `-- practicalunittesting
                    |-- MoneyTest.java ❹
```

❶   `src/main/java` is where all your production code is located,
❷   an exemplary production class - `Money`,
❸   `src/test/java` is where all your test code resides,
❹   an exemplary test class - `MoneyTest`.

The main thing to notice is that code and tests reside in different subtrees. This way your production JARs will not be polluted with unnecessary test classes. Most tools (that I am aware of) recognize this layout, and will treat both subtrees accordingly.

You probably have also noticed that test classes follow the `SomethingTest` name format (in our case, here, it is `MoneyTest`). The `Something` prefix will usually be the name of a class being tested by this particular test. This is a very common pattern, definitely worth following, as it enables developers to understand at once which class is being tested. Some tools also take advantage of this naming format[1].

We will be following this layout and naming format throughout the book.

3.2. Class To Test

For our first unit-testing experience we will use a `Money` class, almost identical to the one used in a popular unit testing tutorial from JUnit[2]. For unit testing, the `Money` class plays a similar role to that played for any programming language by the famous `HelloWorld`

---

[1]For some discussion of test-naming approaches, please refer to Section 9.3
[2]See http://junit.sourceforge.net/doc/testinfected/testing.htm

example: it just has to be there[3]. ;) We will begin with a very simple (and, to be honest, quite useless) class. Later on it will be extended.

Listing 3.2. Money class to be tested

```
public class Money {
    private final int amount;
    private final String currency;

    public Money(int amount, String currency) {
        this.amount = amount;
        this.currency = currency;
    }

    public int getAmount() { return amount; }

    public String getCurrency() { return currency; }

    public boolean equals(Object o) {
        if (o instanceof Money) {
            Money money= (Money) o;
            return money.getCurrency().equals(getCurrency())
                    && getAmount() == money.getAmount();
        }
        return false;
    }
}
```

As you can see, the `Money` class is immutable. It has two final fields set by the constructor. The only method with some logic is the implementation of `equals()`.

3.3. Your First TestNG Test

Before you write a test, you need to have a list of test cases ready. You can write it down somewhere, if you feel it helps, but keeping it in your head should usually be enough.

Looking at the code of the `Money` class you will probably notice two things that can be tested:

* the constructor,

---

[3]This reminds me of the first time I put to the test the examples from this tutorial. It took me a few weeks to really digest these ideas about unit testing, which were completely new to me back then.

- the `equals()` method.

Testing of the constructor seems like a trivial matter, and this is exactly why we will start with it. The only thing we can check here is if `amount` and `currency` have been properly set[4].

Listing 3.3. First TestNG unit test

```
import org.testng.annotations.Test; ❶
import static org.testng.Assert.assertEquals; ❷

@Test ❸
public class MoneyTest { ❹

    public void constructorShouldSetAmountAndCurrency() { ❺
        Money money = new Money(10, "USD"); ❻

        assertEquals(money.getAmount(), 10); ❼
        assertEquals(money.getCurrency(), "USD"); ❽
    }
}
```

❶   `@Test` annotation is required, so TestNG (and other tools) will recognize this class as a test class.

❷   The static import of the `Assert` class method(s) makes assertion checking more concise.

❸   `@Test` annotation used at class level signifies that all public methods of this class count as test methods[5].

❹   The test class does not have to extend any base class or implement any interfaces. Its name is also not important, though using the `Test` suffix leaves no doubt as to its purpose.

❺   The test method can take any name.

❻   An SUT is created.

❼❽   The SUT is put to the test and the results are verified using the static `assertEquals()` methods of the `Assert` class.

    Only `void` methods are treated by TestNG as test methods!

---

[4]It is questionable whether such code is worth testing in code-first manner. Please see the discussion in Section 10.5.
[5]Please see Section 9.2 for additional information.

That is quite a lot of information for such a simple class! Much more could be written about each line of this code, but that is enough for now. We will discuss it step by step in the course of considering subsequent examples. Let us run the test now.

 There are many ways to run tests written with TestNG. Please consult Appendix B, *Running Unit Tests*, which contains detailed description of how to run tests with Eclipse, IntelliJ IDEA, Gradle and Maven.

After you have run this first test, TestNG will print a short summary. It might vary, depending on the way you run it (in particular, your IDE will probably present it in some nicer way), but it will always contain information about executed, passed and failed tests. An example is shown below:

Listing 3.4. TestNG summary test result

```
===============================================
Custom suite
Total tests run: 1, Failures: 0, Skips: 0
===============================================
```

Remember to always look at the status line and react immediately if you see failed or skipped tests. Also, take note of the number of tests executed. It can happen, especially at the beginning of your testing journey, that your test will not run at all!

3.3.1. Test Results

Tests executed by hand (see Section A.1 for some discussion of this) can end up with a plethora of results, ranging from *"it works for me"*, through *"I am not sure, but I do not have time to investigate it any further"*, to *"it works… and this exception has always been there"*. In the case of automated tests things look different. There are only a few possible outcomes. Let us take a closer look at them.

An automated test ends up in one of two states: as **passed** or **failed**. Two other outcomes are less frequent - a test can be **skipped** or finish with **error**. There is no place for *"I think it should work now"* in automated tests!

If all assertions of a test are met, and no unexpected exceptions are thrown, then that test **passes**. A passed test is usually marked with a green color by IDEs and test reports.

If an unexpected exception is thrown then the test **fails**. This happens if some assertion is unmet, or you have a bug in your code which results in, for example `ArraysOutOfBoundsException`. Your IDE and test reports will mark such a failed test with a red color.

A test can be **skipped** (which means it was not run at all) if another test that it depended on failed (see Section 7.2), or if the user decided explicitly that it should be skipped. Such a test is usually marked with a yellow color.

Finally, a test can end up as an **error**, if some unexpected condition occurred that interrupted its execution. This is rather an uncommon situation and usually indicates that something is wrong with your test code. It can happen, for example, if the number of test parameters passed by a data provider (see Section 3.6) is different from the number of parameters accepted by the test method. Just like failed tests, tests which have ended in an error state are also marked with a red color. They are usually grouped with failed tests on reports.

3.4. TestNG Assertions

We have already encountered one assertion - `assertEquals()`. Let me remind you what it looked like:

Listing 3.5. assertEquals() in action

```
assertEquals(money.getAmount(), 10);
assertEquals(money.getCurrency(), "USD");
```

Table 3.1 shows all of the assertion methods of the `org.testng.Assert` class. Most of the methods displayed come in multiple variants with different parameters (e.g. `assertEquals()` accepts two parameters of type `boolean`, `double`, `String`, `Set`, and others, too). Please refer to TestNG Javadocs for detailed information on available assertion methods.

Table 3.1. TestNG assertions

assertion method	description
`assertTrue()`	Checks if the condition **is true**.

assertion method	description
`assertFalse()`	Checks if the condition **is false**.
`assertNull()`	Checks if the object **is null**.
`assertNotNull()`	Checks if the object **is not null**.
`assertEquals()`	Uses the `equals()` method to verify that objects **are identical**.
`assertNotEquals()`	Uses the `equals()` method to verify that objects **are not identical**.
`assertEqualsNoOrder()`	Checks if two arrays **contain the same objects**, but does not care about the order[a].
`assertSame()`	Uses `==` to verify that objects **are the same**.
`assertNotSame()`	Uses `==` to verify that objects **are not the same**.

[a]If you also want to verify the order, use the `assertEquals(Object[] actual, Object[] expected)` method

Some of the above methods (e.g. `assertTrue()`, `assertNotNull()`) take only one parameter and an optional message (see Section 3.5). Others – e.g. `assertEquals()` and `assertSame()` – take two parameters and an optional message. In such a case, the order of parameters is the following:

1. actual value,

2. expected value,

3. (optional) message.

 This order might be quite surprising for users of JUnit, as it uses quite the opposite order of actual and expected values. If you are addicted to JUnit's assertions you can still use them with TestNG. Simply import `org.testng.AssertJUnit` instead of `org.testng.Assert`.

You might ask what difference the order of the first two parameters makes. Is there any difference between comparing A to B and comparing B to A? Of course, there is no difference in terms of result. They are the same/equal, or they are not, right? You will notice the difference only when the test fails. We will get to that soon.

Another point is that you should really learn all of the above assertions and make use of them. At first you might be tempted to stick with just the simplest: i.e. `assertTrue()` and `assertFalse()`. They will allow you to verify just about anything, provided that you write a condition which evaluates to true or false. True, but verifying results with `assertSame()`, `assertNull()` or `assertNotEquals()` will make your test code much more readable. Remember, *"use the right tool for the job"*! This holds on every level.

 If you are not satisfied with the existing assertions you can always add your own custom ones. See Section 6.5 for more information.

3.5. Failing Test

Let us see what happens when a test fails. It is inevitable that you will see many failing tests, so we had better get well acquainted with it.

To make our test fail, we need to introduce a small change into the constructor of the `Money` class.

Listing 3.6. Breaking the code so the test fails

```
public Money(int amount, String currency) {
    this.amount = 15; ❶
    this.currency = currency;
}
```

❶   No matter what was passed by argument, `amount` will be set to 15.

Of course, this change will make one of the assertions in our test (`assertEquals(money.getAmount(), 10);`) fail. After rerunning the test, the following message and stacktrace will appear:

Listing 3.7. Failing test output

```
java.lang.AssertionError: ❶
Expected :10 ❷
Actual   :15

    at org.testng.Assert.fail(Assert.java:89)
    at org.testng.Assert.failNotEquals(Assert.java:480)
    at org.testng.Assert.assertEquals(Assert.java:118)
    at org.testng.Assert.assertEquals(Assert.java:365)
    at org.testng.Assert.assertEquals(Assert.java:375)
    at com.practicalunittesting
        .MoneyTest.constructorShouldSetAmountAndCurrency(MoneyTest.java:18) ❸
```

❶   This line informs us that an assertion has failed.

❷   The values of both parameters of the `assertEquals()` assertion are printed: `10` was expected, but `15` was returned.

❸   The first line of the stack trace which starts with something other than `org.testng` points to the offending line in your test code. In this case, it is the line which threw `AssertionError`: `assertEquals(money.getAmount(), 10);`

One thing we should notice is that the order of assertions' parameters is really important. The printed information about the reason for the test failure is based on the assumption that we kept to the default order (remember: first actual value, then expected value). In any other circumstances, the printed information would have been misleading.

 We will discuss the assertions' messages in details in Section 8.4.

3.6. Parametrized Tests

It is often advisable to test the same method with many different input values, expecting various outcomes[6]. In this section we will learn how TestNG can help us with this task.

3.6.1. The Problem

Let us assume, that apart from testing the `Money` class constructor with `10` `USD`, we also want to test it with `20` `EUR`. That can be done like this:

---

[6]We will discuss the problem of what values should be verified in Section 6.1

Listing 3.8. Testing the Money class with 10 USD and 20 EUR

```
public void constructorShouldSetAmountAndCurrency() {
    Money money = new Money(10, "USD");

    assertEquals(money.getAmount(), 10);
    assertEquals(money.getCurrency(), "USD");

    money = new Money(20, "EUR");

    assertEquals(money.getAmount(), 20);
    assertEquals(money.getCurrency(), "EUR");
}
```

This approach will work, but its drawbacks are clearly visible. First of all, there is a lot of repetition and a clear violation of the DRY[7] principle. Secondly, such code is usually created using the **copy&paste** technique, which is a sure recipe for getting into trouble by copying the whole section while only changing a part of it. Thirdly, the `money` variable is a kind of "global" variable here, which can also bring with it some problems, if its state has been unintentionally preserved[8]. Fourthly, the test class will grow with every new set of arguments. Enough! There must be a better way!

You can use various techniques to avoid repetitions such as those presented above. or example, you could introduce a `for` loop. That would make it better, but at the same time would result in the introduction of logic into your test (albeit of a very basic kind), which is not advisable (see Section 10.2). You could also divide the `constructorShouldSetAmountAndCurrency()` method into a number of smaller methods, each checking only one set of parameters. Yes, but that would have similar unwanted features to those of the naive approach discussed previously.

3.6.2. The Solution

Fortunately, you do not need to invent your own solution here. This requirement is so common, that TestNG offers some very handy support for exactly these sorts of case. It is called "parametrized tests".

With TestNG you can pass arguments to tests by putting them into an XML configuration file, or by using **data providers**. We will concentrate on this second technique.

---

[7]See http://en.wikipedia.org/wiki/Don't_repeat_yourself.
[8]However, in this case `money` is "cleaned" with the construction of the new object, so that as long as this step is not omitted all its "memory" will be gone.

A data provider is a method whose purpose is to act as a source of arguments that will be passed to a test method. We will introduce such a method and call it `getMoney()`. If you look at the code at Listing 3.9, you will see that a clear separation of concerns is achieved: `getMoney()` method provides the data, and `constructorShouldSetAmountAndCurrency()` provides the testing algorithm. The linking of these two methods is achieved thanks to the `dataProvider()` attribute of the `@Test` annotation on the testing method.

Listing 3.9. Parametrized test

```
@DataProvider ❶
private static final Object[][] getMoney(){ ❷
    return new Object[][] {❸
        {10, "USD"}, ❹
        {20, "EUR"} ❺
    };
}


@Test(dataProvider = "getMoney") ❻
public void constructorShouldSetAmountAndCurrency(
                        int amount, String currency) { ❼
    Money money = new Money(amount, currency); ❽

    assertEquals(money.getAmount(), amount); ❾
    assertEquals(money.getCurrency(), currency); ❿
}
```

❶ The `@DataProvider` annotation means, that the `getMoney()` method will provide argument values which will be used as arguments for some of the test methods.

❷ Data providers are expected to return an `Object[][]` array.

❸❼ The `constructorShouldSetAmountAndCurrency()` method expects two parameters: amount and currency. Each row of the array returned by the data provider contains them both.

❹ The first set of arguments will consists of the number `10` and the currency `USD`.

❺ The second set of arguments will consists of the number `20` and the currency `EUR`.

❻ If a method uses the data provider, it will have to be annotated with a `@Test` annotation with the `dataProvider` attribute.

❽❾❿ Instead of hardcoded values both arguments are used to create an object of the `Money` class and to verify it.

If you run the test on Listing 3.9, you will notice that TestNG has created two test cases "under the hood", and now it reports that two tests have been executed. What is more important, you will receive detailed information about what happened: i.e. what values were used for each test. Figure 3.1 compares the output of the two test: MoneyTest from Listing 3.8 and MoneyDataProviderTest from Listing 3.9[9]. With respect to MoneyTest, all you know is that the test passed. As regards MoneyDataProviderTest, you also know what parameters were involved. In the case of a successful test run this might not be a big deal, but in the case of a failure you will instantly know what combination of data caused it.

Figure 3.1. Results of a test with and without data provider

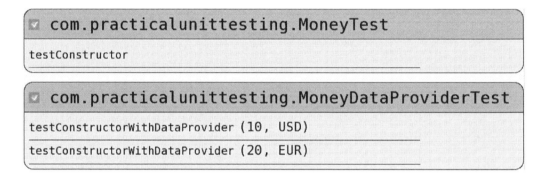

3.6.3. Reusing Data Providers

It is not unusual to have more than one test method use the same data provider. In fact, there is no limit to the number of test methods that can be fed with data from a single data provider.

What is more, you can also reuse data providers amongst test classes. This is possible, providing that you declare the data provider as a public method, and use another attribute of the @Test annotation: dataProviderClass. This is shown in Listing 3.10.

---

[9]We have not yet discussed the test reports which are covered in Chapter 8, *Getting Feedback*.

Listing 3.10. Data provider declared in another class

```
public class DataProviders { ❶

    @DataProvider
    public static final Object[][] getMoney(){ ❷
        return new Object[][] {{10, "USD"}, {20, "EUR"}};
    }

    // some more data providers declared here
}

public class MoneyTest { ❸

    @Test(dataProvider = "getMoney",
            dataProviderClass = DataProviders.class)
    public void constructorShouldSetAmountAndCurrency(
                        int amount, String currency) { ❹
        Money money = new Money(amount, currency);

        assertEquals(money.getAmount(), amount);
        assertEquals(money.getCurrency(), currency);
    }
}
```

❶   A separate class for data provider(s).
❷   A public access modifier makes this data provider accessible from other test classes.
❸   A separate class with test method(s).
❹   This method uses the `getMoney()` data provider by specifying not only its name, but also its class (the `dataProviderClass` attribute of the `@Test` annotation).

It is a matter of personal taste whether to create separate classes for data providers, or to keep them, instead, close to the test code (i.e. within the same test class as the methods which use it). I favor the second option, because:

• reuse of data providers is much less common than you might expect,

• it is easier to read code without moving to and fro amongst several classes.

3.6.4. Dynamic Data Providers

There is one more thing we should all know about data providers. Up until now, they have all returned an `Object[][]` array. This is fine for the majority of cases, but not for all of them. For example, imagine a test method which creates an array of 100000 very complex objects… and dies with OutOfMemoryError! Also, if the creation of objects is costly, then maybe it makes no sense to create all of them up front. If we create them one by one, pass them to the test method, and proceed only if the test does not fail, we save some time in cases of failure[10].

Both situations described above are relatively rare, but TestNG supports them, too. Data providers can return an Iterator, which can create test data lazily. Listing 3.11 illustrates such behaviour, showing how objects of some bogus ComplexObject class can be created, one by one, by a data provider. Let us assume that objects of this class are huge, and the creation of its multiple instances might cause an OutOfMemoryError exception.

Listing 3.11. Lazy data creation by data provider

```
public class LazyDataProviderTest {

    @DataProvider
    private final Iterator<Object[]> getLazyData(){ ❶
        return new Iterator<Object[]>() { ❷

            private int counter = 1; ❸

            @Override
            public boolean hasNext() {
                return counter < 4; ❹
            }

            @Override
            public Object[] next() { ❺
                return new Object[] {new ComplexObject(counter++)};
            }

            @Override
            public void remove() { // not important }
        };
    }

    @Test(dataProvider = "getLazyData") ❻
    public void testLazyData(ComplexObject object) { ❼
        System.out.println("lazy data: " + object);
    }
}
```

---

[10]The implementation of such a scenario would also require the use of a skipFailedInvocations attribute of the @Test annotation. Please refer to the TestNG documentation for details.

❶   The data provider is returning `Iterator<Object[]>`.

❷   There is an anonymous iterator class within the `getLazyData()` method.

❸❹   Let us say that we need only 3 objects to be returned by this data provider.

❺   The execution of the `next()` method occurs before each single value has been passed to the test method. This is where the laziness comes in.

❻❼   There is nothing different within the test method, when it is compared to data providers that are returning `Object[][]`.

Listing 3.12. ComplexObject class

```
public class ComplexObject { ❶

    public ComplexObject(int number) {
        // some costly creation logic here
    }
}
```

❶   Objects of this class should be passed to the test method by the data provider.

3.6.5. Conclusions

Summing up, the advantages of using data providers over any custom code are the following:

- none of one's own, potentially flawed, logic is introduced (e.g. for loop),

- adding another set of arguments is very easy, and does not make the code grow,

- a single data provider can be used to feed multiple test methods (and can do so across multiple test classes), making the code even more concise,

- there is no copy&paste coding, there are no "global" variables, and the DRY principle is faithfully honored,

- there is a clear separation between test logic (how the code is expected to work) and test data (what values are tested),

- we get more detailed results of the tests' execution.

In case your test classes (not test methods!) are parametrized, you should use another feature of TestNG: **factories**. Their purpose is to create multiple instances of test classes. A common use of factories is to run web tests (written with, for example, Selenium) against different web browsers (Firefox, Opera, Safari, Chrome etc.), or some DAO layer tests against different databases. Because factories are rarely used in unit tests, we will not discuss them. Please refer to the TestNG documentation for a detailed description.

3.7. Checking Expected Exceptions

From time to time your code needs to throw an exception. Maybe a method received an unexpected (illegal) value as an argument. Maybe some third-party component that it cooperates with has thrown an exception. Maybe... Anyway, exceptions are a vital part of how your methods behave. They are equally important to the results that are returned. They belong to the interface of your class, and therefore should be tested.

Fortunately, checking for expected exceptions is very easy, these days. The following code snippet illustrates this:

Listing 3.13. Expected exceptions testing pattern

```
@Test(expectedExceptions = ExceptionClass.class)
public void shouldThrowExceptions() {
    // some implementation here which is expected
    // to throw an exception of ExceptionClass
}
```

The `expectedExceptions` attribute of the `@Test` annotation specifies exceptions that are expected to be thrown by this test. It can take one exception, as in the example above, or many (e.g. `@Test(expectedExceptions = {ExceptionA.class, ExceptionB.class})`). In the latter case, the test method is expected to throw one of the exceptions from the list.

Think of the `expectedExceptions` attribute as about another way of writing a `try-catch` statement, and apply the same rules. In particular **do not** catch exceptions of class the `Exception` when something much more specific (e.g. an exception of type the `IllegalArgumentException`) is expected.

Let us have a look at an example now. We will introduce a change to the `Money` class. Let its constructor throw an `IllegalArgumentException` if:

- `amount` is less than 0,

- `currency` is `null` or empty.

The updated constructor is displayed in Listing 3.14.

Listing 3.14. Money class constructor with arguments checking

```
public Money(int amount, String currency) {
    if (amount < 0) {
        throw new IllegalArgumentException(
            "illegal negative amount: [" + amount + "]");
    }
    if (currency == null || currency.isEmpty()) {
        throw new IllegalArgumentException(
            "illegal currency: [" + currency + "],
                it can not be null or empty");
    }
    this.amount = amount;
    this.currency = currency;
}
```

Now, we would like to test it[11]. The test can look as shown in Listing 3.15. In this test we used data providers that you are already familiar with. They make the code very concise and allow for multiple values to tested without encountering difficulties.

Another thing worth noticing is the lack of assertions in the test methods shown in Listing 3.15. In fact there is no need to write any code to check whether expected exceptions have occurred. TestNG will take care of this, on the basis of information contained within the `expectedExceptions` attribute of the `@Test` annotation. So we can say that in fact there is an implicit assertion, or maybe rather an implicit `try-catch` statement, added automatically by TestNG.

 All of the tests shown in Listing 3.15 are one-liners, but this is only because we don't need more lines to invoke the constructor of the `Money` class. Obviously, TestNG does not limit the length of test methods!

---

[11]Personally, I feel slightly uneasy about this code-first approach. We shall soon be introducing the test-first technique, and will be adhering to it throughout the rest of the book.

Listing 3.15. Money class constructor expected exceptions test

```
public class MoneyIAETest {

    private final static int VALID_AMOUNT = 5;
    private final static String VALID_CURRENCY = "USD";

    @DataProvider
    private static final Object[][] getInvalidAmount(){
        return new Integer[][] {{-12387}, {-5}, {-1}};
    }

    @Test(dataProvider = "getInvalidAmount", ❶
        expectedExceptions = IllegalArgumentException.class) ❷
    public void shouldThrowIAEForInvalidAmount(int invalidAmount) {
        Money money = new Money(invalidAmount, VALID_CURRENCY); ❸
    }

    @DataProvider
    private static final Object[][] getInvalidCurrency(){
        return new String[][] {{null}, {""}};
    }

    @Test(dataProvider = "getInvalidCurrency", ❹
        expectedExceptions = IllegalArgumentException.class) ❺
    public void shouldThrowIAEForInvalidCurrency(String invalidCurrency) {
        Money money = new Money(VALID_AMOUNT, invalidCurrency); ❻
    }
}
```

❶❹ both test methods use data providers,

❷❺ both tests will succeed only if a given exception is thrown,

❸❻ there are no explicit assertions in this test.

What I would like to stress here is the importance of giving **meaningful names to methods and variables**[12]. They make the test readable and leave no room for doubts as to the role played by each method or variable. Let's take a look at this line:

```
Money money = new Money(invalidAmount, VALID_CURRENCY);
```

By using meaningful names for variables, we have achieved a highly readable test. Just read it: *"this line of code creates a new object of the class Money, using an invalid amount and a valid currency"*. All perfectly clear.

---

[12]This issue is further discussed in Section 9.3 and Section 11.6.1

More information on expected exceptions testing can be found in Section 6.3.

3.8. Test Fixture Setting

The term *"test fixture"* refers to the notion of a *"well known and fixed environment in which tests are run so that results are repeatable"*[13]. The steps required to set up such an environment differ, depending on the types of test and tool used, but the basic idea is always the same.

It is time to make sure that all elements are in place prior to an SUT's methods' being executed. In this section we will learn the basics of TestNG support for test fixture creation. We will learn some new annotations, and discuss the optimal test code structure.

3.8.1. Test Fixture Examples

The automation of the environment set up process is often the most challenging part of testing. This is especially true for integration and end-to-end tests. In the case of unit tests things are usually much simpler, but there are still some issues which should be taken care of (see Section 9.7 for further discussion). The following table gives examples of test fixtures for different types of test.

Table 3.2. Test fixture examples

type of test	test fixture example
unit test	• creation of new objects (SUT and test doubles), • preparation of input data,
integration test	• resetting the database to the initial state (e.g. so it contains one user with required privileges whose account can be used to perform tests), • copying of files that will be used during tests,
end-to-end test	• installation of a virtual machine that provides the runtime environment for the application,

---

[13]Citation from Wikipedia, http://en.wikipedia.org/wiki/Test_fixture.

type of test	test fixture example
	• installation (or cleaning to some initial state) of the web server and database used by the application.

3.8.2. Test Fixture in Every Test Method

Let us go back to the example of the `Client` and `Address` classes that were introduced in Section 3.9. Suppose we want to verify that the objects of the `Client` class are able to store a collection of addresses. Our first approach to the testing of this class might be the following:

Listing 3.16. Client object created in each test method

```
@Test ❶
public class ClientTest {

    private Address addressA = new Address("street A");
    private Address addressB = new Address("street B");

    public void afterCreationShouldHaveNoAddress() {
        Client client = new Client();

        assertEquals(client.getAddresses().size(), 0);
    }

    public void shouldAllowToAddAddress() {
        Client client = new Client();

        client.addAddress(addressA);

        assertEquals(client.getAddresses().size(), 1);
        assertTrue(client.getAddresses().contains(addressA));
    }

    public void shouldAllowToAddManyAddresses() {
        Client client = new Client();

        client.addAddress(addressA);
        client.addAddress(addressB);

        assertEquals(client.getAddresses().size(), 2);
        assertTrue(client.getAddresses().contains(addressA));
        assertTrue(client.getAddresses().contains(addressB));
    }
}
```

❶   The class-level @Test annotation makes TestNG treat all public void methods as test methods.

This test is fine, yet it certainly has a lot of repeated code related to the creation of objects. The client variable is created in each test method. If only we could have it being created in advance of each test method being executed… Well, it comes as no surprise that such a common concern is addressed by TestNG.

3.8.3. Annotations for Test Fixture Creation

Let us introduce a setUp() method[14] responsible the for creation of all objects. By annotating it with the @BeforeMethod annotation, we tell TestNG to do exactly that: to execute this method before each test method is executed.

After introducing the setUp() method the code looks as shown in Listing 3.17. It is functionally equivalent to the previous test (Listing 3.16), but a little bit shorter.

As can be seen, the creation of the client variable is no longer dispersed across multiple methods, but is grouped in the setUp() method. Also, there is no repetition. Had more test methods been available, the advantages of this approach would have been even more pronounced.

---

[14]Named setUp() for historical reasons (JUnit 3.x had a special method setUp() responsible for setting up the test fixture). As stated before, TestNG does not care about the name, what it responds to are method annotations.

Listing 3.17. ClientTest with @BeforeMethod annotation

```
@Test
public class ClientTest {

    private Address addressA = new Address("street A");
    private Address addressB = new Address("street B");
    private Client client;

    @BeforeMethod ❶
    public void setUp() {
        client = new Client(); ❷
    }

    public void afterCreationShouldHaveNoAddress() {
        assertEquals(client.getAddresses().size(), 0);
    }

    public void shouldAllowToAddAddress() {
        client.addAddress(addressA);

        assertEquals(client.getAddresses().size(), 1);
        assertTrue(client.getAddresses().contains(addressA));
    }

    public void shouldAllowToAddManyAddresses() {
        client.addAddress(addressA);
        client.addAddress(addressB);

        assertEquals(client.getAddresses().size(), 2);
        assertTrue(client.getAddresses().contains(addressA));
        assertTrue(client.getAddresses().contains(addressB));
    }
}
```

❶ The `@BeforeMethod` annotation makes TestNG execute this method before each test method is executed.

❷ Objects are only created in one dedicated method.

The order of method execution of code from Listing 3.17 is the following[15]:

```
setUp()
afterCreationShouldHaveNoAddress()
setUp()
```

---

[15]In fact, the order of execution of the test methods is not guaranteed. What is guaranteed is that methods annotated with `@BeforeMethod` will be invoked before each of the test methods.

```
shouldAllowToAddManyAddresses()
setUp()
shouldAllowToAddAddress()
```

TestNG offers more similar annotations, which helps to control test fixture creation. They are discussed in Section 9.7.

3.9. Phases of a Unit Test

Now that we have encountered some unit tests we may take a closer look at their structure. As you will probably have noticed, a unit test takes care of three things: firstly, it creates an object to be tested (the SUT), along with other required objects (the SUT's collaborators), then it executes the SUT's methods, and finally it verifies the results. This pattern is so common for unit tests that such tests are often described as **"arrange, act, assert"** tests.

Table 3.3. Phases of a unit test

phase	explanation
arrange	creation of all objects (except for the SUT) that are necessary for test execution
	creation of the object whose functionality will be tested, and setting it in some initial state
act	execution of SUT methods to be tested
assert	verification of the test results

The first phase relates to the preparation of **test fixture** (see Section 3.8). As we have already discussed, this functionality is often (at least partially) contained within utility methods shared by many tests, to avoid duplication of such set-up code across multiple test classes. You might have noticed that, in the table above, there is no "cleaning" step (or, to use JUnit nomenclature, tear-down method). Such a step is rarely used in unit tests where fresh objects are created in the beginning of every test method.

Let us now analyze the `ClientTest` class which we have been discussing in the previous section. Table 3.4 shows how this test fits into the **arrange, act, assert** structure.

Table 3.4. The phases of ClientTest

phase	code example

arrange	```Address addressA = new Address("street A");```
	```Address addressB = new Address("street B");```
	```Client client = new Client();```

act	```client.addAddress(addressA);``` ```client.addAddress(addressB);```

assert	```assertEquals(client.getAddresses().size(), 2);```
	```assertTrue(client.getAddresses().contains(addressA));```
	```assertTrue(client.getAddresses().contains(addressB));```

As we have seen in the previous examples, not all of the phases will necessarily be contained within a test method. For example, in the last version of the ClientTest class that we discussed (see Section 3.8.3), both instances of the Address class were created as private fields, and the SUT (an object of the Client class) was created within a setUp() method. However, this does not alter the fact that during the test execution the order of their creation was exactly as shown in Table 3.4.

Opinions are divided within the testing community as to what constitutes an adequate number of assertions per test method (see Section 7.3 for some discussion of this topic). However, it is recommended that all assertions within a single test method verify properties of a single object: the SUT. Asserting on many objects within a single test method is considered bad practice, and should be avoided!

3.10. Conclusions

In this section you have met TestNG and learned:

• about the default project structure that will be used throughout the book,

• how to write test classes and test methods,

• how to run tests,

• what assertions TestNG provides,

• how to use data providers,

- how to verify expected exceptions,

- how to use annotations for test fixture management.

What we have discussed in this section is good enough if you want to write really nice and useful unit tests. We have not gone into greater detail concerning these features, however, for two reasons: firstly, in many cases there are no more details, because testing frameworks (TestNG included) are rather simple, and secondly, we shall be adding a thing or two in subsequent parts of the book to what you have already learned about TestNG, and this will make more sense in the specific contexts that arise.

As you might expect, TestNG offers many other features which we have not yet covered. Some of them will be discussed in the ensuing sections, while others lie beyond the scope of this book, inasmuch as they have no real use in connection with unit tests. Once again, please make sure you at least browse the TestNG documentation, so that you know about its various capabilities.

 If you were to ask me about the most important thing from this section, I would point to data providers (see Section 3.6). Their correct use is hugely advantageous, allowing you to write very concise tests which cover many cases. The use of data providers eliminates redundancy and adds to the readability of tests.

In the following sections we will be making use of the knowledge you have acquired here, so please make sure to practice it a little bit, before reading further.

3.11. Exercises

The goal of the exercises presented below is twofold: firstly, they are here to help you get used to the idea of unit testing your code, and secondly, by carrying them out, you will preserve your knowledge of TestNG features.

3.11.1. TestNG Run

This exercise will help you get up and running with TestNG.

1. Create a new empty project using the build tool of your choice (Ant, Maven, Gradle, …). Add dependency to TestNG. Create a simple test class with a single test method containing some assertions.

2. Compile and run the test using:

   - your build tool,

   - your IDE.

3. Browse the test results.

3.11.2. String Reverse

A developer attempted to write an utility String reversing method. The outcome of his attempts is displayed below:

Listing 3.18. String reverse

```
public static String reverse(String s) {
    List<String> tempArray = new ArrayList<String>(s.length());
    for (int i = 0; i < s.length(); i++) {
        tempArray.add(s.substring(i, i+1));
    }
    StringBuilder reversedString = new StringBuilder(s.length());
    for (int i = tempArray.size() -1; i >= 0; i--) {
        reversedString.append(tempArray.get(i));
    }
    return reversedString.toString();
}
```

Now go ahead and write unit tests (using TestNG framework) which will verify that the method works properly!

Additional requirements and hints:

- think about the possible input parameters (see Section 6.1),

- use data providers (see Section 3.6) to make the test code concise,

- write tests for expected exceptions (see Section 3.7),

- if the method on Listing 3.18 does not work properly, then fix it,

- refactor (after all the tests pass).

3.11.3. HashMap

Write unit tests which will verify the following properties of the `java.util.HashMap` class:

- an object stored with the `put()` method can be retrieved with the `get()` method,

- adding a second object with the same key results in the old value being replaced ,

- the `clear()` method removes all its content,

- the `null` value can be used as a key,

Additional requirements and hints:

- use the appropariate TestNG annotations to create a fresh, empty map before each test method is called (see Section 3.8),

- javadocs of the `java.util.HashMap` class can be accessed at http://download.oracle.com/javase/6/docs/api/java/util/HashMap.html.

3.11.4. Fahrenheits to Celcius with Data Providers

A simple test class is shown in Listing 3.19. Your task is to introduce data provider(s), so there will be no repetition in the test code.

Listing 3.19. Fahrenheit to Celcius conversion test

```
@Test
public class FahrenheitCelciusConverterTest {

    public void shouldConvertCelciusToFahrenheit() {
        assertEquals(FahrenheitCelciusConverter.toFahrenheit(0), 32);
        assertEquals(FahrenheitCelciusConverter.toFahrenheit(37), 98);
        assertEquals(FahrenheitCelciusConverter.toFahrenheit(100), 212);
    }

    public void shouldConvertFahrenheitToCelcius() {
        assertEquals(FahrenheitCelciusConverter.toCelcius(32), 0);
        assertEquals(FahrenheitCelciusConverter.toCelcius(100), 37);
        assertEquals(FahrenheitCelciusConverter.toCelcius(212), 100);
    }
}
```

3.11.5. Master Your IDE

Make sure you spend some time learning about the support your IDE can give you in terms of effective unit testing. In particular, there are two features you should get accustomed with.

Templates

Every decent IDE allows you to create custom templates for quickly creating larger code structures. For the sake of efficient unit testing, you should at least learn how to:

- create a test class template (so, for example, you have all the required imports already included),

- create some typical code constructs - i.e. data providers methods and set-up methods.

Quick Navigation

It is very handy to able to quickly navigate between the production class (e.g. Money) and the corresponding test classes (e.g. MoneyTest). Find out the proper keyboard shortcut for doing this.

Chapter 4. Test Driven Development

At the beginning of testing, things were simple. You wrote code, then you wrote tests to verify its validity. This seemed to be reasonable and brought good results. However after some time a few troublemakers ;) decided to turn things on their heads, and insisted on writing tests before implementation. This rather surprising idea got quite popular, and is claimed to bring even better results.

Initially, writing tests before writing the actual code was a way to verify it as soon as possible. As more and more people started to follow the **test-first** approach, they soon discovered that immediate verification is only a part of what you gain when writing tests first (and maybe not even the most important part). It turned out that thinking about the tests before any implementation has actually been written is a powerful design technique. Code not only worked better (thanks to being thoroughly tested), but also "looked and felt" better, in terms of its architecture, maintainability, and API ease of use.

Thus, test-first is now rather called **Test Driven Development** (TDD)[1]. There is still some discussion regarding the relation of TDD and test-first. However, it seems that the general understanding of these terms is that they really mean the same. Because of this, I will alternate between using one or other of the two terms throughout the book.

 This book concentrates on testing aspects, even though you will get a decent dose of the TDD approach here. The best book on TDD that I know of is [freeman2009]. However, I would suggest that you gain some experience in testing techniques before you start reading it. And, by the way, even though it is really great, it won't "teach" you TDD. Practice, practice, practice!

In this section we are going to take a closer look at what it means to write tests before implementation. Apart from giving some theoretical background, we will concentrate on practice. One important thing to remember is that even though the test-first approach will be demonstrated solely on unit tests, this does not mean that the applicability of TDD is confined to this particular kind of test! On the contrary, this approach can (and should) be used on every testing level.

But first, let us consider various answers to the following question: *"when to write tests?"*.

---

[1] It is also called Test Driven Design, which stresses the **design** aspect of this technique.

4.1. When to Write Tests?

In the previous paragraphs, we have already mentioned two answers to this question:

- write tests after implementation (test-last AKA code-first),

- write tests before implementation (test-first).

Obviously, they are contradictory. You will have to choose which rule to follow, for a given piece of code. However, it is possible to use both of them for the whole coding process, choosing the more suitable one for each implementation task or code part.

 In spite of being a huge supporter of the TDD approach, in Section 4.8 I will discuss some reasons for choosing test-last over test-first.

But there is yet another answer to the "when to write tests?" question, which complements the two given previously: "write a test every time a bug is found". Let us describe each approach in more detail.

4.1.1. Test Last (AKA Code First) Development

In the "test last" approach, tests are written after the production code has been finished. It is a "traditional" approach to testing, pre-existing the more recent "test first" approach.

Writing the tests after the code has advantages and disadvantages. The main advantage is that the tests are written when the functionality of the tested object is well understood. The main disadvantage is that the developer concentrates on testing the implementation (which he/she wrote only a few minutes earlier) instead of testing the interface (behaviour) of the SUT. This can lead to tests which:

- are tightly coupled to the implementation (and as such will need to be rewritten every time it changes),

- encourage developers to (sub)consciously select the sort of test cases they expect to pass successfully.

Additionally, when using the "test last" approach there is always a temptation to not write tests at all. Why bother, if you are pretty sure the code works as expected? Why bother, if you have run the thing and seen for yourself that the log messages are exactly as you wanted them to be? It requires a lot of self-discipline to write tests after you have a working code. And when the deadline comes, the temptation to save some time by avoiding this extra, seemingly unnecessary step, will grow. In my opinion, this is a serious reason to follow the test-first approach.

In some cases, i.e. when working with legacy code, the "test last" approach is the only possible one, as the code already exists.

4.1.2. Test First Development

This whole chapter is devoted to "test first" development, so let us start with a brief description of its most important characteristics.

Writing the tests before the actual code makes developers think about the behaviour of the tested object as opposed to its implementation (which does not exist at this point). It cuts down the functionality of each implemented class to the bare minimum determined by the test cases - no superfluous functionalities are added. It also results in a very high (if not 100%) level of code coverage (see Section 11.3), which, in general, is desirable.

This approach can be applied to any level of testing. In particular, it is very popular for and suited to unit tests.

4.1.3. Always after a Bug is Found

The first thing you should do after a bug has been found is to restrain your natural urge to fix it right away. If you fix it "just like that", you lose an opportunity to get rid of it once and for all. The bug may reappear later (because someone reverts the changes, for example when fixing another bug). If you write a test before fixing it, you will strengthen your safety net of tests, and the same bug will not come back.

So, no matter if you code test-first or test-last, you should write a test immediately after a bug is encountered. The test should expose the bug, that is, it should expect the right thing to happen, and at first it should fail, thus repeating the observed buggy behaviour. Later on, you should fix the code so the test passes.

If you think about it, you will realize that writing a test after a bug has been found really amounts to a test-first approach. You write a test which fails (because you want to mimic the bug), and then you implement the code.

The big issue here is to pinpoint the bug precisely, so that you are able to write a unit test which exposes it. This might be really tricky. It may be that multiple bugs are turning up in your business logic in the course of your clicking the UI of your application. It is not so easy to tell exactly which class is responsible for some particular bit of erroneous behaviour. This is usually solved by first writing a higher-level test (i.e. an end-to-end test), and then gradually gathering information on the cause, narrowing the search field by writing more focused tests: first integration, and then eventually unit, tests.

4.2. TDD Rhythm

The nice thing about test-first coding is that it consists of a few very simple steps repeated over and over again. And – which comes as quite a surprise the first time one encounters it – these simple steps lead to a great coding experience and great results. Pure magic, isn't it?

Now, I would like you to take a look at Figure 4.1. This picture is simplified. It does not tell the whole truth. We will enhance it further to include some more details. Yet, this is **THE** picture that should hang over your desk[2]. It gives you the rhythm of your work:

1. Write a test that fails (RED).

2. Make the code work (GREEN).

3. Eliminate redundancy (REFACTOR).

It also gives you a simple rule to follow: **never write code without failing test**!

---

[2]If I had to choose one thing that I would like you to remember from this book, it would be this picture!

Figure 4.1. The most important picture

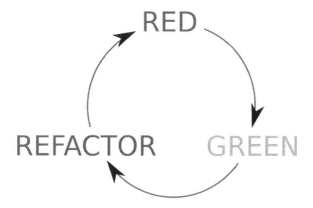

The next picture - Figure 4.2 - gives some more insight into the TDD rhythm. It shows how you start with a list of tests, choose one of them, and then follow the red-green-refactor cycle, making sure you end up with green.

The whole work is finished (i.e. some particular functionality is implemented), when there are no more tests to be written.

Figure 4.2. TDD rhythm explained

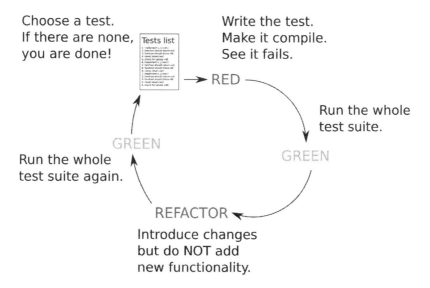

In the following sections we shall discuss each element of the TDD rhythm in details.

4.2.1. RED - Write a Test that Fails

Think about some functionality that should be implemented and write it down in the form of a test. This functionality is not yet implemented, so the test will inevitably fail. That is okay. Now you know that:

- the functionality really does not work,

- once it is implemented, you will see it, because the test result will turn from red to green.

At first you might feel awkward when writing tests for something which is not even there. It requires a slight change to your coding habits, but after some time you will come to see it as a great design opportunity. By writing tests first, you have a chance of creating an API that is convenient for a client to use. Your test is the first client of this newly born API. This is what TDD is really all about: the design of an API.

When thinking like a client of your own soon-to-be-written code, you should concentrate on what is really required. You need to ask questions like: *"do I really need this getter that returns this collection, or would it be more convenient to have a method which returns the biggest element of this collection?"*. And you need to answer such questions by writing tests. This book is not devoted to API design, but even if we were to just scratch the surface of this topic, it could entail a revolutionary change in your coding style. No more unnecessary methods, written because *"they might just possibly be useful for someone someday"*, no more auto-generated getters/setters, when an immutable class is much more appropriate. Concentrate on what the client (the test code) really needs. And write tests which test exactly this, and nothing more.

Writing a test first will make you think in terms of the API of the object. You won't yet know what the implementation is going to look like (even if you have **some** vision of it). This is good: it means your tests will have more chances of testing the external behaviour of the object, and not its implementation details. This results in much more maintainable tests, which are not inseparably linked to the implementation.

 Always start with the failing test, and always observe it failing. Do not neglect this step! It is one of the few ways to learn about the quality of your test (see Chapter 11, *Test Quality*).

Of course, you cannot run the test right after having written it. Why? Because if you truly followed the *"never write code without a failing test"* rule, then your test would be using some non-existent classes and methods. It simply would not be able to compile. So, as part of this first step you will also need to make the test compile. Usually IDE will make this a breeze, by creating a default (empty) implementation of classes and methods which are used from the test code.

 In reality, writing a failing test might sometimes be more trouble than it is worth. Please refer to Section 4.9 for a discussion.

How To Choose the Next Test To Write

Telling you to simply go and write a failing test "just like that" is kind of unfair. It sounds easy, but how should one go about it? Say we have a list of functionalities to be implemented, and a list of tests which cover them. The question we have to deal with right now is how to choose the first test. And then, after you implement it, and finish the TDD circle by implementing the code and refactoring, how to go about the next test? And the next one?

This is a standard problem and, as far as I know, no "standard" answer exists. There is no heuristic that is commonly recognized as the right way to determine the next test to be implemented. However, there are some tips shared amongst the community that might be helpful. Let us have a look at them.

The Low-Hanging Fruit. This rule says: *"Start with something really simple. Implement an obvious test case."*

This technique is especially useful if you are stuck. Writing something, even something trivial or of only minimal importance, might be helpful to overcome this sort of "writer's block". When you have doubts about what tests to write and how the tested method should behave, then making the first step might be the best thing you can do. Even if the functionality implemented in this way is not so important, you will at least get some of the pieces of the puzzle (the SUT class and some of its methods) in place. It might help you to move forward.

An example of writing a simple test case just to get you started would be:

- writing a parameter-checking test for a function (no matter what the purpose of the function in question might be),

- or, when writing a parser, starting with the test case of passing an empty String to the parsing method and receiving `null` in return[3].

In neither case would you touch the main logic (probably quite complex) which is to be tested and implemented. However, you would end up with some classes and methods that might give you some insight into the real task ahead. This could be really handy, if you are feeling lost and do not know how to proceed further.

The Most Informative One. Another approach is to start with the test which gives you the most information about the implemented functionality. This is like striking the ball with the sweet spot: it yields the maximum possible return in terms of knowledge.

However, this usually means facing up to the most difficult dilemmas. Well, you are going to have to deal with them anyway, so maybe instead of circling around, why not simply jump right into the action?

 This approach is like saying *"it does not matter that my first match is against the world champion - if I am going to win the whole tournament, I will have to beat him anyway"*. Some people like this kind of motivation.

All good and well, but haven't we just answered a riddle with another riddle? The question, now, is how to know which test will furnish you with the most knowledge about the implemented functionality? Well, this is not so hard to answer. This is probably the test which you know you still do not know how to make pass. You will simply know which one that is.

In the case of the preceding parser example, had you adopted this approach, then you would probably have started out by parsing a full sentence. This would definitely teach you a lot about the functionality being implemented.

First The Typical Case, Then Corner Cases. It seems quite reasonable to start with a "typical case". Think about how you would expect this function to be most frequently used. When writing a tokenizer, start with a valid sentence as an input. When implementing a

---

[3]This example is taken from Ash Kim's discussion of TDD techniques on StackOverflow http://stackoverflow.com/questions/3922258/when-applying-tdd-what-heuristics-do-you-use-to-select-which-test-to-write-next

vending machine, begin with a client inserting a 1$ coin and selecting a product which the machine has. Later on, you will implement corner cases.

Also, this approach guarantees that you have something valuable working from the very beginning. Even if you get dragged away from your computer (e.g. to some very urgent meeting of the highest importance) you will have already implemented something which is useful for the clients of the SUT. That will be nice.

 This approach represents a "natural" order of testing, as discussed in (see Section 6.1).

Listen To Your Experience.   Probably the most valuable way to deal with the "next test" dilemma is to listen to your experience. It should tell you which one of the above approaches is the most suitable for this particular case. Personally, I like to go with the typical cases first, but it happens that I use other approaches as well.

Readable Assertion Message

After you have a failing test and **before** you start implementing the code to fix it, it is advisable to take care of one additional detail: make sure that the message printed by the failing test indicates precisely what is wrong. Sometimes, in fact quite often, the default information printed by TestNG is good enough. If not, work on the error message (see Section 8.4 for some hints) until you are satisfied with the result. Then, move on to the next step.

4.2.2. GREEN - Write the Simplest Thing that Works

Now that you have a failing test, and a clear assertion message, you need to make the test pass – by writing code, of course!

The point here is not to go too far. It is to **write the smallest amount of code that will satisfy the test**. Concentrate on the task in hand. You have to make the bar green. That is it. Do not think (too much) about possible enhancements, do not worry about all the potential uses of your class, do not dwell on features that it would be "nice to have". Do not try to fulfil those requirements of the tests that have not yet been implemented (but which you can already envisage in your mind). The single failing test makes your current task clear: make it green, and nothing more.

Remember, there will be other tests. They will cover other requirements. And when their time comes, you will add all those cool features that are screaming out to you in your head *"implement me now!"*. Ah, just let them scream for a while. Maybe they really will be required, maybe not. Your tests will tell. **Concentrate on the task at hand**.

On the other hand, do not fall into the opposite trap. "Simple" and "silly" are not synonyms! The "simplest thing that works" should be simple, but reasonable. Concentrating on the task at hand is not an excuse for writing sloppy code.

I am not encouraging you to shut your ears to all of your experience gained from working as an architect or a designer. I am not saying that you should not think about the broader picture. What I am saying is "listen to your code". Have your own ideas, but listen to your code. It can guide your design. Listen to your tests also. They will tell you what is really important. They will not let you roam through the endless realm of exciting possibilities.

4.2.3. REFACTOR - Improve the Code

The question is, won't adding simple features one by one make your final code look like a pile of randomly laid elements? The code will work, but will it be easy to enhance, will it be flexible, will it adhere to all OO principles (KISS[4], DRY, SRP[5] and others)? And this is how we arrive at the next step of the TDD rhythm: refactoring.

Once the test passes you can make some changes to your code. The safety net of tests gives you the confidence that you will not break anything as long as you "keep the bar green". Go on then, refactor! Remove duplicated code, change method names, update variables scope, move chunks from one place to another! And rerun your tests frequently. They will tell you precisely what damage, if any, your refactorings have caused.

And why is this step required? As some people say, *"if it works, don't fix it"* – so why burden yourself with the task? The answer is that during the previous step (writing the least amount of code to satisfy a test) you focused on the task in hand, and the code implemented

---

[4]KISS, *"Keep It Simple Stupid"*, see http://en.wikipedia.org/wiki/KISS_principle
[5]SRP, Single Responsibility Principle, see http://en.wikipedia.org/wiki/Single_responsibility_principle

might not be clear enough. It works, but it might be a nightmare to maintain. And above and beyond this, when coding "only enough to pass the test" you were thinking only about that particular piece of code. Now is the time to look at the broader picture and refactor all the code you have, not just the few lines written a minute or so ago. Maybe there is some redundancy, maybe some functionality should be moved to a private function, maybe some variables should be renamed. Now is the time to do this.

 If you had "refactored", and the tests still passed, but the application is broken now, it means that you were not really refactoring. You were just changing your code. Refactoring is moving around above a safety net of tests. It means working with code which is thoroughly tested. You are being unfair to "refactoring" when you accuse it of having broken something. You had simply done it badly (i.e. not tested well enough).

Refactoring the Tests

Should you also refactor the tests? Yes, you should! Remember, they are a valuable asset. You will be executing them, reading them and updating them often. They are the foundation upon which your code is built and, as such, should be robust and of the highest quality. The quality of your code depends strongly on your tests, so you had better have confidence that they are really, really good.

Refactoring is a way of restructuring the code without changing its functionality. In terms of tests, this means that the refactored tests exercise the same paths of code, call the same methods, use identical arguments, and verify the same assertions, as they were doing before you commenced the refactoring.

An obvious issue with test refactoring is that there are no tests for tests themselves, so you might accidentally introduce some unwanted changes instead of performing a refactor. Such a danger exists, but is not as serious as it might at first glance seem. First of all, unit tests, if written correctly, are really simple (see Section 10.2). They contain no complex logic such as might be prone to breaking down when changes are introduced. When you refactor tests you are more involved in just moving things around - e.g. moving some common functionality to set-up methods[6] - than you are in working with test logic. Also, if you do something wrong, it is very probable that the green bar will turn to red, warning you immediately that something has gone wrong.

---

[6]See Chapter 11, *Test Quality* for more information on refactoring of the test code.

In summary, proceed with caution, but do not be afraid to refactor your tests. Make sure the number of executed tests has not changed, and if you do not feel confident with the changes introduced while refactoring, take a look at the code coverage report (see Section 11.3).

Adding Javadocs

During a refactoring phase I will also be taking care of Javadocs - both for production code and tests. This raises two issues:

1. First of all, your design is still not fixed. Is there a point in writing any documentation now, when the things may still be about to be changed?

2. Writing documentation now can interfere with the flow of thoughts you have. Your brain is already focusing on the next test to be written. Is it a good idea to interrupt this so-called "flow" and switch to a different activity?

 These valid questions are reinforced by the natural aversion of developers to writing documentation. This results in postponing the act of its creation… which, of course, leads to there being no documentation at all. This seems really cool in the short term, but is deadly in the long run.

What I suggest is the following:

1. Keep it short - it will hurt less this way. Write only about the business purpose of the classes and methods, and about any important design decisions.

2. If you really, really do not want to break the coding flow, leave a note to yourself - by putting some TODO or FIXME marks within the code, on a scrap of paper (some kind of Post-it note on your monitor) or only a mental note (be careful here, they tend to vanish, you know!). Obviously, you'll need to devote some time to fixing the issue, after you've finished some larger chunks of functionality.

 Do not forget that you should aim to write code that is self-documenting. Use descriptive method names, and write good, readable tests. This will leave you with virtually nothing to put into Javadocs (except for some higher-level explanations).

4.2.4. Here We Go Again

After the code has been refactored, run the tests again to make sure that no harm has been done. Remember, run all the unit tests - not just the ones you have been working with recently. Unit tests execute fast: no time is gained by only running selected ones. Run them all, see that they pass, and so be confident that you can move on to the next test. Repeat the process till there are no more tests to be written.

4.3. Benefits

> TDD helps with, but does not guarantee, good design & good code. Skill, talent, and expertise remain necessary.
>
> — Esko Luontola

So now you know the theory behind the TDD cycle. Before we move on to a practical example, let us again list the benefits of this approach:

- all of the code is unit tested,

- the code is written to satisfy the tests – there are no superfluous parts of the code that have been written just because they "could possibly be useful" or "will surely be required one day" (YAGNI),

- writing the smallest amount of code to make the test pass leads to simple solutions (KISS),

- thanks to the refactoring phase the code is clean and readable (DRY),

- it is easy to go back into the coding, even after interruptions; all you have to do is take the next test from the list and start the next cycle.

 Once you get into a test-first habit, writing any code without failing tests will make you feel uncomfortable. :)

4.4. TDD is Not Only about Unit Tests

Even though this book is devoted to unit tests, this section is to remind you that TDD is much broader than this. In fact, you can, and you are encouraged to, use TDD on every level. Figure 4.3 illustrates this idea.

As you can see, there are two TDD loops here[7]. The outer loop relates to working with end-to-end tests in the same test-first manner as we have adopted for unit tests. For example, the outer loop could include tests executed against the GUI, written with the Selenium web testing tool. In order to satisfy such a test, many smaller functionalities must be implemented, which takes us into the inner loop. This, in turn, symbolizes the implementation of unit tests, and pertains to the implementation of much smaller functionalities.

Figure 4.3. TDD on different levels

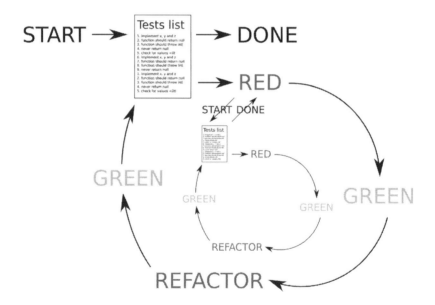

There is a huge difference between the two loops. A developer will finish many cycles of the inner loop each day, while one cycle of the outer loop might even take him a few

---

[7]There might be more of them - i.e. three - if other tests, like integration tests, were also to be taken into account. However, for the sake of simplicity I have decided to put only two of them on the picture.

days. However, both are identical when it comes to the rhythm of work. In both cases you move from red to green, and then you keep it green while refactoring. This approach to development, based on the TDD method, has also gained a degree of popularity and even has its own name – ATDD, which stands for Acceptance Test Driven Development.

We will not be spending any more time on this broader use of TDD, but after you have mastered TDD at the unit-testing level it is advisable to also try it with different types of test. Once again, [freeman2009] is a must-read.

4.5. Test First Example

Now we are so well educated about test-first, let's get down to business and do some coding! We shall code a simple class using – surprise, surprise! – the test-first approach.

Take a look at the TDD cycle shown previously. We shall be following its phases one by one. We will start with a failing test. Then, after we have made sure that the error message is informative enough, we will move on to fixing the code. After the test passes we shall concentrate on making the code better by refactoring.

Even though we shall try to follow precisely the steps described in the preceding sections, you will see that in real life some additional work is required. Well, moving from theory to practice is never a painless process.

 The example shown in this section is simplified – I realize that. I have made it that simple on purpose, so we can see test-first in practice without being distracted by the complexity of the domain model.

4.5.1. The Problem

Let us play some football, okay? We will implement a FootballTeam class, so we can compare different teams and see who takes first place in the league. Each team keeps a record of the number of games won.

Now we have to think about this. Let us imagine the functionalities of the class and the expected outcomes. All we need is a rough idea, and some guesses regarding the implementation. The details will come later – we do not need to think too hard right now.

We should have at least some ideas regarding tests, so we can make the first move. Ok, let us think about this.

> So, in our example we have two teams and we need to compare them. It seems like I can use a Comparable interface. Yes, this is a common Java pattern for comparison... no need to think about anything fancy here....Good... Now, if we are to compare them, each team needs to remember the number of games it has won, and the comparison mechanism will use them. So a FootballTeam class needs a field in which to keep this information, and this field should somehow be accessible... Okay... and the most important thing is the comparison.... We need a few tests here: we need to see that teams with more wins are ranked first, and we need to check what happens when two teams have the same number of wins.
>
> — Tomek *Dump of a Train of Thought (2011)*

All right, I guess this is enough to get us started.

4.5.2. RED - Write a Failing Test

In order to compare two teams, each of them has to remember its number of wins. For the sake of simplicity let us design a FootballTeam class that takes the number of games as a constructor parameter[8]. First things first: let us make sure that this constructor works.

We start by creating a new class - FootballTeamTest - somewhere in the src/test/java/ directory. It can look like the following:

Listing 4.1. Testing number of games won

```
@Test
public class FootballTeamTest {

    public void constructorShouldSetGamesWon() {
        FootballTeam team = new FootballTeam(3); ❶
        assertEquals(team.getGamesWon(), 3); ❷
    }
}
```

---

[8]In a more real-life scenario, a team would probably start with 0 games won, and then, based on the results of games played, it would incrementally adjust its score.

❶   Whoa, wait! At this point, your IDE will mark FootballTeam with a red color, as the class does not exist.

❷   Similarly, at this point your IDE will complain about the lack of a getGamesWon() method.

Obviously, you need to create a FootballTeam class and its getGamesWon() method before proceeding any further. You can let your IDE create the class, its constructor and this one method for you, or you can write them yourself.

There are two things to remember when writing code that is necessary in order for a test to compile:

- All production code should be kept in a different directory tree from the tests. I suggest following the previously described pattern and putting it in src/main/java.

- **Do nothing more than the minimum required for the test to compile**. Create the necessary classes and methods, but do not fit them out with any business logic. Remember, we want to see our test **fail** now!

It does not matter whether we created the required code ourselves or let IDE do it (which I recommend): either way, we will end up with an implementation of the FootballTeam class along similar lines to the following:

Listing 4.2. Autogenerated FootballTeam class

```
public class FootballTeam {

    public FootballTeam(int gamesWon) {
    }

    public int getGamesWon() {
        return 0;
    }
}
```

It is quite interesting that we get this code "for free". And I am not just referring here to the IDE's being able to generate it on the basis of the test. Even if we wrote it by hand, it was still hardly an intellectual challenge! Writing the test might have been demanding, but creating the code was very, very simple. That is not always the case, but it does often happen like that.

Since the test compiles, and has an assertion which verifies an important functionality belonging to our class, it is worth running. Once we run it, it fails miserably, with the following message:

Listing 4.3. Failing tests message

```
java.lang.AssertionError:
Expected :3
Actual   :0

    at org.testng.Assert.fail(Assert.java:89)
    at org.testng.Assert.failNotEquals(Assert.java:480)
    at org.testng.Assert.assertEquals(Assert.java:118)
    at org.testng.Assert.assertEquals(Assert.java:365)
    at org.testng.Assert.assertEquals(Assert.java:375)
    at com.practicalunittesting.
            constructorShouldSetGamesWon(FootballTeamTest.java:19)
```

Let us be clear about this – a failing test at this point is a good thing. Now we know that our test has been executed, and that some important functionality is not ready yet. We will implement it till we see the green light (that is, the test passes).

But first, let us resist the urge to fix the code right away. Instead, we should take care of the error message. Does it say precisely what is wrong here? If the answer is *"no"*, then add a custom error message (see Section 8.4). If you are happy with the current message, then proceed further.

Let us say that I have decided that the test will be better if enhanced with the following custom error message:

```
assertEquals(team.getGamesWon(), 3,
    "3 games were passed to constructor, but "
    + team.getGamesWon() + " were returned");
```

Now, after we have rerun the test, the output will be more informative (stacktrace omitted):

```
java.lang.AssertionError: 3 games were passed to constructor,
            but 0 were returned
Expected :3
Actual   :0
```

If we ever break our code, so this test fails, the assertion message will tell us precisely what is wrong and the fix should be easy.

All right then, it is time to move on to the next phase of TDD – we should make the test pass now – by fixing the code, of course.

4.5.3. GREEN - Fix the Code

The fix is straightforward this time: all we need to do is store the value passed as the constructor parameter to some internal variable. The fixed FootballTeam class is presented below.

Listing 4.4. Fixed FootballTeam class

```
public class FootballTeam {
    private int gamesWon;

    public FootballTeam(int gamesWon) {
        this.gamesWon = gamesWon;
    }

    public int getGamesWon() {
        return gamesWon;
    }
}
```

The test should pass now. However, no celebrations yet! This is the time to polish the code, to refactor and to add comments. No matter how small the changes you have made, rerun the test to make sure that nothing has accidentally been broken.

4.5.4. REFACTOR - Even If Only a Little Bit

In the case of something as simple as this FootballTeam class, I do not see anything worth refactoring. However, let us not forget about the refactoring of the test! The least we should do is to get rid of the magic number 3 – for example, by introducing a THREE_GAMES_WON variable:

Listing 4.5. Refactored FootballTeamTest

```
@Test
public class FootballTeamTest {

    private final static int THREE_GAMES_WON = 3;

    public void constructorShouldSetGamesWon() {
        FootballTeam team = new FootballTeam(THREE_GAMES_WON);

        assertEquals(team.getGamesWon(), THREE_GAMES_WON,
            THREE_GAMES_WON + "were passed to constructor, but "
                + team.getGamesWon() + " were returned");
    }
}
```

4.5.5. First Cycle Finished

We have just finished the first TDD cycle. Everything started with that failed test. Then we worked on the error message and fixed the code. After the test passed, we refactored the code (and rerun the test), thus completing the cycle.

The main challenge here is to restrain yourself from implementing too much. You might have a very precise view from the very beginning about how the FootballTeam class should be implemented. You might be tempted to go ahead and just write it, because you think the code to be written is trivial. The feeling that this is "a piece of cake" that is not worth the trouble of writing tests for is normal. After all, up until now you have been writing code without tests and it has worked pretty well, right? However, I would like to encourage you to follow the test-first pattern, even if it feels a little bit awkward at first. Get to know it, use it for a few hours, and then decide if you like it or not. First impressions might be misleading.

'The Simplest Thing that Works' Revisited

Let us take another look at what we did to satisfy the failing test from Listing 4.1. Did we really do the "simplest thing" to make the tests pass? Not really. One could argue that what should have been done is the following:

Listing 4.6. The simplest thing that satisfies the failing test

```
public class FootballTeam {

    public FootballTeam(int gamesWon) {
    }

    public int getGamesWon() {
        return 3;
    }
}
```

This snippet of code really **does satisfy** the failing test. You could call it an absurdity, but there is wisdom in this folly. What it does is prove that your test is not good enough to cover a certain functionality. It says, *"Look, your test is so pathetic, that I can make it pass by doing such a silly thing. You need to try harder.".* And it really makes you write more tests.

The next test could, for example, be to verify whether the same test passes with a different number of games won – say, 5 instead of 3. Such a test would obviously fail, and then you would have to make the code smarter, so it supports both cases.

I'll leave it to you to decide whether this way of code-teasing yourself is something you want to practice. I would encourage you to give it a try, because this kind of exercise will help to sharpen your understanding of what good tests really involve.

4.5.6. More Test Cases

The constructor seems to work fine, …at least for this one value! We should add tests for more values, and also make the constructor throw an exception if an inappropriate number of wins is passed to the constructor (see Section 6.1). We will use data providers (discussed in Section 3.6) in both cases.

The following code snippets illustrate both cases:

Chapter 4. Test Driven Development

Listing 4.7. Testing valid values using data providers

```
@DataProvider
public Object[][] nbOfGamesWon() {
    return new Object[][]{ {0}, {1}, {2} };
}

@Test(dataProvider = "nbOfGamesWon")
public void constructorShouldSetGamesWon(int nbOfGamesWon) {
    FootballTeam team = new FootballTeam(nbOfGamesWon);

    assertEquals(team.getGamesWon(), nbOfGamesWon,
        nbOfGamesWon + " games were passed to constructor,
        but " + team.getGamesWon() + " were returned");
}
```

Listing 4.8. Testing invalid values using data providers

```
@DataProvider
public Object[][] illegalNbOfGamesWon() {
    return new Object[][]{ {-10}, {-1} };
}

@Test(dataProvider = "illegalNbOfGamesWon",
        expectedExceptions = IllegalArgumentException.class)
public void shouldThrowExceptionForIllegalGamesNb(
        int illegalNbOfGames) {
    new FootballTeam(illegalNbOfGames);
}
```

But is It Comparable?

The constructor works fine. Now we can move on to the main problem: that is, to the comparing of football teams. First of all, we have decided that we are going to use the `Comparable` interface. This is an important decision which will influence not only the implementation of this class but also its API and expected behaviour. If `FootballTeam` is comparable, then the client can expect that once he has put a few teams into a collection, he will be able to use the `Collections.sort()` method to order them. If so, then there should be a test for this behaviour. The only one I can think of is the following:

78

Listing 4.9. Is FootballTeam comparable?

```
private static final int ANY_NUMBER = 123;

public void shouldBePossibleToCompareTeams() {
    FootballTeam team = new FootballTeam(ANY_NUMBER);

    assertTrue(team instanceof Comparable,
        "FootballTeam should implement Comparable");
}
```

This is a rather uncommon test: I rarely write tests which use an `instanceof` operator. However, in this case it seems legitimate, as it covers an important characteristic of the `FootballTeam` class, required by its clients.

 Please note the name of the static value passed to the constructor: ANY_NUMBER. That indicates that this argument is not important. The real value of the argument does not influence the test in any way.

The test will fail. Your IDE is surely capable of fixing the code. After the IDE has generated the default implementation of the `compareTo()` method, the `FootballTeam` class will look like this:

Listing 4.10. FootballTeam implements Comparable interface

```
public class FootballTeam implements Comparable<FootballTeam> {
    private int gamesWon;

    public FootballTeam(int gamesWon) {
        this.gamesWon = gamesWon;
    }

    public int getGamesWon() {
        return gamesWon;
    }

    @Override
    public int compareTo(FootballTeam o) {
        return 0;
    }
}
```

Rerun the test to check that it passes now. It does. Good.

Before we move on to the next tests, let us make one thing clear: it is essential to run the whole test suite, and **NOT** only the last failed tests. Make sure that while working on a certain feature you do not break other features. Remember, always run all unit tests you have. If they are really "unit", they will run fast - no problem running them often, right?

Comparison Tests

If you are not familiar with the `Comparable` interface, please take a look at the description of the `Comparable.compareTo()` method Javadocs.

Now let us write the first comparison test. The idea is simple: take two teams with different numbers of wins and compare them.

Listing 4.11. The first comparison test

```
@Test
public void teamsWithMoreMatchesWonShouldBeGreater() {
    FootballTeam team_2 = new FootballTeam(2);
    FootballTeam team_3 = new FootballTeam(3);

    assertTrue(team_3.compareTo(team_2) > 0);
}
```

After running, the test will fail. Once again, the error message is cryptic, and needs to be updated. After it has been changed, the failed tests can print something more informative:

Listing 4.12. Comparison test failure

```
java.lang.AssertionError:
    team with 3 games won should be ranked before the team with 2 games won
Expected :true
Actual    :false

    at org.testng.Assert.fail(Assert.java:89)
    at org.testng.Assert.failNotEquals(Assert.java:480)
    at org.testng.Assert.assertTrue(Assert.java:37)
    at com.practicalunittesting.FootballTeamTest
        .teamsWithMoreMatchesWonShouldBeGreater(FootballTeamTest.java:36)
```

Let us fix the production code, but **do not** implement more than the test requires us to! The `compareTo()` method shown below is a minimal (reasonable) implementation which will make the test pass:

Listing 4.13. compareTo() method recognizes better teams

```
@Override
public int compareTo(FootballTeam o) {
    if (gamesWon > o.getGamesWon()) {
        return 1;
    }
    return 0;
}
```

After running all tests, we should:

- refactor (e.g. change the o variable to otherTeam),

- rerun the tests so we are sure nothing is broken,

- and, finally, proceed with the next test.

Listing 4.14. Another comparison test

```
@Test
public void teamsWithLessMatchesWonShouldBeLesser() {
    FootballTeam team_2 = new FootballTeam(2);
    FootballTeam team_3 = new FootballTeam(3);

    assertTrue(team_2.compareTo(team_3) < 0,
        "team with " + team_2.getGamesWon() +
        " games won should be ranked after the team with "
        + team_3.getGamesWon() + " games won");
}
```

Run, see it fail, then introduce changes to the FootballTeam class so the tests pass. The implementation which makes this test pass is, once again, trivial:

Listing 4.15. compareTo() method recognizes lesser team

```
public int compareTo(FootballTeam otherTeam) {
    if (gamesWon > otherTeam.getGamesWon()) {
        return 1;
    }
    else if (gamesWon < otherTeam.getGamesWon()) {
        return -1;
    }
    return 0;
}
```

All tests pass, so we can move on to an equality test:

Listing 4.16. Testing for equality

```
@Test
public void teamsWithSameNumberOfMatchesWonShouldBeEqual() {
    FootballTeam teamA = new FootballTeam(2);
    FootballTeam teamB = new FootballTeam(2);

    assertTrue(teamA.compareTo(teamB) == 0,
        "both teams have won the same number of games: "
        + teamA.getGamesWon() + " vs. " +
        teamB.getGamesWon() + " and should be ranked equal");
}
```

Well, this test passes instantly, because our implementation has already returned 0 in cases of equality. So, what should we do now? We have definitely skipped one step in the TDD rhythm. We have never seen this equality test failing, so we do not know why it passes. Is it because the FootballTeam class really implements the expected behaviour, or is it because our test has been badly written and would always pass?

For the time being, let us assume that the test is flawless, and that the implementation of FootballTeam also is. We will come back to this discussion later on, when examining some corner cases of TDD (see Section 4.9).

Now that we have a safety net of tests we can really refactor the tested method. After having thought through the matter carefully, we have ended up with much simpler implementation:

Listing 4.17. compareTo() method simplified

```
public int compareTo(FootballTeam otherTeam) {
    return gamesWon - otherTeam.getGamesWon();
}
```

The rerunning of the tests now tells us that this implementation satisfies all the requirements (written in the form of tests) so far.

4.6. Conclusions and Comments

The actual implementation of the test is rather a detail of TDD. Much more important is the mindset of practicing baby steps, the mindset of gaining insights and evolving through rapid feedback, the mindset of leveraging trial & error as a methodology, where errors are not failures but valuable insights that guide the evolution of the project.

— Jonas Bandi

So we have just implemented a class using the test-first approach. We moved in very small steps. We paid attention to the details. We polished the code. We even dealt with assertion messages. And all the time we were making sure that no functionality was broken – by rerunning the tests over and over again. And all the time we were moving forward… step by step… always forward.

I have a lot of questions to ask you now. How did you like it? Did you enjoy the red-green-refactor rhythm? Did it help you with writing the code, or did you feel it got in the way of your style of thinking and coding? Are you confident that the created code really works? Would you have done it better or faster without testing, or – maybe – would you have preferred to have written the tests after the implementation had finished? Did you feel you were wasting time by writing tests even for trivial cases? Did you feel confident refactoring the code?

Such a simple example might not be enough to demonstrate its usefulness. The problem was so trivial that you surely would have had an implementation ready in your mind from the outset, and would not have benefitted much from having written the tests first. However, it will be different when you start using test-first "in the wild". You will be writing tests for features that you have no idea how to implement. Then you will see how having tests helps you come up with a solution.

Personally, I feel I owe so much to the test-first technique that I would be delighted if you also were to like it. However, it is up to you to decide whether test-first really suits you. Throughout the rest of this book I will be relying solely on the test-first technique. If you like it, great! If not, well, please do bear with it anyway!

It would be sensible to have a look at the benefits of TDD as listed in Section 4.3. Have you taken note of them? Is your code 100% covered by your tests? Any "possibly important" features implemented? Is it simple? Is it clean and readable? Have you noticed the difference when continuing your work after an interruption? If so, maybe TDD is worth the effort!

One additional comment regarding our tests written using test-first. As you have probably noticed, each test created its own object of the `FootballTeam` class. Usually a good idea is to create the SUT in a set-up (which is an example of **extract method** refactoring) so that each test automatically gets a new one (in a clean, well-known state). However, in this case it was not possible, because each test method required a football team that had been created differently.

4.7. How to Start Coding TDD

We are all the same, under pressure we fall back on what we know; hit a few difficulties in TDD and developers stop writing tests.

— Ian Cooper

So now you have read about the wonders of the TDD approach! And you like it! It seems a little bit awkward, but at the same time sensible. You have heard about some great programmers writing tests before code. You have heard about some projects written test-first and renowned for their superior quality. You have spent some time reading about TDD techniques, you know the rhythm, you are getting more and more excited about the whole idea (up to the point of tattooing a "red-green-refactor" mantra on your back). Eventually… you have made up your mind about it: you want to try it… you want to be a step ahead of your team mates. You are eager to try it right now, with the very next job that you are given!

And you do try it. And it feels like… like trying to break a wall with your own head! Databases, Spring context, static classes, ORM tools, JNDI calls, web services, global variables, deep inheritance hierarchy and console output jump out at you all at once. Nothing looks like it did in the test-first tutorials; none of the good advice you read seems of any help. It is just plain impossible to proceed!

But of course you do not give up without a fight. Struggling, with gritted teeth, you somehow overcome one issue after another, one at a time. It takes time. You need to read some blogs, talk with your colleagues about the necessary design changes, but somehow it works. But at the end of the day, you look at the amount of written code, and you know that this is not good. You would have achieved 10 times more by using the code-first approach that you are accustomed with. You are not even proud of your tests - you know what dirty hacks you had to use to be able to write them.

Let us stop here, before we sink into despair. Dear TDD-Wannabe-Programmer, you were simply trying to do too much at once! You were trying to change your habits (which is hard enough in itself) and, at the same time, to solve multiple problems existing in your codebase. Even if you did have some tests (as I hope you did), your code was probably never written with testability in mind. Trying to add new features in test-first manner is like challenging the old codebase: it will fight back, as you have just experienced. It will attempt to thwart your efforts. Those same solutions that once you were so proud of are now stopping you from moving forwards.

What I would suggest is exactly what TDD itself promotes. Move in small steps. Start with the simplest things. Implement easy tasks using the test-first approach. Cherish every TDD success. Learn from every TDD failure. If you find something that you cannot tackle using the test-first approach, then do not worry too much about it. After a few weeks (hours, days, months?) you will be able to deal with such tasks. Build up your experience in small steps. Day by day… This way it will work – you will see!

It will get easier and easier every day. Firstly, because you are getting better and better at coding test-first. You "feel the rhythm", you concentrate on the task in hand, you stop thinking about possible and useful issues that are merely hypothetical, etc. Secondly, because you stop doing things you were doing, and start thinking in terms of testing. Thirdly, your design is much more testable now, and the next parts of your code are easier to test. Fourthly, some colleagues have joined you and stopped producing tons of untestable code. …and now you can see the light at the end of the tunnel. Good. :)

4.8. When not To Use Test-First?

TDD works like a charm, and it is very probable that once you get a good grip on it, you will be reluctant to code in any other way. However, there are some circumstances where this approach does not seem to be the best option. This section discusses this.

As explained in the previous section, it is really not advisable to jump at the deep end after just reading a "how-to-swim" tutorial. :) I do have faith in your programming skills (and so on), but it might just happen to be the case that you are **not yet ready** to implement any real-life programming tasks using the test-first approach. Start with something simple, gain experience and then move on.

This means that the first anti-test-first situation is **attacking all possible problems at the same time, while lacking experience, skills and confidence**. Do not do that.

And even then, when you have some experience, you will still find yourself stuck with TDD. Like Kent Beck[9], who tried to implement a new Eclipse plugin without prior knowledge of the technology:

---

[9]Do I really have to introduce Kent Beck? If so… see http://en.wikipedia.org/wiki/Kent_Beck

> For six or eight hours spread over the next few weeks I struggled to get the first test written and running. […] If I'd just written some stuff and verified it by hand, I would probably have the final answer to whether my idea is actually worth money by now. Instead, all I have is a complicated test that doesn't work, a pile of frustration, [and] eight fewer hours in my life […].
>
> — Kent Beck *Just Ship, Baby (2009)*

Writing tests usually requires a **good understanding of the technologies used, and knowledge of the problem domain**. If you lack these, you will probably be better off starting with the code-first approach - especially if you lack the time to acquire the necessary knowledge and know you will spend time struggling with the (unknown) testing framework instead of writing real code. As usual, use common sense and learn from your mistakes.

Another TDD stopper is when you apply it to some **legacy code**. You might not be able to go with TDD without some serious refactoring - thus, hitting the "chicken and egg" problem, because you cannot refactor for real without a safety net of tests… But then you'll have a few dirty tricks up your sleeves: tools which allow you to deal with all the weirdness of your legacy code[10]. Sadly, there will be a time when you will need to use them, even if you would gladly rewrite the whole code from the scratch.

However, all this applies more to integration tests than unit tests. My experience with test-first coding of unit tests is that it is always possible to do at least some state testing this way. As for testing of interactions between objects, this is sometimes significantly harder (because of some legacy non-easily-testable code structure).

4.9. Should I Follow It Blindly?

> I am not apt to follow blindly the lead of other men.
>
> — Charles Darwin

TDD is based on a set of very simple rules: first write a test, then see it fail, make it pass, refactor, and then… repeat the cycle. Moreover, their beauty is magnified by their wide scope of applicability – you can tackle almost any programming dilemma with them. However, these rules are not carved in stone. You will encounter some situations where it make sense to omit some steps. This section gives some examples of such situations.

---

[10]This takes us back to the distinction between "tools for verification" and "tools for design" discussed in Section 1.3.

4.9.1. Write Good Assertion Messages from the Beginning

After you have gained some experience with TestNG you will just know when the default assertion message is good enough, and when it should be corrected. I do not see any point in waiting for the test to fail, only to see that my experience was telling me the truth and that I should, indeed, fix the message.

That is why I often write good assertion messages without waiting for the test to fail.

4.9.2. If the Test Passes "By Default"

IDEs are great. However, they can interfere with your TDD habits. Sometimes they will not let you see a failing test, by auto-generating the required functionality. Let us have a look at an example. Suppose you start writing a test, as shown in Listing 4.18.

This might not be the best possible test, but it is good enough to illustrate the case in point. When writing it, your IDE will probably suggest auto-generating an empty implementation of the required methods in order to make the test compile.

Listing 4.18. A simple getter/setter test

```
Client client = new Client(); ❶
client.setAge(20); ❷
assert(client.getAge(), 20) ❸
```

❶   First the IDE will suggest creating a client class with a default constructor – and this is good!

❷❸   When it comes to the `setAge()` and `getAge()` methods, IntelliJ IDEA will offer two options: to create a method, or create a getter/setter.

If you choose the second option – generating getters and setters – IntelliJ IDEA will generate the following code:

Listing 4.19. Code autogenerated by IDE

```java
public class Client {
    private int age;

    public void setAge(int age) {
        this.age = age;
    }

    public int getAge() {
        return age;
    }
}
```

Now, if you run the test, you will see it pass. Ups… seems like we have just skipped the first step of TDD! This code will not only compile, but pass the first test, so you have no chance to see the failing test!

In the case of such trivial code, I would suggest dropping your TDD habits for a minute and believing that IDE is capable of doing things correctly. However, there is one thing that we **have to do**. If the test fails, we will be 100% sure it was executed. But if all we see is a green color, then we have to be certain about whether it was executed at all. In cases of larger test suits it might be easy to overlook a test that was not run. So at least **make sure your was test actually executed**.

Unfortunately, there are some subtler cases, where extra care is required. Remember the tests of the `compareTo()` method that we created for the `FootballTeam` class (see Section 4.5.6)? The default return value which the IDE put into the `compareTo()` method was 0. Given that, if we were to compare two football teams with equal numbers of wins, such a test would pass instantly. The code of the `compareTo()` method is much more complicated than the getters/setters discussed previously, and I would not recommend taking it for granted that "everything is just fine". Instead, I would suggest the following: **break the code so you see the test fail**.

In our case, that would mean changing 0 to some other value, like this:

Listing 4.20. Breaking the code on purpose

```
public int compareTo(FootballTeam otherTeam) {
    if (gamesWon > otherTeam.getGamesWon()) {
        return 1;
    }
    else if (gamesWon < otherTeam.getGamesWon()) {
        return -1;
    }
    return 18723;
}
```

Now rerun the test, and see it fails Good. Revert the change of compareTo() method (so it returns 0 again). Rerun the test to see it pass. Good. This means that your test really verifies this behaviour. And that is exactly what we wanted to know.

 I know this advice might sound extreme, but this is the only way to make sure you do not make any silly mistakes at all when writing tests.

4.10. Exercises

You have just got acquainted with a new development method, which promotes writing tests before actual implementation. It is time to see, in practice, what you have learned. The exercises in this section are not so hard from the point of view of the complexity of the tasks. The point is to focus on the TDD rhythm and not on the algorythmic gotchas. When doing your homework, be extra careful about following the TDD, and doing everything in really small steps. Good luck!

 When working on these exercises, remember to obey the *"never write code unless you have a failing test"* rule!

4.10.1. Password Validator

When creating an account, it is often required that the password should fulfil some strength requirements. It should be X characters long, have at least Y digits, contain underscore, hash, and a mixture of lower and capital letters, etc. Your task is to write a method that will validate a given password. The set of rules (requirements) with which you will be verifying the passwords is up to you.

4.10.2. Regex

> If you have a problem, which can be solved with regular expression, then you have two problems.
>
> — Wisdom of the Internet ;)

This example requires you to write a method which, given a `String`, returns a list of all numbers which have more than 3 digits. Table 4.1 gives some examples of expected results for various input strings.

Table 4.1. Expected outputs of regex method

input	output
abc 12	
cdefg 345 12bb23	345

input	output
cdefg 345 12bbb33 678tt	345, 678

4.10.3. Booking System

Your task is to write a (very) simplified version of a booking system. In fact, it can be written as a single class, which should:

- return a list of booked hours,

- not allow a particular hour to be double-booked,

- deal in a sensible manner with illegal values (provided as input parameters).

On the constraints side (to make the task more appropriate for practicing TDD), the system:

- has only one resource that can be booked (e.g. a classroom, a lawn mower, a restaurant table, or anything else that makes sense to you),

- has no notion of days, or to put it differently, it assumes all reservations are for today,

- should only permit booking of regular whole clock-hours (e.g. it should not allow a booking from 4:30 pm. to 5:30 pm.),

- is not required to remember any additional information concerning the reservation (who booked it, when etc.).

Chapter 5. Mocks, Stubs, Test Spies

No man is an island.

— John Donne *Devotions upon Emergent Occasions (1624)*

Classes are like people: only some of them thrive living in solitude. In the previous part of the book we took on board the very unrealistic assumption that the classes we test have a life of their own. It is time to get more real and dive into the troubled waters of relationships. As you will see, this has a serious impact on the testing techniques we will use.

Things are going to get interesting from now on. Pessimists will probably complain about things getting much harder, while optimists will be thrilled at the prospect of new, exciting challenges. Whichever one you are, read carefully, question what you learn, and practise a lot, because this is where the real challenges of unit testing begin.

Section 2.2 showed various types of interaction between an SUT and DOCs. We have already discussed how to deal with direct inputs and outputs. In this section we will be learning about ways to deal with the remaining SUT-DOCs interactions. We will do this by introducing **test doubles**, which will help us in many ways.

In general, test doubles are used to replace DOCs, where this allows us to:

- gain full control over the environment in which the SUT is running,

- move beyond state testing and verify interactions between the SUT and its DOCs.

Before we encounter the test doubles, we must learn about a tool which will greatly facilitate our task: it is time to meet **Mockito**. We will not spend too much time on theory right now – only introduce it briefly. Later, we will discover more about Mockito by watching it in action – it will be used in every example in this chapter. Anyway, some preliminary knowledge is required, so let us begin.

5.1. Introducing Mockito

Let me start by remarking that there are, at the very least, several good tools which could help us create and use test doubles in our test code. The choice is not an easy one, as they all have slightly different characteristics, which make them more suitable for different, specific scenarios. Moreover, some JVM languages - e.g. Groovy[1] - come with some mocking capabilities built into the language itself, which further widens the field of choice. But because we are using Java, and because this is the beginning of our journey into the world of test doubles, Mockito seems like the best option.

Mockito is a relatively new framework[2]. It was originally based on EasyMock, a very successful and popular mocking framework. Mockito differs from its predecessor by promoting the use of test-spies over mocks, offering much cleaner API and very readable error messages. Thanks to the fact that it focuses on test-spies, it allows you to retain the natural test code order - arrange, act and assert - which you are already familiar with[3]. Its use is very intuitive – the learning curve is rather flat – but, at the same time, Mockito can serve you for a long time, as it is perfectly appropriate, even for complicated scenarios.

Fortunately, the syntax of Mockito is very simple to understand, so we can avoid lengthy explanations and simply enjoy its readability. Later on we will be learning more about it, but right now let us look at, and briefly explain, some code snippets.

 As was the case with TestNG, this chapter introduces Mockito, but does not aim at being a complete reference source for this framework. Please consult the original documentation of Mockito to learn about all of its features.

5.1.1. Creating Test Doubles

You can think about a test double just as you would about a normal Java object. Its uniqueness results from the fact that it pretends to be something else: i.e. an object of some specific type[4]. The point is that you will have much more control over this imposter than you would over an object of the original class. This is why test doubles are so very useful in tests.

Listing 5.1 shows a very simple interface, which we will be using for the rest of this section.

---

[1]See http://docs.codehaus.org/display/GROOVY/Groovy+Mocks
[2]Tools like Mockito are commonly called *'mock frameworks'*. This term is slightly misleading, because Mockito is really a test-spy framework. However, you will hear it used a lot, so you had better get used to this flawed way of referring to it.
[3]Other mock-focused frameworks use a slightly different order, which is less friendly, especially if you are a beginner.
[4]I use the term `type` to denote both classes and interfaces.

Listing 5.1. Car interface

```
public interface Car {

    boolean needsFuel();

    double getEngineTemperature();

    void driveTo(String destination);
}
```

Let us imagine that our SUT uses a DOC of type `Car`, and that, for the purpose of our tests, we need to fully control the behaviour of this DOC. Obviously, to be able to use a test double we must first create it (as mentioned earlier, test doubles are normal Java objects, after all). However, we do not use the `new` keyword to bring them to life. Instead, we ask Mockito, or another specialized framework, to create them. This is shown in Listing 5.2.

Listing 5.2. Creation of a test double

```
Car myFerrari = Mockito.mock(Car.class);
```

This code uses the `org.mockito.Mockito` class to create a test double. The static `mock()` method takes a `class` as an argument, and returns an object of this class. In the listing above, an object of the `Car` type is created. Mockito allows us to create test doubles of both classes and interfaces. If you were to try checking the type of object created, by means of the `instanceOf` operator, you would learn that this is a legal instance of the type `Car`. Listing 5.3 demonstrates this.

 I will be using tests to demonstrate the various capabilities of Mockito.

Listing 5.3. myFerrari is of type Car

```
import org.testng.annotations.Test; ❶

import static org.mockito.Mockito.*; ❷
import static org.testng.Assert.assertTrue; ❸

@Test ❹
public class FirstMockitoTest {

    private Car myFerrari = mock(Car.class); ❺

    public void testIfCarIsACar() {
        assertTrue(myFerrari instanceof Car); ❻
    }
}
```

❶❹   It is a normal test using TestNG `@Test` annotation.
❷❺   The static import of the `Mockito` class makes the code more concise.
❸   Normal TestNG assertions are used within the test code.
❻   As this test proves, the test-double object (`myFerrari`) is an instance of the type `Car`.

 I will omit static imports of the `org.mockito.Mockito` class in the consecutive listings to make them shorter. However, do bear in mind that they are really all the time there.

Mockito uses the same method - `mock()` - to create all types of test double. No distinction between them is made at the time of their being created. The `myFerrari` object shown in Listing 5.2 can become a dummy, stub or test spy (we will discuss all of these in the next section). You, as a programmer, decide which role it plays, by expressing its expected behaviour and verifying (or not verifying) its actions.

The point of having a test double is to tell it what it should do. Now, if you were to use the `myFerrari` object, you would discover that it actually can do something without any intervention from your side. In particular, it is able to return some canned (default) values when we call its methods. Listing 5.4 demonstrates this[5].

---

[5]For complete information concerning default returned values please refer to Mockito's Javadocs of `org.mockito.internal.stubbing.defaultanswers` package.

Listing 5.4. myFerrari returns default values

```
public class MockitoDefaultValuesTest {

    private Car myFerrari = mock(Car.class);

    @Test
    public void testDefaultBehaviourOfTestDouble() {
        assertFalse(myFerrari.needsFuel(),
            "new test double should by default return false as boolean");
        assertEquals(myFerrari.getEngineTemperature(), 0.0,
            "new test double should by default return 0.0 as double");
    }
}
```

This feature – the returning of some default values by test doubles - is specific to Mockito. In fact, this is just a manifestation of a certain deeper philosophy underlying this tool. Test doubles created by Mockito are considered to be *'nice'*, which means their behaviour is not strictly verified (by default). When using Mockito, you must explicitly ask it to verify interactions. This has some deeper implications, discussion of which lies outside the scope of this book.

 Other popular tools - i.e. EasyMock and JMock - take the opposite approach by using *'strict'* test doubles by default. This difference between Mockito and the rest of the world is a source of endless, heated, but at the same time very interesting and informative debate. Please refer to Appendix C, *Test Spy vs. Mock* for some information on this topic.

5.1.2. Expectations

Of course, an object which can only return zeros and falseys is not much use to our tests. It is time to teach our myFerrari object to do as we say.

Let us say we need our myFerrari test double to return true when asked if it needs some fuel. Listing 5.5 shows how this can be done.

Listing 5.5. myFerrari returns what we want it to return

```
public class MockitoReturningDesiredValuesTest {

    private Car myFerrari = mock(Car.class);

    @Test
    public void testStubbing() {
        assertFalse(myFerrari.needsFuel(), ❶
            "new test double should return false as boolean");

        when(myFerrari.needsFuel()).thenReturn(true); ❷

        assertTrue(myFerrari.needsFuel(), ❸
            "after instructed test double should return what we want");
    }
}
```

❶   This is what we already know - the default return value for the Boolean is `false`.
❷   Now we tell `myFerrari` what to do when asked about the fuel. The `when()` method is another static method of the `org.mockito.Mockito` class.
❸   The behaviour has changed. This time `myFerrari` has returned `true`. All consecutive executions of `needsFuel()` will also return `true`.

Listing 5.5 also illustrates a very nice feature of Mockito: the fact that code written using it is very readable. The crucial fragment:

```
when(myFerrari.needsFuel()).thenReturn(true)
```

can be read "just like that". Let us try it: *"when someone asks* `myFerrari` *if it* `needsFuel()` *then it should return* `true`*"*. Voila!

Using a similar syntax, we can also instruct test doubles to throw exceptions. This is shown in Listing 5.6.

 This feature of mocking frameworks - throwing exceptions on demand - is extremely useful for simulating all kinds of errors that can happen during the execution of your application. It is especially important when testing possible scenarios involving cooperation with some third-party components - e.g. databases or web services.

Listing 5.6. myFerrari throws an exception

```
public class MockitoThrowingDesiredExceptionsTest {

    private Car myFerrari = mock(Car.class);

    @Test(expectedExceptions = RuntimeException.class) ❶
    public void throwException() {
        when(myFerrari.needsFuel()).thenThrow(new RuntimeException()); ❷
        myFerrari.needsFuel(); ❸
    }
}
```

❶❸   The test passes, because myFerrari throws the expected exception as instructed.

❷   Expectations set.

This test also passes, as myFerrari obediently throws an exception when its needsFuel() method is executed.

 You need to use a different syntax when setting expectations on void methods. This is discussed in Section 6.4.

5.1.3. Verification

Now we know that using Mockito, we can tell our test double to return some values that are required by our tests. This is great, and we will be making use of this knowledge very soon. However, for testing purposes we need something more. We want to make sure that the SUT has executed certain methods of the DOCs (represented by test doubles). To do this we need to also verify whether some methods of test doubles have been called. Or, to put it differently, we want to verify the indirect outputs of the SUT.

 Watch out now, because this is the moment we enter the world of interactions testing for real! Up till now, our tests have only mentioned other collaborators. Expectations could be construed along the lines of *"if a certain call to the collaborator happens, then this collaborator should do X or Y"*. Now things are different. We are starting to demand that certain methods of collaborators are executed. This makes our tests very much linked to the production code, which in turn spells trouble, as it makes them fragile - **if the implementation of the SUT changes, our tests will need to be rewritten**. The rule of thumb to follow here is: **write an interactions test only if some of the SUT's features cannot be tested using state testing**.

The first example, shown in Listing 5.7, presents a successful attempt at verification of a test double's behaviour. First it invokes some of the methods of `myFerrari`, then it verifies whether they have been called. A different, static method of the `org.mockito.Mockito` class, called `verify()`, is used to check the behaviour of `myFerrari`. The test in Listing 5.7 passes, because the requested methods have really been invoked.

Listing 5.7. Expectations met, verification passed

```
public class MockitoVerificationTest {

    private Car myFerrari = mock(Car.class);

    @Test
    public void testVerification() {
        myFerrari.driveTo("Sweet home Alabama"); ❶
        myFerrari.needsFuel(); ❷

        verify(myFerrari).driveTo("Sweet home Alabama"); ❸
        verify(myFerrari).needsFuel(); ❹
    }
}
```

❶❷ Calling the methods of the test double. Nothing fancy here: no Mockito syntax of any sort, simply normal method calls

❸❹ The verification part. Checking has occurred of whether `myFerrari` has really been asked to drive to Alabama, and whether someone has requested it to answer a *"Do you need fuel?"* question.

Once again the code is quite readable: *"`verify()` that `myFerrari` was asked to `drive()` to Alabama"*.

Now let us take a look at another example. This time the expectations are not met. The test is shown in Listing 5.8.

Listing 5.8. Different methods executed than expected

```
public class MockitoFailedVerificationTest {

    private Car myFerrari = mock(Car.class);

    @Test
    public void testVerificationFailure() {
        myFerrari.needsFuel(); ❶

        verify(myFerrari).getEngineTemperature(); ❷
    }
}
```

❶   The `needsFuel()` method of a test double of type `Car` was called,

❷   …but invocation of `getEngineTemperature()` is what had been expected! This cannot possibly work and will surely fail.

…and fail it does, as displayed below.

Listing 5.9. The output of a failed verification test

```
Wanted but not invoked:
car.getEngineTemperature(); ❶
-> at com.practicalunittesting.FailedVerificationTest
            .testVerificationFailure(FailedVerificationTest.java:22)

However, there were other interactions with this mock: ❷
-> at com.practicalunittesting.FailedVerificationTest
            .testVerificationFailure(FailedVerificationTest.java:21)
```

❶   the `getEngineTemperature()` method had been expected, but did not occur. Hence the failure.

❷   Mockito informs us, that some other methods of `myFerrari` were invoked. This might be a good debugging hint.

The error message is quite clear. Mockito also provides detailed information on code lines, so finding the problem is rather simple.

The next listing - Listing 5.10 - presents another situation where expectations are not fulfilled. It illustrates the fact that Mockito not only can verify methods which have been invoked, but is also sensitive to the parameters passed.

Listing 5.10. Method invoked with different parameters than expected

```
public class MockitoFailedVerificationArgumentsTest {

    private Car myFerrari = mock(Car.class);

    @Test
    public void testVerificationFailureArguments() {
        myFerrari.driveTo("Sweet home Alabama");  ❶
        verify(myFerrari).driveTo("Sweet home Honolulu");  ❷
    }
}
```

❶   `myFerrari` headed towards Alabama
❷   …but we wanted to get to Honolulu!

Once again the error message is very clear.

Listing 5.11. The output of failed verification test - arguments do not match

```
Argument(s) are different! Wanted:
car.driveTo("Sweet home Honolulu");
-> at com.practicalunittesting.FailedVerificationArgumentsTest
    .testVerificationFailureArguments(FailedVerificationArgumentsTest.java:22)
Actual invocation has different arguments:
car.driveTo("Sweet home Alabama");
-> at com.practicalunittesting.FailedVerificationArgumentsTest
    .testVerificationFailureArguments(FailedVerificationArgumentsTest.java:21)
```

 Readable error messages are one of the selling points of Mockito. This feature is really important!

5.1.4. Conclusions

So far we have looked at a bit of Mockito, and we know that it can help us to write tests with test doubles. In particular, Mockito can:

- create various test doubles (e.g. `Car myFerrari = Mockito.mock(Car.class)`),

  - …which   by   default   return   some   canned   values   (e.g. `assertFalse(myFerrari.needsFuel())`),

- tell them how they should behave (e.g.
  `when(myFerrari.needsFuel()).thenReturn(true)` or
  `when(myFerrari.needsFuel()).thenThrow(new RuntimeException())`),

- verify that some of their methods have been called (e.g.
  `verify(myFerrari).needsFuel()`).

 For the sake of a more complete picture, we should mention here that Mockito also has some limitations. In particular, it will not help you when working with code which does not adhere to certain design standards (in particular, Mockito works well with loosely coupled code). This will be further discussed in Section 7.5.

5.2. Types of Test Double

Now that we know the basics of Mockito, we can move on to the real topic of this chapter. It is time to learn more about test doubles and start using them for some testing.

The point of unit tests is to verify the correctness of our own code. What we want is to shield a particular piece of code from distractions introduced by web services, a file system, other modules, databases or third-party software, and then check if it works as expected. In order to achieve such a state, strict control over the SUT's collaborators must be achieved. In this way it will be possible to **test the SUT in isolation**, which is an important characteristic of unit tests (see Section 2.1). Right now we are going to take a look at the various types of testing objects that can be used to replace the real collaborators of a class.

All such objects are grouped under just the one umbrella term – namely, **test doubles**. We will encounter four types of such objects. They are briefly described in Table 5.1. Do not worry if the descriptions sound a little bit cryptic. Everything will be clear once we have discussed each test-double type alongside some sample code.

Table 5.1. Types of test doubles

test-double type	also known as	description
dummy object	dummy	needs to exist, no real collaboration needed
test stub	stub	used for passing some values to the SUT ("indirect inputs")

test-double type	also known as	description
test spy	spy	used to verify if the SUT calls specific methods
mock object	mock	of the collaborator ("indirect outputs")

Figure 5.1 shows how test stubs, test spies and mocks cover a different aspect of communication between the test class, the SUT and its DOCs.

Figure 5.1. Test doubles covering inputs and outputs

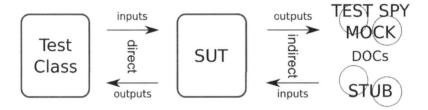

Based on this data, we may arrive at the following observations:

- **Dummies** and **stubs** are used to **prepare the environment for testing**. They are not used for verification. A dummy is employed to be passed as a value (e.g. as a parameter of a direct method call), while a stub passes some data to the SUT, substituting for one of its DOCs.

- The purpose of **test spies** and **mocks** is to **verify the correctness of the communication between the SUT and DOCs**. Yet they differ in how they are used in test code, and that is why they have distinct names[6]. Both can also participate in test-fixture setting; however, this is only their secondary purpose.

- No test double is used for direct outputs of the SUT, as it can be tested directly by observing its responses.

Let us mention, here, that even though in theory all test doubles have well defined roles and responsibilities, this is not the case in real-life programming. You will often encounter, and probably even yourself write, test code in which a test double plays more than one role. Typically, this happens with test spies and mocks, which are also frequently used in order to provide indirect inputs to the SUT, thus also playing the role of stub.

---

[6]Please refer to Appendix C, *Test Spy vs. Mock* for a detailed comparison of test spy and mock.

Fake

For the sake of completeness, let us describe another type of test double: a **fake**. Fake works almost as good as the real collaborator, but is somehow simpler and/or weaker (which makes it not suitable for production use). It is also usually "cheaper" in use (i.e. faster or simpler to set up), which makes it suited to tests (which should run as fast as possible). A typical example is an in-memory database that is used instead of a full-blown database server. It can be used for some tests, as it serves SQL requests pretty well; however, you would not want to use it in a production environment. In tests, fake plays a similar role to dummy and stub: it is a part of the environment (test fixture), not an object of verification. Fakes are used in **integration tests** rather than in unit tests, so we will not be discussing them any further.

5.2.1. Code To Be Tested with Test Doubles

Now that we know what types of test double there are, we can start using them. First, let us discuss a few lines of code, which will be used to demonstrate the role of test doubles in testing.

The code in Listing 5.12 is responsible for the sending of messages. It retrieves some data (i.e. the `email` of a client) from the parameters of `sendMessage()` method, then it tells its collaborators to perform certain actions. The code is trivial, yet quite close to reality (the real one would probably do some arguments checking and exception handling - we will skip both for the sake of simplicity).

The idea is to present the usefulness of each test double using some realistic example. Testing such a class with unit tests is almost never enough: you should also have some higher-level (i.e. integration) tests. However, that lies beyond the scope of this book. The issue is discussed further in Section 5.3.

Listing 5.12. Class to be tested with test doubles

```
public class Messenger {

    private TemplateEngine templateEngine;
    private MailServer mailServer;

    public Messenger(MailServer mailServer,
            TemplateEngine templateEngine) { ❶
        this.mailServer = mailServer;
        this.templateEngine = templateEngine;
    }

    public void sendMessage(Client client, Template template) { ❷
        String msgContent =
            templateEngine.prepareMessage(template, client);   ❸
        mailServer.send(client.getEmail(), msgContent);  ❹
    }
}
```

❶   All collaborators injected using constructor.

❷   This method returns `void`, and does not change the state of the `Messenger` object, which means there is no way we can test it using the state-testing approach.

❸❹   This is what we are really interested in: the cooperation between the `Messenger` and its collaborators. Our SUT invokes some methods on each of its collaborators and also retrieves some data from the `client` parameter of the `sendMessage()` method.

This code illustrates pretty well our previous discussion about OO systems. The `Messenger` class takes care of transforming and passing messages rather than doing any real work. `mailServer`, a collaborator of our class, is expected to perform the real work, but it probably also passes the message to some third-party library. According to the previous discussion, our class is a **manager**, as it tells others what to do rather than getting its own hands dirty.

Figure 5.2. Interactions of Messenger with the test class and DOCs

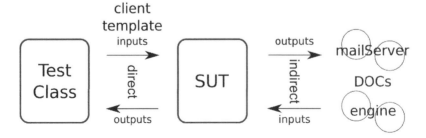

As shown in Figure 5.2 collaborators interact differently with the SUT.

The testing of this `sendMessage()` method is problematic. It does not return anything, so the results of its work cannot be directly observed. It does not even change the state of the `client` or `template` object, so we cannot use these for verification. What we could do is use it to implement a real template processing engine and to set up a real mail server. We could also use a real mail client to verify the delivery of an e-mail. Such a thing is possible, but it takes us far away from unit tests, into the realm of integration tests. Such an integration test would require a great deal more preparation (a test fixture), and would run more slowly. In cases of failure, it would also be much harder to decide where the bug is – in the SUT, in collaborators' code, or maybe in the database storage implementation.

Right now our goal is to **test this class in isolation**, so we need to think about something other than integration tests. If only we could verify the interactions of the SUT and DOCs… Then we could make sure that it works as expected. Well, thanks to test doubles this is possible. Using them, we can:

- fully control the context of the working of the SUT,

- eavesdrop on communication between the SUT and DOCs.

We will start with the simplest one - the **dummy** - and then proceed with the more interesting test doubles - the **stub**, **test spy** and **mock**. Eventually we will see how they all play together and form a valid test case. Our goal is not really to test the class in question, but rather to understand how each of the test doubles can help us in testing.

 ## What should be unit-tested?

When discussing unit tests that verify behaviour it is quite important to grasp what it is that is supposed to be verified. As regards the `Messenger` class, we can verify only one thing: whether the `send()` method of `mailServer` is invoked with the same argument value as that provided by the `client` parameter and by the `templateEngine` collaborator. Why only this? Because that is the whole logic of the tested class! As discussed previously, our SUT is a "manager" – it coordinates the work of others, doing very little by itself. And with a unit test, the only thing we can test is this coordination part.

5.2.2. The Dummy Object

Take a look at the `template` parameter of the `sendMessage()` method presented in Listing 5.12. It is used only as an input parameter to another method - `templateEngine.prepareMessage()`. This is where a **dummy** can be used.

We are already familiar with the static `mock()` method of the `org.mockito.Mockito` class (see Section 5.1.1). It takes a `Class` as an argument and returns an object of this class - in this case of the `Template` type. Now we can use the `template` object in our tests: it is a perfect replacement for a real `Template` object.

Listing 5.13. Using a test double as a dummy object

```
Template template = mock(Template.class); ❶

sut.sendMessage(client, template); ❷
```

❶   Creation of a dummy object. We assign a real object to it, generated using the `mock()` method.
❷   Execution of the SUT's method using a dummy `template` object as one of the parameters.

To sum up, a **dummy object** is required just to execute the test, but not really needed for anything useful. It simply has "to be there". In some cases `null` will suffice, but in general it would be more far-sighted to use a mocking framework to generate an object of the requested type.

You probably will not use **dummies** a lot. In my experience they are rarely required.

 Maybe you have already noticed that it is enough to pass a `null` value as a `template` parameter. That would work, but in general it is not recommended. It is probable that the method being tested will sooner or later be extended with some arguments checking functionality, so `null` values will not be accepted. Then your test will break, which is always frustrating. Instead of using this short-term solution, I would suggest using a non-null value from the very beginning.

5.2.3. Test Stub

Now let us take a look at the `templateEngine` collaborator. This object is used to provide some value (the content of an email), so that, later on, `mailServer` will be able to send an email. The **stub** is meant for exactly this kind of collaboration: it allows us to take care of the "indirect inputs" of a class, by providing some values to the SUT.

In the case of the dummy we only have to create it. Its methods are not invoked at all, or the result of calling them is of no importance. With a stub, we also need to instruct it about what values to return when its methods are invoked. Listing 5.14 illustrates how we can create a stub and give orders to it. It uses Mockito's `when()` method, which we are already familiar with (see Section 5.1.2).

 An inquisitive reader may notice that Mockito also offers a `stub()` method, which at first glance may seem more appropriate. However, a glance at Mockito Javadocs will show that the `stub()` method is deprecated, and that the `when()` method should be used instead.

Listing 5.14. Use of a test stub

```
TemplateEngine templateEngine = mock(TemplateEngine.class); ❶

Messenger sut = new Messenger(mailServer, templateEngine); ❷

when(templateEngine.prepareMessage(template, client)) ❸
    .thenReturn(MSG_CONTENT);

sut.sendMessage(client, template); ❹
```

❶ Stub creation - as usual, via the `mock()` method.
❷ The `templateEngine` test stub is injected into SUT, so it can be used.
❸ Describing behaviour which the `templateEngine` test double should perform using the `when()` method.
❹ The execution of the SUT's method will result in the SUT calling the `prepareMessage()` method of our stub.

This is exactly what we discussed in Section 5.1.2. We create a stub, and then we give it the following order: *"Whenever someone asks you to return a value for the `12345L` parameter, please return the value `some@email.com`"*. Mockito will make sure that the stub will do what we want it to. Hip, hip, hurray! We have just gained control over the indirect input of our class. Now we can write tests which pass any value from `templateEngine` to the SUT.

Test stubs are often used to simulate exceptions thrown by collaborators. [meszaros2007] introduces a distinct name for such an exception-oriented test double - a **saboteur**. I have not noticed this name gaining any popularity among developers and testers, so I will only use the term test stub.

5.2.4. Test Spy

The only thing we still lack, now, is an extension of our control so that it will also take in **indirect outputs**. This means we do not yet know how to control messages sent by the SUT to its collaborators. Both **mocks** and **test spies** can help us with this task. We shall take a look at test spy first.

Let us discuss our sample code (Listing 5.12) some more. The only indirect output of the SUT is its communication with the `send()` method of `mailServer`. This is something we can verify using test spy. Listing 5.15 shows how it can be done using Mockito's `verify()` method, exactly as discussed in Section 5.1.3.

Listing 5.15. Taking control over indirect inputs

```
MailServer mailServer = mock(MailServer.class); ❶

Messenger sut = new Messenger(mailServer, templateEngine); ❷

sut.sendMessage(client, template); ❸

verify(mailServer).send("some@email.com", msgContent); ❹
```

❶   Creation of a test spy using the `mock()` method.
❷   The `mailServer` test spy is injected into SUT, so it can be used.
❸   Execution of the SUT's `sendMessage()` method.
❹   Verification of what happened during the execution of the SUT's `sendMessage()` method. Has the SUT really invoked the `send()` method of `mailServer` with given parameters? Once again the code which does the verification is really easy to read: *"verify that the `send()` method of `mailServer` was invoked with given email and message content"*.

In the case of our example we can use the **test spy** to actually verify the actions of the SUT. This is where real testing takes place: we check whether the SUT is behaving as we expect it to.

5.2.5. Mock

I feel I should say at least something about **mocks**, even though we do not really need them. Let me repeat that in functional terms, there is little difference between a mock and a test spy. What a test spy can do, a mock can also do (and vice versa). The difference lies in the syntax and in the flow of code within your test methods. The main purpose of the mock and the test spy are the same: to verify that some communication between objects has taken place: i.e. that some methods have been called. I have decided to devote Appendix C, *Test Spy vs. Mock* to a detailed discussion of the differences between test spies and mocks. But this is not something you need to know about. If you have grasped the idea of test spies, you can write perfect tests without knowing about mocks.

 Do not worry that we haven't really covered mocks! You can still put in your CV that you know how to mock classes. This is because mocking is about verifying the collaboration between the SUT and DOCs, and you are perfectly capable of doing this.

As regards our example, we could use a mock to cover exactly the same area that we decided to use a test spy for: to verify the expected behaviour of the SUT.

5.3. Putting it All Together

Once again, we go back to the code presented on Listing 5.12. In the previous sections we have been discussing the role of each test double – dummy, stub, test spy and mock – in testing this code. Now it is time to show them working together. But before the code is shown, a few words of warning.

It is very good that we are able to test such code using unit tests. It is really great, that we know how to isolate the SUT from the environment, how to control its direct and indirect inputs and outputs. It is perfect, that we have learned the difference between stubs, test spies, dummies and mocks. We will – well, you will – make use of this knowledge many, many times, and it will make you a better developer - I am quite sure of this. However, the decision about what should be tested on which level (with which type of test) is not an easy one. In fact, it requires one thing: experience. And the problem is that this can only be gained through blood, sweat and tears.

If I were to test the example shown in Listing 5.12, I would opt for a mixture of unit and integration tests. I would certainly use unit tests - in a manner that will be shown in a minute - to check for all the strange things that can happen, and which are hard to trigger when using real components. So, for example, I would make `clientDAO` return all kinds of unexpected result - e.g. throw an exception of the `NoSuchUserInDatabase` kind, and the like. Unit tests in conjunction with test doubles are just perfect for this kind of verification.

In parallel, I would use integration tests to see that my code really results in e-mails being sent. This means that I would:

- prepare an e-mail template and implement the `TemplateEngine` class, so that it really could then prepare a nice e-mail message,

- implement the `MailServer` class, so the e-mails really would be sent.

And only then, thanks to having written a few unit and integration tests, would I be able to sleep peacefully in my bed, resting assured that everything is fine with my code.

Having said that, let us now turn to a good example of a unit test, which is shown below. This will demonstrate our ability to write unit tests for such code. It proves that we know how to use the test doubles. But let us bear in mind that this is only a single test, chosen from many other tests - unit, integration and end-to-end - which would have to be written to fully cover the functionality considered here.

Listing 5.16. MessengerTest

```
public class MessengerTest {

    private static final String CLIENT_EMAIL = "some@email.com"; ❶
    private static final String MSG_CONTENT = "Dear John! You are fired."; ❷

    @Test
    public void shouldSendEmail() {
        Template template = mock(Template.class); ❸
        Client client = mock(Client.class);
        MailServer mailServer = mock(MailServer.class);
        TemplateEngine templateEngine = mock(TemplateEngine.class);

        Messenger sut = new Messenger(mailServer, templateEngine); ❹

        when(client.getEmail()).thenReturn(CLIENT_EMAIL); ❺
        when(templateEngine.prepareMessage(template, client))
            .thenReturn(MSG_CONTENT); ❻

        sut.sendMessage(client, template); ❼

        verify(mailServer).send(CLIENT_EMAIL, MSG_CONTENT); ❽
    }
}
```

❶❷ Some static value to be used within the test code.

❸ Creation of test doubles using static `mock()` method. At this point they do not differ from each other (except for the type they are pretending to be).

❹ Creation of the SUT. No `mock()` method here, we want to test the real one! Dependency injection of DOCs into the SUT.

❺❻ Stubbing of DOCs in order to satisfy the SUT (have a look at the `Messenger` class to understand what is required of each DOC).

❼ Execution of the SUT method.

❽ Verification of the behaviour of the SUT: *"was the `send()` method invoked on `mailServer` DOC with the same `CLIENT_EMAIL` and `MSG_CONTENT` that were obtained from other collaborators?"*.

5.4. Example: TDD with Test Doubles

Let us now discuss an example which integrates two techniques we have already learned: TDD and test doubles.

This example shows how we can test and implement a service whose role is to inform interested parties about the results of races. The idea of the implementation is pretty obvious. There is a notification service, which allows clients to subscribe. The service should send out messages to all of its subscribers. And, basically, that is it.

In general, it is a good thing to avoid tight coupling between components of the system. In line with this rule, we want to make sure that the subscribers know as little as possible about the service, and vice versa. To achieve this result, we can use a publish/subscribe design pattern[7] which does exactly this: it decouples publisher(s) from subscribers.

First, let us discuss some requirements for our class - `RaceResultsService`:

- It should allow clients to subscribe (which means they start receiving messages),

- It should allow subscribers to unsubscribe (which means they stop receiving messages),

- Every time a new message comes, it should be sent to all subscribers.

These simple requirements, along with some common sense, already furnish us with a lot of test cases. In the ensuing sections we will be implementing the following:

- If the client is not subscribed, it should not receive any messages,

- If client is subscribed, it should receive each incoming message once (and only once),

- If multiple clients are subscribed, each of them should receive each incoming message,

- Consecutive subscribe requests issued by the same client will be ignored (nothing happens),

- If the client unsubscribes, then it should be the case that no more messages are sent to it.

We shall test `RaceResultsService` (the SUT) and make sure it sends messages to the right subscribers (DOCs). At first glance, it seems like we must have at least three types to implement the discussed functionality. First of all, we have to have an object of class `RaceResultService` (our SUT). Then, we must create a `Client` type which can subscribe, unsubscribe and receive messages (objects of this type will play the role of DOCs). We

---

[7]See http://en.wikipedia.org/wiki/Publish/subscribe.

will also need a `Message` type, which will be being passed from the race results service to subscribed clients.

We will follow the TDD approach to implementing this functionality. Along the way we will also learn a thing or two about Mockito.

5.4.1. First Test: Single Subscriber Receives Message

The first test is meant to verify whether, if a single client has subscribed to the `RaceResultsService`, it receives messages.

This test also plays another important role, as writing it helps us to set everything in its proper place. Before we do any real testing, writing some test code will allow us to come up with the basic structure of `RaceResultService` and the interfaces of the DOCs. In fact, it will be some time before we are actually able to test anything.

We begin our test with the creation of the SUT, as displayed below.

Listing 5.17. Creation of an SUT

```
@Test
public class RaceResultsServiceTest {

    public void subscribedClientShouldReceiveMessage() {
        RaceResultsService raceResults = new RaceResultsService();
    }
}
```

This simple test code results in the `RaceResultsService` class being (auto)generated by the IDE, as shown in Listing 5.18.

Listing 5.18. The RaceResultsService class autogenerated by IDE

```
public class RaceResultsService {
}
```

To test the functionality under consideration, we must introduce the two remaining types: `Client` and `Message`. Listing 5.19 shows this next step – creating the DOCs.

Listing 5.19. Creation of DOCs

```
@Test
public class RaceResultsServiceTest {

    public void subscribedClientShouldReceiveMessage() {
        RaceResultsService raceResults = new RaceResultsService();
        Client client = mock(Client.class); ❶
        Message message = mock(Message.class); ❷
    }
}
```

❶❷ Test doubles of `client` and `message` are both created using the `Mockito.mock()` method. At this point, their role is not yet defined - they could become dummies, stubs or test spies.

At this juncture the IDE complains that `Message` and `Client` types do not exist yet, and suggests creating both types. The question is, should they be created as interfaces or as classes? Following the basic rule of *"code to an interface, and not to a implementation"* ([gof1994]), I would choose the first option. This results in the creation of two empty interfaces – as shown in Listing 5.20.

Listing 5.20. Empty Client and Message interfaces

```
public interface Client {
}

public interface Message {
}
```

Now it is time to write the actual test. I would like it to present the following functionality:

- the client subscribes to the service,

- the service sends a message to the subscribed client.

This test is displayed in Listing 5.21.

Listing 5.21. Test: messages sent to a single subscribed client

```
@Test
public class RaceResultsServiceTest {

    public void subscribedClientShouldReceiveMessage() {
        RaceResultsService raceResults = new RaceResultsService();
        Client client = mock(Client.class);
        Message message = mock(Message.class);

        raceResults.addSubscriber(client); ❶
        raceResults.send(message); ❷

        verify(client).receive(message); ❸
    }
}
```

❶ the client subscribes to the service,
❷ the race results service sends a message (to all subscribers),
❸ verification part: making sure that the subscribed client has received the message.

 The verification part here clearly indicates that the `client` test double is a test spy. Its behaviour is verified after the execution of the tested code. Another test double - `message` object - is a dummy. Its behaviour is not verified, and the SUT does not require `message` to return any information. It is only being passed between other objects.

Once again, the code does not yet compile. Use IDE help to generate the required methods. You will end up with the following empty implementations of the `RaceResultService` and `Client` types (Listing 5.22).

Listing 5.22. Empty implementation of methods required for the first test

```
public interface Client {
    void receive(Message message);
}

public class RaceResultsService {

    public void addSubscriber(Client client) {
    }

    public void send(Message message) {
    }
}
```

The test compiles, so let us run it. The error message – as shown in Listing 5.23 - clearly indicates that the functionality does not work. The client has not received any message.

Listing 5.23. The first test has failed: the client has not received any message

```
Wanted but not invoked:
client.receive(
    Mock for Message, hashCode: 23894119
);
-> at com.practicalunittesting.RaceResultsServiceTest
    .subscribedClientShouldReceiveMessage(RaceResultsServiceTest.java:32)
Actually, there were zero interactions with this mock.
```

Very good! This means we really are into the RED phase of TDD. Following the TDD approach, let us implement "the simplest thing that works" (see Section 4.2.2) that satisfies the failing test. Listing 5.24 shows such an implementation.

Listing 5.24. The first test has passed: a single subscriber receives a message

```
public class RaceResultsService {

    private Client client;

    public void addSubscriber(Client client) {
        this.client = client;
    }

    public void send(Message message) {
        client.receive(message);
    }
}
```

Once again, even though I can imagine this code being changed, and can even suspect how it would be changed (e.g. using a collection of clients instead of a single client field), I do not make use of this knowledge. Coding it now would be an example of YAGNI. What I really need to do is make the test pass (move in small steps, remember?). And the implementation shown in Listing 5.24 achieves this goal. So, for the time being it counts as perfect and does not call for any changes.

The execution of the test assures me that this implementation will be good enough for now.

Before implementing the next test, I spend a bit of time refactoring and making the code more readable. In the case of the code written so far, there is not much to be done. The classes and interfaces are very short (no copied code fragments, etc.), and I like the current method and class names. At this point I would only suggest writing some Javadocs: namely, for the RaceResultService class, as this is the crucial part of the code (from the business point of view)[8].

5.4.2. The Second Test: Send a Message to Multiple Subscribers

The decision concerning which test to perform next comes naturally: since I know that a message has been sent to one single client, I now wish to test whether this functionality will also work for more than one subscriber. The test is shown in Listing 5.25.

---

[8]Please see the notes on writing Javadocs in Section 4.2.3

I created the second test method (`allSubscribedClientsShouldRecieveMessages()`) by copying the content of the first test method (`subscribedClientShouldReceiveMessage()`). Then I introduced some changes there. **Copy & paste** technique is potentially dangerous, so I must double-check that the test does what I intended it to do.

Listing 5.25. The second test: messages sent to multiple subscribed clients

```
@Test
public class RaceResultsServiceFirstAndSecondTest {

    public void subscribedClientShouldReceiveMessage() { ❶
        RaceResultsService raceResults = new RaceResultsService();
        Client client = mock(Client.class);
        Message message = mock(Message.class);

        raceResults.addSubscriber(client);
        raceResults.send(message);

        verify(client).receive(message);
    }

    public void messageShouldBeSentToAllSubscribedClients() { ❷
        RaceResultsService raceResults = new RaceResultsService();
        Client clientA = mock(Client.class); ❸
        Client clientB = mock(Client.class); ❹
        Message message = mock(Message.class);

        raceResults.addSubscriber(clientA);
        raceResults.addSubscriber(clientB);
        raceResults.send(message);
        verify(clientA).receive(message);
        verify(clientB).receive(message);
    }
}
```

❶ The old test (the one verifying the sending of messages to a single subscriber) is left untouched, even though it seems to be redundant. However, I am going to keep it, so I can always be sure that this functionality will work for a single subscriber.

❷ The second test verifies whether the service works for more than one subscriber.

❸❹ In order to implement the new test, I need more test doubles of the `Client` class.

As in the case of the test discussed earlier (see Listing 5.21), both client objects (`clientA` and `clientB`) are test spies, and `message` is a dummy.

After the test has been run it prints the following error (Listing 5.26).

Listing 5.26. Error - client has not received the message

```
Wanted but not invoked:
client.receive(
    Mock for Message, hashCode: 11746570
);
-> at com.practicalunittesting.RaceResultsServiceTest
    .allSubscribedClientsShouldReceiveMessages(RaceResultsServiceTest.java:39)
Actually, there were zero interactions with this mock.
```

Well, obviously the `addSubscriber()` and `send()` methods of the `RaceResultsService` class are not able to operate on more than one client. A possible fix is shown below.

Listing 5.27. The second test passed: multiple subscribers receive the message

```
public class RaceResultsService {

    private Collection<Client> clients = new ArrayList<Client>(); ❶

    public void addSubscriber(Client client) {
        clients.add(client); ❷
    }

    public void send(Message message) {
        for (Client client : clients) { ❸
            client.receive(message);
        }
    }
}
```

❶❷❸ This implementation uses a list of subscribers instead of one subscriber.

The test passes now. The main functionality – that of sending messages to subscribers – works. Good.

Refactoring

The production code looks fine, but the test code really calls out to be refactored. There is an obvious redundancy relating to the creation of the SUT and DOCs in every test method. We can expect that subsequent test methods will also require a fresh SUT and DOCs, so it seems a good idea to move this redundant code into a specialized method[9]. The result of this refactoring is shown below.

Listing 5.28. setUp() method introduced

```
@Test
public class RaceResultsServiceFirstAndSecondRefactoredTest {

    private RaceResultsService raceResults;
    private Message message;
    private Client clientA;
    private Client clientB;

    @BeforeMethod ❶
    protected void setUp() throws Exception {
        raceResults = new RaceResultsService();
        message = mock(Message.class);
        clientA = mock(Client.class);
        clientB = mock(Client.class);
    }

    public void subscribedClientShouldReceiveMessage() { ❷
        raceResults.addSubscriber(clientA);
        raceResults.send(message);

        verify(clientA).receive(message);
    }

    public void allSubscribedClientsShouldReceiveMessages() { ❸
        raceResults.addSubscriber(clientA);
        raceResults.addSubscriber(clientB);
        raceResults.send(message);

        verify(clientA).receive(message);
        verify(clientB).receive(message);
    }
}
```

---

[9]We will discuss the issues related to test fixture creation in Section 9.7.

❶ The SUT and all of the DOCs have now been created within the `setUp()` method, annotated with `@BeforeMethod` annotation.

❷❸ Both test methods are guaranteed to receive all objects (the SUT and all DOCs) in a "fresh" state, as created by the `setUp()` method.

5.4.3. The Third Test: Send Messages to Subscribers Only

The next step is to make sure that clients who are not subscribed do not receive any messages. Looking at the code written so far, I suspect the test will pass instantly; still, it needs to be tested (so that later on, if some changes are made to the code, this functionality will not be broken). The implementation of such a test method is shown in Listing 5.29.

Listing 5.29. The third test: clients not subscribed do not receive any messages

```
public void notSubscribedClientShouldNotReceiveMessage() { ❶
    raceResults.send(message);

    verify(clientA, never()).receive(message); ❷
    verify(clientB, never()).receive(message); ❸
}
```

❶ Such a test method is possible thanks to the creation of both the SUT and DOCs within the `setUp()` method (annotated using `@BeforeMethod` annotation). This way, the SUT does not remember that some clients were subscribed (as happens in other test methods), and the DOCs (`clientA` and `clientB`) do not remember receiving any messages in other methods.

❷❸ This test presents a new feature of Mockito: its ability to check that something **has not occurred**. This is done using the static `never()` method. As usual with Mockito, the code is very readable (*"verify that `clientA` has never received a message"*).

As expected, the new test passes instantly.

 The fact that the last test passed instantly should make us feel just a little uneasy. This is a warning sign. It might mean that **the test repeats what other tests**

have already verified. But in fact this is not the case here. Another possibility is that we are testing very "defensively". This means we are trying to protect ourselves from bad things which are really outside the scope of the original requirements. Testing whether the SUT **does not** make something is often questionable. In our case, there is no direct requirement that clients who are not subscribed should not receive the message; however, I find it logical to add this one, and in my opinion such a test is legitimate. But this is a subjective matter, and you might well hold a different view here.

Now I spend some time looking at the test code. I see some kind of a pattern there. The consecutive tests verify what happens when there are one, two or no clients subscribed to the SUT. I have made this pattern more visible by rearranging the order of the tests, as displayed in Listing 5.30 (for the sake of brevity, only method signatures are shown).

Listing 5.30. Refactored tests: order changed

```
@Test
public class RaceResultsServiceTestBeforeCombining {

    @BeforeMethod
    public void setUp() { .... }

    // zero subscribers
    public void notSubscribedClientShouldNotReceiveMessage() { ... }

    // one subscriber
    public void subscribedClientShouldReceiveMessage() { ... }

    // two subscribers
    public void allSubscribedClientsShouldReceiveMessages() { ... }
}
```

I like the new version better. It shows how things are progressing. Good.

5.4.4. The Fourth Test: Subscribe More Than Once

Let us now verify the behaviour of the `RaceResultsService` when subscribers subscribe more than one time. This situation is a little bit outside of the "path of normal, reasonable usage" of the SUT; however, it is possible, and should be tested.

Listing 5.31 shows a test which verifies that a subscriber who subscribes again still receives only one message (only the new test method is shown, for the sake of simplicity – the rest of the test class has not changed).

Listing 5.31. The fourth test: subscribed client subscribes again

```
@Test
public void shouldSendOnlyOneMassageToMultiSubscriber() {
    raceResults.addSubscriber(clientA);
    raceResults.addSubscriber(clientA);
    raceResults.send(message);

    verify(clientA).receive(message); ❶
}
```

❶   By default, Mockito verifies that the method has been invoked exactly once.

After running the test, it transpires that our implementation is not behaving as expected (Listing 5.32).

Listing 5.32. Error - client subscribed more than once

```
org.mockito.exceptions.verification.TooManyActualInvocations:
client.receive(
    Mock for Message, hashCode: 28652556
);
Wanted 1 time:
-> at com.practicalunittesting.RaceResultsServiceTest
    .shouldSendOnlyOneMassageToMultiSubscriber(RaceResultsServiceTest.java:59)
But was 2 times. Undesired invocation:
-> at com.practicalunittesting.RaceResultsService
    .send(RaceResultsService.java:22)
```

This can be fixed by replacing List with Set within the RaceResultsService class, as shown in Listing 5.33.

Listing 5.33. The fourth test has passed!

```
public class RaceResultsService {

    private Collection<Client> clients = new HashSet<Client>(); ❶

    public void addSubscriber(Client client) {
        clients.add(client);
    }

    public void send(Message message) {
        for (Client client : clients) {
            client.receive(message);
        }
    }
}
```

❶   A set does not allow for duplicates. The older version - which used a list - did not
     work properly.

Mockito: How Many Times?

Let us go back to Listing 5.31 for a minute, so that we can learn something new about
Mockito. This code contains a single line, which verifies whether the `receive()` method
of the client has been called. To be more precise, it makes Mockito verify whether this
method has been called exactly once.

```
verify(clientA).receive(message);
```

If you want to specify another value, you could use another static method of the `Mockito`
class: `times()`, e.g.:

```
verify(clientA, times(3)).receive(message);
```

5.4.5. The Fifth Test: Remove a Subscriber

What remains is to make sure that once a client has unsubscribed, it will not receive any
messages. Such a test can be built upon the existing tests - i.e. those tests that prove that a
subscribed client does receive messages. Its implementation is presented in Listing 5.34.

Listing 5.34. The fifth test: unsubscribed client stops receiving messages

```
@Test
public void unsubscribedClientShouldNotReceiveMessages() {
    raceResults.addSubscriber(clientA); ❶
    raceResults.removeSubscriber(clientA); ❷
    raceResults.send(message);

    verify(clientA, never()).receive(message); ❸
}
```

❶ We know that after this line of code `clientA` should start receiving messages. Our knowledge is based on other tests (i.e. `subscribedClientShouldReceiveMessage()`), which verify this behaviour.

❷ …but we want the `removeSubscriber()` method to alter this behaviour (we let IDE auto-generate this method),

❸ …so `clientA` will not receive any message. Again, this "negative" verification is done using the `never()` method.

After we let the IDE create an empty implementation of the `removeSubscriber()` method of the `RaceResultsService` class, the test will fail, as shown in Listing 5.35.

Listing 5.35. Error - unsubscribed client still receives messages

```
org.mockito.exceptions.verification.NeverWantedButInvoked:
client.receive(
    Mock for Message, hashCode: 32801378
);
Never wanted here:
-> at com.practicalunittesting.RaceResultsServiceTest
    .unsubscribedClientShouldNotReceiveMessages(RaceResultsServiceTest.java:66)
But invoked here:
-> at com.practicalunittesting.RaceResultsService
    .send(RaceResultsService.java:24)
```

Proper implementation of the `removeSubscriber()` method is shown in Listing 5.36. Now the test passes.

Listing 5.36. The fifth test has passed: client unsubscribes successfully

```
public class RaceResultsService {

    private Collection<Client> clients = new HashSet<Client>();

    public void addSubscriber(Client client) {
        clients.add(client);
    }

    public void send(Message message) {
        for (Client client : clients) {
            client.receive(message);
        }
    }

    public void removeSubscriber(Client client) {
        clients.remove(client); ❶
    }
}
```

❶   The client is removed from the subscribers list.

This functionality completes the task in hand. All of the planned tests have been written, and all of them pass. It is time to summarize what we have learned.

 There are still some tests which ought to be written, but which have been omitted (on purpose, so this book does not end up being 1000 pages long). I would, nevertheless, encourage you to implement them as a practice exercise. Some of them are listed in the exercises part of Section 5.7.

5.4.6. TDD and Test Doubles - Conclusions

The RaceResultsService example showed how to use test doubles to verify interactions between objects. Thanks to our using them - i.e. thanks to the test spies - we were able to implement the given functionality. We followed the TDD approach by coding test-first and refactoring along the way. There are some interesting points connected with the way we coded and the results of our efforts.

More Test Code than Production Code

One interesting thing was the amount of written code. We ended up with roughly twice as much test code as production code (counted with JavaNCSS[10]). With more tests written - and, as stated previously, it would be sensible to add a few additional ones - the result would be even more favourable as regards test code. This is nothing unexpected. When coding test first, and testing thoroughly, you can expect this sort of test-to-code ratio. In fact, this is rather a good sign.

The Interface is What Really Matters

An interesting fact about the code we have just written is that we did not implement any of the collaborating classes. Neither `Message` nor `Client` were implemented. This is kind of weird, considering the number of times they were used. However, we did just fine with only their interfaces.

Now, this is important! It means that you can work on `RaceResultsService` while your teammates are coding the `Message` and `Client` classes in parallel – so long as you have agreed on the interfaces and stick to them. That need not mean you should necessarily spread such simple tasks between team members, but it is worth being aware of the fact that it opens up some possibilities of doing this sort of thing. It might not be a big deal when working on simple classes like `Client` and `Message`, but it surely helps to be able to code your services and DAO layers separately (even in parallel).

Starting with an interface also brings with it another advantage: by analogy with road works, there is no danger of building two halves of a bridge that do not ultimately meet. In fact, you will have actually started out with a meeting point in place, so there can be no risk of such a situation arising.

To conclude, we have done pretty well without any implementation of DOCs (the `Client` and `Message` classes) at all. That is because at this stage all that matters is their interfaces.

Interactions Can Be Tested

The example of `RaceResultsService` has proved – once more – that verification of interactions is possible. I even hope that it has demonstrated that they are not as scary as they might seem at first glance. :)

---

[10]http://javancss.codehaus.org

In fact, we had no choice. There is nothing else we could have tested, as the `RaceResultsService` is all about interactions with other entities. There are simply no observable outputs of its activities. And remember, the `Client` class is still not implemented yet, so there is no way to verify the quality of the `RaceResultsService` implementation by looking at the behaviour of clients.

Some Test Doubles are More Useful than Others

In the case of the `RaceResultsService` tests, only two test doubles were used - a **dummy** and a **test spy**. There is nothing special about this: we have simply been using what was required, and this time there was no role that stubs could have played.

We haven't made any use of mock objects, either: because, as mentioned previously, they can be used interchangeably with test spies.

Test Dependencies are There, whether You Like It or Not

Another point to make here is that there are some test dependencies out there, even if we have not explicitly named them. For example, let us take the first test (the one which verified sending messages to a single subscriber - see Listing 5.21). Is there any point in checking the functionality of sending messages to many subscribers (the second test - see Listing 5.25) if this first test fails? Probably not, as the second one is based on the functionality tested by the first one. So, there seems to be some link between the two tests.

We will discuss this topic some more in Section 7.2, but for now, let us go no further than this simple observation.

5.5. Always Use Test Doubles… or Maybe Not?

One feature of a decent unit test is isolation (see Section 2.1). Testing in isolation allows one to find out whether the SUT behaves properly, independently of the implementation of other classes. This is an important property of unit tests, that should not be recklessly abandoned. In previous sections we have learned how to use test doubles to fully control the SUT's collaborators.

But does this mean that you should always create a test double for every collaborator of a class?

If it should turn out that using a real collaborator means involving database connections, third-party frameworks or costly computations in the conducting of unit tests, then have no choice: you must use a test double – otherwise it will not be a unit test anymore[11]. Using a real class would make your (supposed) unit test depend on too many external components – ones that could, in turn, make the test fail unexpectedly, even if your code has worked fine. This is unacceptable for unit tests.

But what if a collaborator is a very simple class with almost no logic? Is replacing it with a test double worth the effort? Let us look for an answer to this question by considering the example of two simple classes shown below.

Listing 5.37. Phone class

```java
public class Phone {
    private final boolean mobile;
    private final String number;

    public Phone(String number, boolean mobile) {
        this.number = number;
        this.mobile = mobile;
    }

    public boolean isMobile() {
        return mobile;
    }
}
```

---

[11]However, it could still be a very important, useful and necessary test. Nevertheless, it would lack some of the properties of decent unit tests: namely, short execution time and good error localization.

Listing 5.38. Client class

```java
public class Client {
    private final List<Phone> phones = new ArrayList<Phone>();

    public void addPhone(Phone phone) {
        phones.add(phone);
    }

    public boolean hasMobile() {    ❶
        for (Phone phone : phones) {
            if (phone.isMobile()) {
                return true;
            }
        }
        return false;
    }
}
```

❶   This is the method that we will be testing in the sections below.

As you can see, the Client class is tightly coupled with the Phone class. There is no interface that would shield Phone from Client.

Now let us think about how we could test the hasMobile() method of the Client class. You would need a few test cases capable of verifying the following:

- if the client has no phones, the hasMobile() method returns false,

- if the client has only stationary (i.e. landline) phones, the hasMobile() method returns false,

- if the client has one or more mobile phones (and any number of stationary phones), the hasMobile() method returns true.

For our purposes, we shall limit the number of phones to one mobile and one stationary one. This will be sufficient to be illustrative of the case in point.

5.5.1. No Test Doubles

In such a simple case you might be tempted to use the classes directly in your test code. The thing is, making Phone a mobile phone is very easy: simply pass true to its constructor. So you can create instances of the Phone class in test code, as shown in Listing 5.39.

Listing 5.39. No test doubles used

```
@Test
public class ClientTest {
    private final String ANY_NUMBER = "999-888-777";
    private final Phone MOBILE_PHONE = new Phone(ANY_NUMBER, true); ❶
    private final Phone STATIONARY_PHONE = new Phone(ANY_NUMBER, false); ❷

    private Client client;

    @BeforeMethod
    public void setUp() {
        client = new Client();}

    public void shouldReturnTrueIfClientHasMobile() { ❸
        client.addPhone(MOBILE_PHONE);
        client.addPhone(STATIONARY_PHONE);

        assertTrue(client.hasMobile());
    }

    public void shouldReturnFalseIfClientHasNoMobile() { ❹
        client.addPhone(STATIONARY_PHONE);

        assertFalse(client.hasMobile());
    }
}
```

❶❷   Real objects are created to be used by the SUT.

❸❹   Both test methods use real objects of the `Phone` class, and both rely on its correctness.

The test code shown in Listing 5.39 is clear and concise. The required DOCs are created using a `Phone` class constructor with the appropriate boolean parameter - `true` for mobiles and `false` for stationary phones.

5.5.2. Using Test Doubles

The alternative approach would be to use test doubles instead of real objects. This is shown in Listing 5.40.

Listing 5.40. Test doubles

```
@Test
public class ClientTest {
    private final static Phone MOBILE_PHONE = mock(Phone.class); ❶
    private final static Phone STATIONARY_PHONE = mock(Phone.class); ❷

    private Client client;

    @BeforeMethod
    public void setUp() {
        client = new Client();
    }

    public void shouldReturnTrueIfClientHasMobile() {
        when(MOBILE_PHONE.isMobile()).thenReturn(true); ❸

        client.addPhone(MOBILE_PHONE);
        client.addPhone(STATIONARY_PHONE);

        assertTrue(client.hasMobile());
    }

    public void shouldReturnFalseIfClientHasNoMobile() {
        client.addPhone(STATIONARY_PHONE);

        assertFalse(client.hasMobile());
    }
}
```

❶❷ Collaborators are created using Mockito's `mock()` method. The creation of DOCs is completely independent from constructor(s) of the `Phone` class.

❸ In contrast to real objects of the `Phone` class, test doubles have no idea about how to behave, so we need to instruct them. This is required for mobile phones (which should return `true`). For stationary phones, there is no need to specify a returned value, as mocks created by Mockito return `false` by default[12].

The code in Listing 5.40 does not differ much from the previously shown Listing 5.39. Constructor calls, which defined how objects of the `Phone` class should behave, were replaced with calls to Mockito's `mock()` and `when()` methods.

---

[12]See Section 5.1.1 for information concerning the default behaviour of Mockito's test doubles.

No Winner So Far

So far, so good. Both approaches seems fine. Using real classes in test code seems to be justified by the close relationship between `Client` and `Phone`. Both test classes are concise and free of any logic. Good.

5.5.3. A More Complicated Example

But let us stir things up a little bit, where this very solid construction is concerned, by introducing a small change to the `Phone` class: let us make it behave more intelligently. `Phone` constructor can recognize if a number belongs to a mobile phone, using pattern matching. Because of this change, there is no need for the constructor's second boolean parameter, as shown in Listing 5.41.

Listing 5.41. Phone class constructor enhanced

```
public Phone(String number) {
    this.number = number;
    this.mobile = number.startsWith("+") && number.endsWith("9"); ❶
}
```

❶ Do not do this at home! This is surely **not** a valid way to recognize mobile phone numbers!

After this change has been introduced, the test, which does not use mocks, needs to be updated. This time, in order to create appropriate phones (mobile and stationary), a knowledge of the internals of the `Phone` class is required. Without it there is no way a developer could construct a phone of the desired type. The test starts to look as shown in Listing 5.42.

Listing 5.42. No test doubles used - enhanced Phone class version

```
@Test
public class ClientTest {
    private final static Phone MOBILE_PHONE = new Phone("+123456789"); ❶
    private final static Phone STATIONARY_PHONE = new Phone("123123123"); ❷

    private Client client;

    @BeforeMethod
    public void setUp() {
        client = new Client();}

    public void shouldReturnTrueIfClientHasMobile() {
        client.addPhone(MOBILE_PHONE);
        client.addPhone(STATIONARY_PHONE);

        assertTrue(client.hasMobile());
    }

    public void shouldReturnFalseIfClientHasNoMobile() {
        client.addPhone(STATIONARY_PHONE);

        assertFalse(client.hasMobile());
    }
}
```

❶❷ The chosen phone numbers must follow the logic of the `Phone`'s constructor.

This version of the `ClientTest` class is coupled with the implementation of the `Phone` class. If the pattern-matching mechanism used in the `Phone` constructor changes, the test code will also need to change. The SRP principle has clearly been breached, because this test class is also coupled with the `Client` class implementation (so `ClientTest` has more than one reason to change). This is a warning signal. The violation of SRP entails that the DRY principle has also been breached. Surely, there must exist a `PhoneTest` class that will make sure that the `Phone` constructor and `isMobile()` method works as expected! To test this functionality, `PhoneTest` needs to create identical (or almost identical) instances of phones, as shown in Listing 5.42. If so, then a change in the `Phone` class will entail changes in two tests - `PhoneTest` and `ClientTest`. This is bad.

Surprisingly (or, rather… perhaps not!), the test class based on test doubles remained unchanged. The stubs did not even notice the change of algorithm within the `Phone` class or the difference in the values of the arguments passed to the constructor, because they do not make use of either of these. They were ordered to return certain values at certain points of execution, and they are still following those orders.

5.5.4. Use Test Doubles or Not? - Conclusion

 This issue is worth discussing only in the case of "real" objects: that is, objects that have some business logic and offer some complex behaviour. In the case of DTOs[13], or Value Objects[14], using a test double will be overkill. Similarly, creating a test double of a `java.util.ArrayList` is **not** recommended.

As has been confirmed in some of the preceding paragraphs, testing without test doubles is possible, but carries some serious consequences. First of all, it may result in cluttering up your test code with logic that belongs to collaborators. This results in tests failing unexpectedly, if and when the code of the collaborators changes. Secondly, it makes you repeat the same code constructs (e.g. the creation of the DOCs) across multiple tests. This brings it about that making just a single change to some class or other has a ripple effect on your tests, with many of them then needing to be changed[15]. Thirdly, it obliges you to develop classes in some specific order (e.g. the `Phone` class must be ready and fully tested before you can start working on the `Client` class), and may lull you into being over-reliant upon the existing implementation of the collaborators.

On the other hand, using test doubles in some situations might be considered overkill. For people who are new to test doubles, writing `new MyClass()` instead of `mock(MyClass.class)` is much more natural, especially if there is no instant gain in using test doubles.

In general, I would recommend using test doubles. The overheads related to their creation and the setting of expectations might seem unjustified at first (especially if a collaborator is very simple). However, when the design of your classes changes, you will benefit from the isolation, and your tests will not break down unexpectedly. Also, current frameworks only call for you to write a very small number of lines of code, so there is no decline in productivity. Using a test double makes it virtually impossible to rely on the DOCs' implementation, as it might not exist yet.

---

[13]Simple containers for data with getters and setters only. See http://en.wikipedia.org/wiki/Data_transfer_object
[14]Small simple objects like dates, money, strings. See http://c2.com/cgi/wiki?ValueObject
[15]Another solution is to extract the DOCs creation parts of the code into some utility method. This solves the problem of multiple changes, but reduces the readability of test code by forcing the reader to jump between different classes.

The only situations where I would consider using a real collaborator instead of a test double are the following:

- the collaborator is very, very simple, preferably without any logic (e.g. some sort of "container" class with only accessors and mutators methods),

- the collaborator's logic is so simple that it is clear how to set it in the desired state (and its logic will not be enhanced in the foreseeable future).

Even then, I would be highly cautious, as changes are inevitable – no matter how very unlikely they may seem!

5.6. Conclusions (with a Warning)

In this section we have discussed an essential – and probably the hardest – part of unit testing. We have learned about the various types of test double, and started using Mockito to create and manage them in tests. Working with an example has enabled us to acquire an overview of what it is like to develop tests using the TDD approach with test doubles. Wow... really a lot of knowledge this time!

By introducing test doubles, and especially test spies, we have entered the realm of interaction testing. Thanks to them, we can test much more than we would be able to with state testing alone. This is definitely a good thing. However, there is always a price to pay, and this is indeed the case with test doubles. So before we start putting our new testing abilities to use, we really ought to try to become aware of the perils awaiting us.

In fact, we are in a trap, even if we have not yet seen it. The problem is as follows: as we already know, if we just stick to state testing, we will not be able to test everything (as discussed in Section 2.2.1). However, if we start testing interactions between objects, we will soon discover that even innocent seeming refactorings may result in broken-down tests. And why is that? Well, with state testing all we attend to is the outcome (of some method calls), and this gives us the freedom to refactor the tested code. With interaction testing things are different, because it is all about methods being called on collaborators. Interaction testing makes some assumptions about the implementation of an object, and thus makes it harder to change this implementation.

We can think about this using a black-box/white-box analogy. With state testing, the SUT is a black box. We put some things inside, and verify what comes out. State testing respects objects' right to privacy, and does not try to make any assumptions about "how" things work inside. It concentrates only on **"what"** the results of actions amount to. With interactions testing the focus changes from "what" to **"how"**. The SUT is no longer a black box. On the contrary, we look inside the SUT (contravening the "information hiding" principle[16], along the way), and verify its internal parts. And, as usual when breaking some sensible rules, we pay a price for this.

 We will discuss issues pertaining to the manageability of tests as these relate to interactions testing in Chapter 11, *Test Quality*.

---

[16]See http://en.wikipedia.org/wiki/Information_hiding

5.7. Exercises

The exercises presented in this section will allow you to practise your knowledge of testing with test doubles through actually using them. They will also allow you to familiarize yourself with the Mockito framework.

5.7.1. User Service Tested

Write a happy-path test for the class presented below. Verify that the user gets his new password, and that the updateUser() method of userDAO is called.

Listing 5.43. The UserServiceImpl class

```
public class UserServiceImpl {
    private UserDAO userDAO;
    private SecurityService securityService;

    public void assignPassword(User user) throws Exception {
        String passwordMd5 = securityService.md5(user.getPassword());
        user.setPassword(passwordMd5);
        userDao.updateUser(user);
    }

    // constructor and/or setters omitted for the sake of brevity
}
```

5.7.2. Race Results Enhanced

Please enhance the Race Results example (see Section 5.4) with the following functionality:

- RaceResultsService should send messages with the results of different categories of race - e.g. horse races, F1 races, boat-races, etc. Subscribers should be able to subscribe to selected categories. Make sure they receive only messages related to the ones they have signed up for.

- Each message sent by RaceResultsService should be logged. Introduce a logging DOC, and make sure that the date and text of each message is logged. Do **not** implement the logging mechanism: concentrate on the interactions between the service and its collaborator.

- In the tests implemented so far, `RaceResultsService` sends only one message. This is unrealistic! Enhance the tests to ensure that subscribers will receive any number of sent messages.

- What should happen if a client that is not subscribed tries to unsubscribe? Make up your mind about it, write a test which verifies this behaviour, and make `RaceResultsService` behave accordingly.

5.7.3. Booking System Revisited

You have already written one booking system (see Section 4.10.3). This time, you are asked to implement a similar application, but testing it using test doubles. Below, you will find a description and some requirements that will help you to start coding. If some details are omitted, simply make them up during the development.

This booking system allows classrooms to be booked. Each classroom has a certain capacity (e.g. for 20 people), and can be equipped with an overhead projector, microphone and whiteboard. It also has a certain "name" (ID, number, whatever you wish to call it…). The API of the system should allow one to:

- list all existing classrooms,

- list all available classrooms (for a given day and hourly time slot),

- book a specific classroom by name (e.g. *"I want to book classroom A1"*: `book("A1")`),

- book a specific classroom by specifying some constraints (e.g. *"I want to book a classroom with a projector for 20 people"*: `book(20, Equipment.PROJECTOR)`).

Here are some additional constraints, so the system is not too complex at first:

- only periodical booking is supported, which means you can book, for example, classroom A1 for **every** Friday from 10 to 11 am, but not just for Friday the 13th of May.

- each booking lasts for 1 hour; no longer or shorter periods are allowed.

Once you have implemented the system specified above, use your imagination and add some more complexity. For example:

- each booking operation should be written to logs[17],

- each classroom has a "cleaning hour", when it is not available,

- the booking time is no longer limited to 1 hour

5.7.4. Read, Read, Read!

This is not so much an exercise as a reminder: namely, that you really should read Mockito's documentation if you plan to use it. This book gives you a good understanding of what Mockito is good for, and explains the core syntax, but does not try to discuss every detail of Mockito's API. Please, spend some time reading the official Mockito documentation, studying its wiki page and browsing Javadocs! Also, reading some online discussions about differences between Mockito and other frameworks (i.e. EasyMock) may be highly instructive.

---

[17]Please read http://www.mockobjects.com/2007/04/test-smell-logging-is-also-feature.html before implementing this feature.

Part III. Hints and Discussions

I really hate this darn machine;
I wish that they would sell it.
It won't do what I want it to,
but only what I tell it.

— from Programmer's Lament

Discussion is just a tool. You have to aim; the final goal must be a decision.
— Harri Holkeri

Chapter 6. Things You Should Know

> You have learned much, young one.
> — Darth Vader *The Empire Strikes Back (1980)*

After having read the previous parts of this book, you should now be capable of writing unit tests. In fact, you should know a lot about things which some people would regard as "advanced" - for example parametrized tests and test doubles. Still, there are a great many other things you should also know, that will make your tasks easier to complete. You could probably figure them out yourself, using your existing knowledge and your general programming experience, but I would encourage you to continue your education here, and to read about custom patterns, frequently arising problems and various aspects of unit testing. There is still so much for you to learn!

In this section we will first discuss a few general aspects of writing tests (namely, advanced expected exceptions handling and the use of matchers), before proceeding with some how-to subsections devoted to such extremely common problems as testing collections, testing time-dependent methods, and the like.

6.1. What Values To Check?

> […] even for a small program, with a relatively simple set of variables and relatively few possible states per variable, the total number of possible valid states in combination is intractably large.
> — Michael Bolton *DevelopSense*

This section discusses a common problem related to the number of tests that should be written for a given function. It does not give an ultimate answer, but definitely sheds some light on this topic.

To test functionality you need to decide what arguments will be passed to methods. In general it is impossible to tests every combination of input arguments (for obvious reasons). This forces us to choose a subset of arguments, that will represent all possible cases. This might sound hard, but is usually quite simple. Let us discuss some tips for selecting the right arguments.

My general advice is as follows. You should select arguments that belong to these three groups: **expected values** (AKA happy path), **boundary values**, and **strange values** (AKA validity or domain).

6.1.1. Expected Values

This is how you expect a reasonable client[1] will use your code. You expect that he will pass "John" as his name, "52" as his age and "yellow" as his favorite color. You expect him to pass values from 1 to 12 to the function that takes month as an input. You expect that he will pass a positive value to a constructor of `circle` class that takes `radius` parameter. You expect that if he asks you to parse an XML file, to find all products with price greater than 30, then the file will at least be a valid XML. And so on…

This is something you absolutely need to check. Call your code with normal, reasonable, sensible, expected values, and make sure that it behaves properly, i.e. that it gives good answers. This is crucial. If your code does not work properly for such decent input arguments, it is useless.

6.1.2. Boundary Values

After you have checked that your code works fine for "normal" values, it is time to look for boundary values. Such values are a typical source of errors. You need to be especially inquisitive when checking for boundary values[2].

In the previous section we chose arguments that represented expected values. It was always clear what your code should do when asked to work on them. In short, it should do its job. Now we choose arguments that are on the borderline. Sometimes we choose those that live inside a box labeled "reasonable arguments", sometimes we choose them from a box labeled "out of scope". When writing tests **we need to decide** which value belongs to which group[3]. This is when we decide whether, for example, -1 should result in an `IllegalArgumentException` or should cause a normal flow of calculations to ensue.

Let us discuss an example. Imagine a method that takes a single integer parameter and returns the number of days in a month. You assume that:

---

[1]In this case *client* is someone or something that calls your code, not necessarily a person.

[2]See http://en.wikipedia.org/wiki/Boundary-value_analysis and http://en.wikipedia.org/wiki/Off-by-one_error for more information.

[3]This is true, when working in test-first manner, see Chapter 4, *Test Driven Development*.

- 1 symbolizes January, 2 means February, ..., 11 - November and 12 December.

Now, let us test the boundary values. What we surely need to check is whether our counter really starts with 1 and not with 0. So we need to check that:

- 0 fails with an error, while 1 returns a value for January.

And similarly, we also need to check "the other end":

- 12 returns a value for December, while 13 fails with an error.

 Analysis of the values that should be checked can lead you to some interesting findings. For example, it seems that the function that takes an integer representing a month could be improved by the introduction of enum Month. That way, passing of bad values will not be a problem anymore. This is an example of what happens when you start thinking about tests, and you consider boundary values. Redesign happens, and better design emerges. And that is a good thing!

6.1.3. Strange Values

So your code is almost bulletproof. It is verified to work well with expected values, and has some border checking capabilities. That is good, but not enough. The code is not yet ready to deal with values that are completely out of order.

No matter what values you expect, you can always meet with something unexpected. So, expect the unexpected, likely one of the following:

- negative values, when only positive ones make sense (e.g. age),

- null or empty values (e.g. empty Strings, empty collections),

- data structures not conforming to some expectations, e.g. unsorted (when sorting is assumed) or with duplicates (when no duplicates are expected),

- corrupted files (another mime-type than expected, not-valid XML, a binary file instead of text, etc.),

- objects of a different type than expected (possible in weakly typed languages).

This kind of testing is especially important if your code deals with values entered by the user – be it directly via some WWW form, or by reading information from a file uploaded from the user. When receiving data directly from users be prepared to expect every possible value!

Let us consider dates for example. Dates are a common source of confusion and error, because:

- they are intrinsically complicated (e.g. leap years, different numbers of days in months),

- we use them differently (i.e. various data formats – e.g. `YYYY-MM-DD` vs. `YYYY-DD-MM`).

So let us say that the function we are testing takes date as String. We expect it to be in YYYY-MM-DD format. The code is already tested to deal with:

- normal values - `2011-01-18`, `1956-07-14`, `2015-12-23`, ...

- boundary values - `2011-02-28` and `2011-02-29`, ...

Now, it should be hardened against unexpected dates. For example, a date entered by a user might be one of the following:

- `2011-28-03` - which is `YYYY-DD-MM`, instead of the required `YYYY-MM-DD`,

- `2011/04/18` - which uses a different group separator,

- `tomorrow` - which is a nice date, but not really what was expected,

- `null` or empty String - this happens all the time,

- `http://some.address/`, `I love you Mom` or `blah (*&$` - it can also happen.

6.1.4. Should You Always Care?

"I will spend my life writing tests for this simple function..." If a dreadful thought like this crossed your mind while you were reading the previous section, maybe the next few paragraphs will cheer you up.

Let us say you write tests for `AgeValidator` class. Your web-based application will use it to check the validity of arguments passed from a web form (probably HTML). You know that this form will allow you to input only two digits in the `age` field. The question is, should you use this knowledge to limit the set of tested values to `[0..99]`? Does it make sense to write tests that pass `100` or `-1` to `validateAge()` method?[4]

If you were to design all your classes and methods so that they did not depend on the context of your application, they would definitely be more robust and reusable, which in turn would certainly be a good thing. But should you strive for this? This is a common problem you will face. Let us discuss it.

In general, you will probably not be expected to write all the code keeping reusability in mind. This would only be the case in some rare situations – i.e. when writing a "library", whose purpose is, precisely, to be reusable. What you are going to be paid for is to build this particular application – not to prepare your code so you can build any application with it. Of course, thinking about reusability is valuable, as it make you code much clean and easier to maintain, so not only your company, but also your own team will surely benefit from the lower maintenance effort. On the other hand, thinking about possible future use breaches the You Ain't Gonna Need It (YAGNI) principle[5]. Try to be pragmatic about it.

And if you code **every** component with reusability in mind, your integrated application may perform suboptimally. For example, each component would repeat the same checks (e.g. `null` values checking). Does it really makes sense to check arguments for being `null` in the web layer, then pass them to the services layer and repeat the same checks, then pass them further to the DAO layer and perform the same checks? I don't think so.

It is a different case with all "utility" classes. They should be context-free, because the chances of reusing them are much higher than for any other code you write. You should test them with special care, knowing that you cannot assume much about the context they will be used in.

As a case in point, the validator class, mentioned previously, falls into the "utility classes" category. As such, I would recommend preparing it for work in any context, without any assumptions about the arguments. That would mean it should be tested taking into account values not from 0 to 9 but from `Integer.MIN_VALUE` to `Integer.MAX_VALUE`. I guess that for this validator that would not mean a lot more work. In other cases, though, it might be different.

---

[4]Let us assume that tampering with POST data is not possible…
[5]http://en.wikipedia.org/wiki/You_ain%27t_gonna_need_it

There are some ways to deal with methods which require many different sets of arguments in order to be properly tested. See Section 3.6 for what TestNG can offer in this respect. If this is something of great importance, you should also look for information on *"pairwise testing"*[6] and tools like quickcheck[7] or feed4testng[8].

6.1.5. Not Only Input Parameters

So far, we have only discussed those sorts of case that have allowed us to freely set input parameters. However, in the real world not every input is passed as a method argument. We have already discussed the issues related to indirect inputs provided by DOCs. In case of such interactions of an SUT with DOCs, the same rules apply as were discussed previously. That is, we should write test cases for:

• the normal behaviour of the DOC (i.e. that it returns reasonable values or throws reasonable exceptions),

• the DOC returning boundary values,

• the DOC returning unexpected values, i.e. throwing exceptions, that are unlikely to happen.

6.2. How to Fail a Test?

Apart from the assertion methods discussed in Section 3.4, there is also one more method in the `Assert` class that deserves our attention: `fail()`. It makes a test fail, and has overloaded versions which allow for an optional message and throwable cause to be specified. A test terminated with the `fail()` method is treated as if it had failed because of an unmet assertion. Historically, the `fail()` method was used for verifying expected exceptions. Currently, TestNG provides a better mechanism for this (see Section 6.3 for more information).

Note that the `fail()` method can usually be replaced with other assert methods. However, it sometimes lets you express more clearly the intent of a test, which is always recommended.

---

[6]See http://en.wikipedia.org/wiki/All-pairs_testing
[7]http://java.net/projects/quickcheck/pages/Home
[8]http://databene.org/feed4testng.html

For example, `fail()` can be used in pre-testing methods, which verify some preconditions, and stop tests if they are not met. Listing 6.1 shows such a use of the `fail()` method. It also uses test dependencies, which are discussed in Section 7.2.

Listing 6.1. Example of use of the fail() method

```
@Test
public void xmlParserAvailable() {
    if ( ... ) { // some verification here
        Assert.fail("No XML parser available."); ❶
    }
}


@Test(dependsOnMethods = {"xmlParserAvailable"}) ❷
public void someXmlParsingTestHere() {
    // xml parsing tests
}
```

❶   The `fail()` method is used here if some condition has not been met.
❷   This test will not run if the `fail()` method has been executed within the `xmlParserAvailable()` method.

To conclude, you will rarely, if ever, find yourself using `fail()` methods in unit tests. However, in some circumstances it can be really useful, so it is good to know about its existence. One possible use of the `fail()` method is discussed in Section 6.3.

6.3. More about Expected Exceptions

In Section 3.7 we learned about the default approach to expected exceptions testing with TestNG using the `expectedException` attribute of the `@Test` annotation. In this section we will be discussing this topic in greater detail and showing how certain more complex requirements with regard to exceptions testing can be met. But first, let us remind ourselves of what we have already learned. An example of the default expected exceptions testing pattern is presented below.

Listing 6.2. Expected exceptions testing pattern - a reminder

```
@Test(expectedExceptions = ExceptionClass.class)
public void shouldThrowException() {
    // calling SUT's method which should
    // throw an exception of ExceptionClass
}
```

There is no explicit assertion anywhere within the test code regarding the expected exception. Everything is handled through the annotation of the test method.

This pattern has two main disadvantages. Firstly, it does not allow us to inspect all the properties of the exception that has been caught – neither does it allow us to examine the properties of the SUT after the exception has been thrown. Secondly, the use of annotation makes the test code diverge from the usual pattern of arrange/act/assert (or, if you happen to be an advocate of BDD, that of given/when/then). In this section we will discuss various ways in which both of these issues might be resolved.

As was previously mentioned, the rules for specifying expected exceptions in tests are the same as for the `catch` clause of a `try-catch-finally` statement: explicitly name the exceptions you expect to catch, and never use general exception classes! Otherwise the exception could be thrown in a different line of code than the one you were expecting it to be thrown in (and the test will still pass…). Keeping this in mind, let us proceed with some further examples.

6.3.1. The Expected Exception Message

On some rare occasions it is important to verify whether the exception has been thrown with a proper message or not. This is rarely the case, because verification of an exception message makes the message difficult to change, and so in general should be avoided. However, the following case - shown in Listing 6.3 - illustrates the need for exception message verification. It presents a `Phone` class constructor which performs various checks on a number given to it.

Listing 6.3. Phone class constructor throwing the same exception twice

```
public Phone(String number) {
    if (null == number || number.isEmpty()) {
        throw new IllegalArgumentException(
                "number can not be null or empty"); ❶
    }
    if (number.startsWith("+")) {
        throw new IllegalArgumentException(
                "plus sign prefix not allowed, number: [" + number + "]"); ❷
    }
    this.number = number;
}
```

❶❷   In both cases, `IllegalArgumentException` is thrown, but with a different message.

The throwing of two exceptions of the same kind could be regarded as being an instance of "code smell"[9]. It would probably be better if two different exceptions were thrown.

Now imagine a test method that verifies the expected exception thrown by the `Phone` class constructor. Relying solely on the exception type (in this case `IllegalArgumentException`) will not suffice. Listing 6.4 shows how another attribute of `@Test` annotation can be exploited in order to write correct tests

Listing 6.4. Verification of an exception message

```
public class ExpectedExceptionMessageTest {

    @DataProvider
    private static final Object[][] emptyNumbers(){
        return new Object[][] {{null}, {""}};
    }

    @Test(dataProvider = "emptyNumbers",
                expectedExceptions = IllegalArgumentException.class,
                expectedExceptionsMessageRegExp = ".*empty.*" ) ❶
    public void shouldThrowIAEForEmptyNumber(String emptyNumber) {
        new Phone(emptyNumber);
    }

    @DataProvider
    private static final Object[][] numbersWithPlus(){
        return new Object[][] {{"+123"}, {"+456 789 012"}};
    }

    @Test(dataProvider = "numbersWithPlus",
                expectedExceptions = IllegalArgumentException.class,
                expectedExceptionsMessageRegExp = ".*plus.*" ) ❷
    public void shouldThrowIAEForPlusPrefixedNumber(String numberWithPlus) {
        new Phone(numberWithPlus);
    }
}
```

❶❷ The test methods differ with respect to the data providers used and the expected message of exception thrown. Both cases involve the same type of expected exception: `IllegalArgumentException`. However, one test expects the word *"empty"* and the other the word *"plus"* to appear in the message.

---

[9]The term "code smell" was coined by Kent Beck; see http://en.wikipedia.org/wiki/Code_smell for more information.

The `expectedExceptionMessageRegExp` attribute of the `@Test` annotation takes a regular expression argument, which affords us great flexibility when we come to specify the expected exception message. As Listing 6.4 shows, the rule of thumb for this says that we should specify a minimal, but crucial, fragment of the exception message. This will make your tests less prone to fail in the event of the exception message being changed.

6.3.2. When Having a Common Pattern is not Enough

Another case where catching expected exceptions with the `expectedExceptions` attribute of the `@Test` annotation is not sufficient is when there is more to be verified than just whether an appropriate exception has in fact been thrown or not. Let us consider the following example:

Listing 6.5. Code to be tested for exceptions and interaction

```
public class RequestHandler {

    private final RequestProcessor requestProcessor;

    public void handle(Request request) throws InvalidRequestException { ❶
        if (invalidRequest(request)) {
            throw new InvalidRequestException();
        }
        requestProcessor.process(request);
    }

    // injection of requestProcessor and implementation of invalidRequest()
    // method not presented for the sake of brevity.
}
```

❶   Method to be tested. This verifies an incoming request and throws an exception, or asks a collaborator - `requestProcessor` - to process it.

]Now let us assume that we want to check to make sure that if an invalid request arrives, it is **NOT** then passed to `requestProcessor`, and that the appropriate exception is thrown. In such a case we will need to use a different pattern. One possibility is to follow the normal approach to exceptions handling, based on a `try-catch statement`.

Listing 6.6. Expected exception and interactions testing

```
@Test
public void shouldNotProcessInvalidRequests() {
    Request request = createInvalidRequest();
    RequestProcessor requestProcessor = mock(RequestProcessor.class);

    RequestHandler sut = new RequestHandler(requestProcessor);

    try {
        sut.handle(request); ❶
        fail("Should have thrown InvalidRequestException"); ❷
    } catch (InvalidRequestException e) {
        Mockito.verifyZeroInteractions(requestProcessor); ❸
    }
}
```

❶   We expect the `handle()` method to throw an exception of the `InvalidRequestException` type.

❷   If we have reached this point, then it means the expected exception has not been thrown – so it is time to fail the test (using a static `fail()` method of the `Assert` class).

❸   We are making sure that the invalid request has not been passed to `requestProcessor`. We have already seen how Mockito can verify that a specific method has not been called on a mock object (with the `never()` method - see Section 5.4.3). Another Mockito method - `verifyZeroInteractions()` - is more general in scope: it verifies whether any calls have been made to some given test doubles, and fails the test if they have.

 I must say that personally I am not so enthusiastic about the test shown in Listing 6.6. It tests two things at once: the expected exception and the lack of interaction with the `requestProcessor` collaborator[10]. However, it would be hard to divide this test into two, because the interaction test would still have to use the `try-catch` pattern, which would make it obscure anyway.

This approach allows us to test what we wanted to test: both that the exception has been thrown and that there has been no interaction with `requestProcessor`. Another advantage is that we could also test the properties of the caught exception (inside the `catch` clause). For example, we could verify its message, or even retrieve the root cause of the `InvalidRequestException` and verify its properties (e.g. its type and exception message).

---

[10]While writing this test method I could not figure out a good name for it – a name that would describe the scenario being tested. That is itself a good indication that the scope of what the test is responsible for may be too broad.

But we can surely all agree that it is hard to be proud of such test code. The test looks ugly because of the `try-catch` statement, while the swallowed exception in `catch` block is something that makes me feel uneasy every time I see it. Moreover, the use of `fail()` as an "inverted" assertion looks strange. If only we could get rid of this `try-catch`...

6.3.3. catch-exception Library

Listing 6.7 proves that it is possible to get rid of the `try-catch` statement while still being able to verify whatever we want, and to do all this adopting a nice, clean arrange/act/assert approach. It uses an additional library - **catch-exception**[11] by Rod Woo, which provides some convenient methods for dealing with expected exceptions in test code.

Listing 6.7. Expected exceptions testing - BDD style

```
import static com.googlecode.catchexception.CatchException.*; ❶

@Test
public void shouldThrowExceptions() throws InvalidRequestException {
    Request request = createInvalidRequest();
    RequestProcessor requestProcessor = mock(RequestProcessor.class);

    RequestHandler sut = new RequestHandler(requestProcessor);

    catchException(sut).handle(request); ❷

    assertTrue(caughtException() instanceof InvalidRequestException, ❸
            "Should have thrown exception of InvalidRequestException class");

    Mockito.verifyZeroInteractions(requestProcessor); ❹
}
```

❶ Importing of static methods of the `CatchException` class from the catch-exception library.
❷ The static method `catchException()` of the `CatchException` class is used to call a method which is expected to throw an exception.
❸ The thrown exception is returned by another static method (`caughtException()`). The assertion verifies whether an appropriate exception has been thrown.
❹ Verification of the absence of any interactions with the `requestProcessor` collaborator.

---

[11]See http://code.google.com/p/catch-exception/

The code in Listing 6.7 fits nicely into arrange/act/assert. It is concise and highly readable. The static methods of the **catch-exception** library make the sequence of the code easy to grasp. Since the caught exception is available after it has been thrown (you can assign it to some variable, e.g. `Exception e = caughtException()`), it is possible to analyze some of its properties. In addition, if some of the methods executed within the test method are capable of throwing the same exception, a developer can specify which of them is expected to do so by wrapping specific lines of code with the `catchException()` method. Thanks to this, no mistakes concerning the provenance of the caught exception are possible.

6.3.4. Conclusions

As this chapter shows, there are many ways to write test code that will verify whether an expected exception has been thrown or not. For 95% of cases the default TestNG pattern (with the `expectedException` attribute of the `@Test` annotation) is good enough. For the remaining few percent you can choose between using a `try-catch` statement and a catch-exception library. Of these two alternatives, the second one seems more appealing. In fact, if you want to have all your tests share the same pattern you should consider relying exclusively on the catch-exception library.

To complete the picture, let me also mention that matcher libraries (which are the topic of Section 6.5) offer many syntactic goodies for writing assertions relating to exceptions. For example, one can replace the following assertions:

Listing 6.8. Standard assertions

```
assertTrue(e instanceOf IllegalArgumentException.class)
assertEquals(e.getMessage(), "number can not be null or empty")
```

with the following one-liner:

Listing 6.9. Assertions using FEST Fluent Assertions library

```
assertThat(e).isInstanceOf(IllegalArgumentException.class)
    .hasMessage("number can not be null or empty");
```

If you find yourself needing to perform such verifications on expected exceptions, consider adding matchers to your testing toolbox.

6.4. Stubbing Void Methods

Sometimes it is required to stub `void` methods. Mockito allows to do it, but there is a small catch: the syntax differs substantially from what we have learned so far. For example, to stub the behaviour of `someMethod()` method you would usually write the following:

Listing 6.10. Stubbing a non-void method

```
when(someObject.someMethod()).thenReturn("some value");
```

However, if a method returns `void`, then the syntax differs (obviously it does not make sens to return anything from `void` method, so in the example below we instruct the `voidMethod()` to throw an exception):

Listing 6.11. Stubbing a void method

```
doThrow(new IllegalArgumentException("bad argument!"))
    .when(someObject).voidMethod();
```

As the original Mockito's documentation states, this different syntax is required, because: *"Stubbing voids requires different approach from when(Object) because the compiler does not like void methods inside brackets...".*

 Apart from the `doThrow()` method, there are two other methods which may help when working with `void` methods: `doNothing()` and `doAnswer()`. Mockito documentation discusses them in detail, giving very good examples for both.

6.5. Matchers

Up to now we have been almost exclusively using standard TestNG assertions. We have used `assertTrue()` to verify some basic boolean expressions, `assertEquals()` to compare two objects with respect to equality, and `assertNull()` or `assertNotNull()` to make sure that a given object is or is not null, etc. These basic assertions are enough to verify any condition you might think of. That is true, but there is still room for further improvement here! In particular, thanks to using matchers we can have more readable test code, which is always a good thing.

In some sections of this book we have already mentioned that there are two aspects to the readability of assertions: how they look within the test code, and what information is given to the developer once an assertion has failed. Matchers are particularly useful for helping with both of these issues.

 The information included in this section is valid across all currently existing implementations of matchers; you can use what you learn here with both FEST and Hamcrest (the two most popular frameworks of this kind). All the examples will be written with FEST, but only because this is my tool of choice.

Matchers makes your tests **more readable**. They provide extra readability at a linguistic level, because the order of words in `assertThat(worker, isA(manager))` resembles natural language much more closely than does `assertEquals(worker, manager)`, the standard `assertEqual()` assertion. This is true both for FEST or Hamcrest matchers available out-of-the box, and for custom matchers that you yourself write. The following example demonstrates this:

Table 6.1. Comparison of default TestNG assertions and FEST matchers

standard TestNG assertions	`book = new Book(TITLE);`
	`assertNotNull(book.getTitle());`
	`assertFalse(book.getTitle().isEmpty());`
	`assertEquals(book.getTitle(), TITLE);`

FEST matchers	`book = new Book(TITLE);`
	`assertThat(book.getTitle()).isNotNull();`
	`assertThat(book.getTitle()).isNotEmpty();`
	`assertThat(book.getTitle()).isEqualTo(TITLE);`

You may also notice that the use of matchers introduces a specific "rhythm" to your assertions: they all read similarly.

But so far this is nothing to get especially excited about. We can do more than this by writing custom matchers, which are designed to verify properties of our domain object. For example, would it not be nice to replace the assertion on a book's title property with a simple `assertThat(book).hasTitle(TITLE)`? Absolutely! This is possible, even though creating such a matcher comes at a certain cost. Listing 6.12 shows the code of a custom matcher that will furnish us with the aforementioned `hasTitle()` method:

Listing 6.12. Implementation of a FEST custom matcher

```java
import org.fest.assertions.*; ❶

public class BookAssert extends GenericAssert<BookAssert, Book> {

    public BookAssert(Book actual) {
        super(BookAssert.class, actual);
    }

    public static BookAssert assertThat(Book actual) { ❷
        return new BookAssert(actual);
    }

    public BookAssert hasTitle(String name) { ❸
        isNotNull();
        String errorMessage = String.format(
                "Expected book's title to be <%s> but was <%s>",
                                    name, actual.getTitle()
                );
        Assertions.assertThat(actual.getTitle()) ❹
                .overridingErrorMessage(errorMessage)
                .isEqualTo(name);
        return this;
    }
}
```

❶   Import of required FEST classes.

❷   Our implementation of `assertThat()` is required, so that we can start assertion lines in the same way as we would start any matchers' assertions. Then we can chain together both the default matchers (e.g. `isEqualTo()`, `isNotNull()`) and our custom `hasTitle()` matcher.

❸   Here we have a custom matcher responsible for verifying equality as regards book title, with respect to any given book. It also contains a null check (`isNotNull()`), so that the test code will be safe from any `NullPointerException` error.

❹   The error message is overridden here, so that if the assertion fails the developer will know exactly what happened (e.g. *"Expected book's title to be <Hobbit> but was <Odyssey>"*). This is yet another advantage of matchers, which can provide **very readable failure messages** in cases of failed assertions.

Now that we have this custom matcher implemented, we can use it in our test code as shown below:

Listing 6.13. The use of a custom matcher

```
import org.testng.annotations.Test;

import static com.practicalunittesting.fest.BookAssert.assertThat; ❶

@Test
public class BookFestTest {

    private static final String TITLE = "My book";

    private Book book;

    public void constructorShouldSetTitle() {
        book = new Book(TITLE);

        assertThat(book).hasTitle(TITLE); ❷
    }
}
```

❶❷   In this case we use the `assertThat()` method provided by the `BookAssert` class.

As shown in the listing above, custom matchers also help to achieve better readability by helping us to **write the tests at a reasonable level of abstraction**. This is possible because custom matchers can contain some assertions within themselves and so act as superordinate assertions under intention-revealing names. The association with private methods, which are often used in test code to achieve exactly the same goal, is justified. However the syntax of matchers makes them even more readable.

Another interesting point about matchers is that they are **highly reusable**. They can be used in connection with a great many test methods and test classes. Moreover, they can be combined together to create complex assertions, as shown in Listing 6.14. This example also demonstrates that it is possible to combine default matchers (`isNotIn()`) with custom ones (`hasTitle()` and `isWrittenIn()`).

Listing 6.14. Combining matchers

```
public void combinedMatchersExample() {
    book = new Book(TITLE);

    assertThat(book).hasTitle(TITLE)
        .isNotIn(scienceFictionBooks)
        .isWrittenIn(ENGLISH);
}
```

Such simple examples hardly reveal the true power and usefulness of matchers. Custom matchers excel particularly when working with **rich domain objects** or **complex data structures**.

It is time to list the advantages of matchers, which are numerous:

- they enhance code readability,

- they help us to write assertions on the right abstraction level,

- they help to remove logic from tests (and encapsulate it within the matchers' classes),

- they are highly reusable, which is very important if your domain objects are complex and are tested with multiple test scenarios,

- many matchers are available directly from matcher libraries - including specific matchers for work with collections (as shown in Section 6.9) or exceptions (see Section 6.3),

- writing custom matchers is a relatively simple task.

In spite of their usefulness, I do not see matchers being used much. I guess the main reasons for this are lack of knowledge about them, a general reluctance to add yet another library to one's project, and the cost involved in implementing custom assertions. Personally, I find them **invaluable**, especially when working with rich domain objects. As soon as I no longer feel comfortable using the default assertions (`assertEquals()`, `assertTrue()`), I write a custom matcher instead. Usually this solves my problem.
In my experience, it quite often happens that the custom matchers one has written for unit tests get reused later for integration and/or end-to-end tests. This increases the "return on the investment" one had to make to implement them.

As a last tip, I would suggest that if you use matchers, you should use them everywhere, so that all your assertions begin with `assertThat()`. This will make your tests very readable indeed.

6.6. Mockito Matchers

Continuing our discussion on matchers, let us take a look at their use in specific, test-double related cases. So far we have been very specific as to the arguments of methods that we have been instructing Mockito to return when stubbing. Similarly, when verifying test doubles' behaviour, we have expected certain methods to be called with certain values. For example, in Section 5.4.5 we verified whether `client` had received a specific `message` object or not. This makes sense, but sometimes expressing the arguments of calls in such detail is too rigid, as well as being simply unnecessary. In this section we will learn how to make our tests more relaxed by using argument matchers provided by Mockito.

But first things first, why bother at all with such a feature? Basically, there are two good reasons for doing so:

- **improved readability** coming from the fact that code with matchers can be read like natural language (well, almost…),

- **improved maintainability** thanks to the omitting of some unimportant details within the test code by means of more relaxed matchers.

Mockito offers a variety of predefined matchers which can be used for verification or stubbing. There are a great many of them, some being just aliases of others, simply for the sake of ensuring the readability of your tests. The list below gives only a subset of all of the matchers available[12]:

- `any()` matches any object (or null),

- `anyVararg()` matches any number and values of arguments,

- `isNull()`, `isNotNull()` match null and not-null values respectively,

- `anyBoolean()`, `anyByte()`, `anyChar()`, `anyDouble()`, `anyFloat()`, `anyInt()`, `anyLong()`, `anyShort()`, `anyString()` match these Java types (or null),

- `isA(Class<T> clazz)` matches any object of a given class,

- `same(T value)` matches an object which is the same (`==`) to a given object,

- `anyCollection()`, `anyList()`, `anyMap()`, `anySet()` matches any kind of instance of each sort of collection (or null),

---

[12]For the full list of available matchers please refer to the Mockito documentation relating to the `Matchers` class.

- `refEq(T value, String… excludeFields)` matches an object that is reflection-equal to the given value; allows us to specify excluded fields, not to be taken into account,

- `eq(boolean value)`, `eq(byte value)`, `eq(char value)`, `eq(double value)`, `eq(float value)`, `eq(int value)`, `eq(long value)`, `eq(short value)`, `eq(T value)` - matches values which are equal to given arguments.

Many of the above methods also exists with additional arguments (of the `java.lang.Class` type) to make them generics-friendly: i.e. to avoid compiler warnings.

There are also some utility matchers for working with `String` arguments:

- `startsWith(String prefix)`, `endsWith(String suffix)` match a string that starts/ends with the prefix/suffix that is given,

- `contains(String substring)` matches a string that contains a given substring,

- `matches(String regex)` matches a string that matches a given regular expression.

Such matchers are useful for specifying some "generic" stubbing behaviour or expectations. For example, such code will make the userDAO stub return the object user every time its getUser() method is called, regardless of what ID parameter is passed there.

Listing 6.15. Use of the anyInt() matcher

```
UserDAO userDAO = mock(UserDAO.class);
User user = new User();

when(userDAO.getUser(anyInt())).thenReturn(user); ❶

assertEquals(userDAO.getUser(1), user);
assertEquals(userDAO.getUser(2), user);
assertEquals(userDAO.getUser(3), user);

verify(userDAO, times(3)).getUser(anyInt()); ❷
```

❶   Stubbing of userDAO using an anyInt() matcher.
❷   Verification that getUser() was called three times with some int argument.

The listing above shows you how to get rid of specific values and use more relaxed arguments when stubbing or verifying your code. This feature of Mockito is highly compatible with the approach that Mockito itself promotes – namely, **only specifying in**

your tests what actually needs to be specified. So, if it is not crucial for your test logic that `getUser()` gets an argument equal to `789`, then maybe `anyInt()` would be good enough? If so, do not hesitate. Work at the right abstraction level, hiding the unimportant details beneath the handy matchers we have just been learning about.

6.6.1. Hamcrest Matchers Integration

Last but not least, the `Matchers` class also provides a set of methods that will facilitate using custom Hamcrest matchers within your Mockito-based test code:

- `argThat(org.hamcrest.Matcher<T> matcher)`, which uses a given matcher,

- `booleanThat(Matcher<Boolean> matcher)`, `byteThat(Matcher<Byte> matcher)`, `charThat(Matcher<Character> matcher)`, `doubleThat(Matcher<Double> matcher)`, `floatThat(Matcher<Float> matcher)`, `intThat(Matcher<Integer> matcher)`, `longThat(Matcher<Long> matcher)`, `shortThat(Matcher<Short> matcher)`, all of which will match on the basis of matchers of the specified type.

By allowing any custom Hamcrest matcher to pass, we gain limitless possibilities for writing highly readable testing code. The use of matcher libraries in test code was discussed in Section 6.5, so right now let us conclude with just one example:

Listing 6.16. Use of Hamcrest matchers with Mockito

```
import static org.mockito.Matchers.argThat; ❶
import static org.hamcrest.Matchers.hasEntry;

User user = new User();
UserDAO userDAO = mock(UserDAO.class);

when(userDAO.getUserByProperties(argThat(hasEntry("id", "2")))) ❷
        .thenReturn(user);

assertNull(userDAO.getUserByProperties(new HashMap<String, String>())); ❸

Map<String, String> properties = new HashMap<String, String>();
properties.put("id", "2");

assertEquals(userDAO.getUserByProperties(properties), user); ❹
```

❶   The necessary static methods are imported.

❷   Our use of the Hamcrest matcher `hasEntry()` must be wrapped in the `argThat()` method of Mockito[13].

❸   This map does not fulfill the requirement - no user will be returned (as discussed previously, Mockito will return null in such cases).

❹   Now the map contains the entry required by the matcher, so a real user will be returned.

"Limitless possibilities" are opened up, in that it is possible to write custom Hamcrest matchers that can then be used within the `argThat()` method in just the same way as the original Hamcrest matchers are used.

6.6.2. Matchers Warning

One thing to remember is that **if you are using argument matchers, all arguments have to be provided by matchers**. This is shown in Listing 6.17 (an example copied directly from the Mockito documentation):

Listing 6.17. The requirement to use matchers for all arguments

```
verify(mock).someMethod(anyInt(), anyString(), eq("third argument")); ❶

verify(mock).someMethod(anyInt(), anyString(), "third argument"); ❷
```

❶   This is correct: all argument are matchers.

❷   This is incorrect: the third argument is not a matcher and will result in an exception being thrown.

6.7. Testing Thread Safe

> Chuck Norris can test multi-threaded applications with a single thread.
> — Wisdom of the Internet ;)

In the real world, the applications we write are often accessed simultaneously. We use specialized tools (e.g. JMeter[14]) to make sure that our software can handle this concurrent

---

[13]This is because all Hamster matcher methods return objects of the `org.hamcrest.Matcher<T>` type, while Mockito matchers return objects of the `T` type.

[14]http://jakarta.apache.org/jmeter/

load. Sometimes it is important that we verify such requirements, even as they relate to cases involving single classes. This section gives an example of such a test.

6.7.1. ID Generator: Requirements

Let us implement a utility class whose task will be to generate unique identifiers (IDs). Its interfaces are shown in Listing 6.18.

Listing 6.18. ID generator interface

```
public interface IdGenerator {

    /**
     * @return unique id
     */
    Long nextId();
}
```

6.7.2. ID Generator: First Implementation

The first, rather naive implementation is shown in Listing 6.19.

Listing 6.19. ID generator implemented using the System.currentTimeMillis method

```
public class SystemIdGenerator implements IdGenerator {

    public Long nextId() {
        return System.currentTimeMillis(), ❶
    }
}
```

❶ The SystemIdGenerator class uses a static method of the System class to obtain unique identifiers.

To test if the returned IDs are really unique, we need to call the nextId() method of our ID generator two times in a row, and compare the results. Such a test is shown in Listing 6.20.

Listing 6.20. Basic test of an ID generator

```
public class SystemIdGeneratorTest {

    private IdGenerator idGen = new SystemIdGenerator();

    public void idsShouldBeUnique() {
        Long idA = idGen.nextId();
        Long idB = idGen.nextId();

        assertNotEquals(idA, idB, "idA " + idA + " idB " + idB);
    }
}
```

Even though some time passes between the generation of idA and idB this test fails every time I execute it. This means that both of the identifiers generated by an instance of the SystemIdGenerator class are equal. Apparently, current CPUs are fast enough to execute the nextId() method two times in every millisecond. However, looking at the test code, I think that in some circumstances the test **might pass**. That would be something extremely unwelcome. A test which sometimes passes and sometimes fails (for no apparent reason) is called a "flickering test". In general, flickering tests are a nightmare to deal with. One time they pass, the next they fail, etc., and there are no clues we can follow up that might shed light on the reason for this non-deterministic behaviour.

Having said that, I do promise we will write a much better test soon. But for now, let us make the ID generator class better, so that it passes the test.

6.7.3. ID Generator: Second Implementation

Another version of an ID generator - the AtomicIdGenerator class shown in Listing 6.21 - uses a unary increment operator. Now it should always return unique values.

Listing 6.21. ID generator implemented using a unary increment operator

```
public class AtomicIdGenerator implements IdGenerator {

    private static Long nextId = System.currentTimeMillis();

    public Long nextId() {
        return nextId++;
    }
}
```

If we run our test in Listing 6.20 against this version of an ID generator, the test will pass. No matter how many times we execute the test, no matter if we add a `for` loop inside the test code to repeat it again and again, it will pass. Yet, it does not mean that our generator class is ready to be used in the real world. In the next step we will prove it is still not robust enough.

 If you expect your code to be used concurrently, then your tests should simulate this.

Even if a unary increment operator were atomic (which it isn't!), it might happen that two threads both execute the `nextId()` method and get the same value. How? Well, two threads might obtain the same "old" value of the `nextId` variable, then both might increment it and subsequently assign a "new" value to the `idA` and `idB` variables. To write a test which exposes such a threat, we would have to create two separate threads and make them access `nextId()` in exactly this way – which is by no means easy. Fortunately, TestNG offers a nice way to solve this dilemma.

The solution, shown in Listing 6.22, relies on two attributes of the `@Test` annotation:

- `threadPoolSize`, which sets the number of threads that are to execute a test method,

- `invocationCount`, which sets the total number of test method executions.

Listing 6.22. ID generator tested simultaneously by multiple threads

```
@Test
public class JVMUniqueIdGeneratorParallelTest {

    private IdGenerator idGen = new AtomicIdGenerator();

    private Set<Long> ids = new HashSet<Long>(100); ❶

    @Test(threadPoolSize = 7, invocationCount = 100) ❷
    public void idsShouldBeUnique() {
        assertTrue(ids.add(idGen.nextId())); ❸
    }
}
```

❶❸ The test uses method add() of the HashSet class, which returns true if, and only if, the element added was not already in the set. In other words, the test will fail if the ID generated is not unique.

❷ The idsShouldBeUnique() method will be invoked 100 times, by 7 threads simultaneously. Please note that we need not create any Thread objects in the code. Everything has already been done, thanks to the @Test annotation attributes.

If you run the test against the AtomicIdGenerator class now, you should see it fail. Apparently, our ID generator is not yet ready to be used by multiple clients at the same time.

6.7.4. Conclusions

Let us leave the implementation of an ID generator as homework for you, dear reader (see Section 6.12.6), and concentrate on the testing side of our example. Here are some comments on what we have seen so far, and also some remarks about further enhancements to the test we have just written.

First of all, we have learned that TestNG allows us to execute tests methods concurrently, through the simple use of annotations. There is no need for you to implement threads yourself. Instead, use the threadPoolSize and invocationCount attributes of @Test annotation. As the examples have shown, this makes testing code very clean and easy to understand. Definitely a good thing!

In addition to what we have done, you can also use the timeOut and invocationTimeOut attributes of @Test annotation. Their role is to break the test execution and fail the test if it takes too long (e.g. if your code has caused a deadlock or entered some infinite loop). These annotations are especially useful for integration testing (when external modules or applications can cause unacceptable delays). Please refer to TestNG documentation for detailed information.

The examples presented in this section do not solve the problem of testing and concurrency. In fact, we have only touched on a part of it. Right now we know how to test our code simultaneously with many threads. However, if production code creates threads, then testing it raises other new and complicated issues. [goetz2006] is **the** book on Java concurrency, and it contains some hints on the testing of concurrent code. JMock library offers some support for multithread code testing[15]. There are also some libraries which can help you with this task.

6.8. Time is not on Your Side

Time is making fools of us again.
— J.K. Rowling *Harry Potter and the Half-Blood Prince (2005)*

Alas, after all the years of software development we still cannot get it right! The number of bugs related to time formatting and storage is horrifying. Wikipedia gives a lot of examples of such issues, with the famous Y2K problem among them[16]. There is definitely something complicated connected with time – something which makes us write code not in conformity with its quirky and unpredictable nature. In this section we will see how to deal with classes whose behaviour is determined by time.

A typical example of a time-dependent class is shown in Listing 6.23. The code itself is trivial, but testing such code is not.

Listing 6.23. Time-dependent code

```
public class Hello {

    public String sayHello() {
        Calendar current = Calendar.getInstance(); ❶
        if (current.get(Calendar.HOUR_OF_DAY) < 12) {
            return "Good Morning!";
        }
        else {
            return "Good Afternoon!";
        }
    }
}
```

❶   Returns the current date (at the time of the test's execution).

   Please do not be offended by this *"HelloWorld"* style example. Its point is that it encapsulates everything problematic about the unit testing of time-dependent code. I have seen complicated business code with exactly the same issue as is

---

[15]See http://www.jmock.org/threads.html
[16]See http://en.wikipedia.org/wiki/Time_formatting_and_storage_bugs

shown in Listing 6.23. If you learn to solve the problem of `Hello` class, you will also know how to deal with much more complicated logic.

Whatever test we write in connection with this simple `Hello` class, its result will depend on the time of execution. An example is shown in Listing 6.24. After execution, one of the tests will fail. This is something we cannot accept. What is expected of unit tests is that they abstract from the environment and make sure that a given class **always** works.

Listing 6.24. Time-dependent code - a failing test

```
@Test
public class HelloTest {

    public void shouldSayGoodMorningInTheMorning() {
        Hello hello = new Hello();

        assertEquals(hello.sayHello(), "Good Morning!");    ❶
    }

    public void shouldSayGoodAfternoonInTheAfternoon() {
        Hello hello = new Hello();

        assertEquals(hello.sayHello(), "Good Afternoon!"); ❷
    }
}
```

❶❷ One of these assertions will fail.

We need to think of something different… And voila! The trick is to make time a collaborator of the `Hello` class. In order to do this, we need to:

- create a new interface - see Listing 6.25,

- redesign `Hello` class a little bit - see Listing 6.26.

Listing 6.25. The TimeProvider interface

```
/**
 * Allows for taking control over time in unit tests.
 */
public interface TimeProvider {

    Calendar getTime();
}
```

A default implementation of the `TimeProvider` interface shown in Listing 6.25 would probably reuse the system calendar (`Calendar.getInstance()`).

Listing 6.26. Time as a collaborator

```
public class Hello {

    private TimeProvider timeProvider;

    public HelloRedesigned(TimeProvider timeProvider) { ❶
        this.timeProvider = timeProvider;
    }

    public String sayHello() {
        Calendar current = timeProvider.getTime(); ❷
        if (current.get(Calendar.HOUR_OF_DAY) < 12) {
            return "Good Morning!";
        }
        else {
            return "Good Afternoon!";
        }
    }
}
```

❶   The `TimeProvider` collaborator has been injected as a constructor parameter, which means it is easily replaceable with a test double.

❷   `timeProvider.getTime()` is used instead of `Calendar.getInstance()`.

Suddenly, the tests of the redesigned `Hello` class have become trivial. Listing 6.28 shows a possible implementation.

Listing 6.27. Testing time - setting the stage

```
public class HelloRedesignedTest {

    private HelloRedesigned hello;
    private TimeProvider timeProvider;

    @BeforeMethod
    public void setUp() { ❶
        timeProvider = mock(TimeProvider.class);
        hello = new HelloRedesigned(timeProvider);
    }

...
```

❶   Here a mock of `TimeProvider` has been created and injected into the SUT[17].

Listing 6.28. Testing time is not an issue anymore

```
...
    @DataProvider
    private static final Object[][] morningHours(){
        return new Object[][] { {0}, {1}, {2}, {3},
                {4}, {5}, {6}, {7}, {8}, {9}, {10}, {11}};
    }

    @Test(dataProvider = "morningHours") ❶
    public void shouldSayGoodMorningInTheMorning(int hour) {
        when(timeProvider.getTime()).thenReturn(getCalendar(hour)); ❷

        assertEquals(hello.sayHello(), "Good Morning!");
    }

    @DataProvider
    private static final Object[][] eveningHours(){
        return new Object[][] { {12}, {13}, {14}, {15},
                {16}, {17}, {18}, {19}, {20}, {21}, {22}, {23}};
    }

    @Test(dataProvider = "eveningHours") ❸
    public void shouldSayGoodAfternoonInTheAfternoon(int hour) {
        when(timeProvider.getTime()).thenReturn(getCalendar(hour)); ❹

        assertEquals(hello.sayHello(), "Good Afternoon!");
    }

    private Calendar getCalendar(int hour) {
        Calendar cal = Calendar.getInstance();
        cal.set(Calendar.HOUR_OF_DAY, hour);
        return cal;
    }
}
```

❶❸   Both test methods take parameters provided by data providers.

❷❹   Here we have stubbing of the `timeProvider` test double.

If you run this new test it should pass. No matter if it is 3 am or 6 pm, it will pass. Apparently, time is not a issue anymore. :)

---

[17]Because the test-fixture setting code grew, I decided to put it into a separate method. See Section 9.7.2 for some discussion.

Redesign Is Not The Only Way. This redesign trick (i.e. implementing time provider as a separate entity) is not the only way of dealing with such time-dependent code. Using tools like PowerMock or JMockit it is possible to convince the `Calendar` class to return whatever value we want. I do not recommend such solutions, because they do not make the SUT's code any better. Instead they make its current implementation fixed, by repeating some of its implementation details within the test code (see Section 7.5 for a discussion of the trade-offs between the redesign option and its alternatives). Nevertheless, I do believe you should know about the different options – which is why I mention them.

6.8.1. Test Every Date (Within Reason)

Now that we know how to deal with time-dependent code - it really is that simple! - it is time for some general, but nevertheless very important, remarks.

Numerous bugs relate to undertested code, which depends on time. Developers seem to share a naive faith that *"if it works today, then it should also work tomorrow"*. Well, not necessarily. The point I want to make is that you should be really, really cautious when dealing with time, which in essence means the following:

- be pedantic when writing unit tests for such code,

- run your tests with at least a few subsequent years in mind.

With unit tests, there really is no excuse for not running tests for all possible dates or hours. Why not run tests for 5 years in advance, if your tests are ultra-fast? Just do it and then you can rest confident that for the next five years you will not encounter any time-related issue in that particular piece of code.

6.8.2. Conclusions

In this section we have discussed how to deal with time-dependent SUTs. The solution is quite simple: make time one of the SUT's collaborators, and then do exactly what you would with other collaborators: replace it with a test double. Once you have done this, your design will be improved (the SUT is freed from time-management knowledge and can focus on business logic), and you can then proceed with a standard approach to all collaborators. Yes, this is enough to triumph over time (at least in unit tests). :)

The technique presented in this section is sufficient to deal with the time problem at the unit-testing level. However, it does not solve many problems related to time that you will encounter when testing applications on a higher level. The different time-zones of servers and databases, triggers in databases, or external processes running only during certain hours of the night, as well as security certificates whose viability expires, will all give you a good deal of trouble. Fortunately, though, none of these affect unit tests!

6.9. Testing Collections

Sometimes the methods of SUTs return collections whose content is the outcome of an SUT's business logic: of course, this is something to be tested. This section provides some information on testing collections and their content.

6.9.1. The TDD Approach - Step by Step

First of all, a few remarks on testing collection content with TDD. It is advisable to do this step by step. Start with a simple assertion which verifies that a returned collection is not null. Watch the test fail (as a default implementation created by your IDE will probably return null). Make the test pass by returning a new collection. Add another assertion verifying whether or not the returned collection has the expected number of elements. Now start verifying the content.

An example of the resulting test code is shown in Listing 6.29. It contains many assertions, each progressively more restrictive than the previous one.

Listing 6.29. TDD collection content testing

```
public class UserTest{

    @Test
    public void shouldReturnUsersPhone() {
        User user = new User();
        user.addPhone("123 456 789");

        List<String> phones = user.getPhones();

        assertNotNull(phones); ❶
        assertEquals(phones.size(), 1);
        assertTrue(phones.contains("123 456 789"));
    }
}
```

❶ Always worth checking, as it defends us from a NulPointerException being thrown in consecutive assertions.

Even though this pattern might seem unnatural at first, the benefit is that if anything goes wrong, you can pinpoint bugs with 100% accuracy. But of course, you do not have to be so meticulous - if you feel like moving in larger steps, then by all means do so. You might save a few seconds here, but on the other hand you might lose much more time later. It is for you to decide.

6.9.2. TestNG Assertions for Collections Verification

As shown in Listing 6.29, it is possible to test collections content using the common assertions of TestNG, e.g. assertEquals(), assertTrue() and assertFalse(). In case you should need to compare the content of two collections, TestNG offers a few specialized versions of assertEquals() that will facilitate this task[18]:

- assertEquals(java.util.Map actual, java.util.Map expected)

- assertEquals(java.util.Set actual, java.util.Set expected)

- assertEquals(java.util.Collection actual, java.util.Collection expected)

- assertEquals(java.lang.Object[] actual, java.lang.Object[] expected) - returns true if two arrays contain the same elements in the same order,

- assertEqualsNoOrder(java.lang.Object[] actual, java.lang.Object[] expected) - returns true if the same elements exists in both arrays, but does not require them to be in the same order.

The first three methods - for Map, Set and Collection - return true if both parameters contain the same elements. No order is considered, even if a particular implementation of the Map, Set or Collection interface backs up ordering. Listing 6.30 presents an example of such a situation: both sets are considered equal, even if the order of insertion (which is taken into account by LinkedHashSet) is not the same.

---

[18]Each of the methods also has an overloaded version which takes a String message as an additional parameter. See http://testng.org/javadocs/org/testng/Assert.html

Listing 6.30. Collection content testing

```
public class SetEqualityTest {

    @Test
    public void twoSetsAreEqualsIfTheyHaveSameContent() {
        Set<String> setA = new LinkedHashSet<String>();
        Set<String> setB = new LinkedHashSet<String>();

        String s1 = "s1";
        String s2 = "s2";

        setA.add(s1);
        setA.add(s2); ❶

        setB.add(s2);
        setB.add(s1); ❷

        assertEquals(setA, setB); ❸
    }
}
```

❶   Set `setA` contains *"s1"* and *"s2"* (in this order).
❷   Set `setB` contains *"s2"* and *"s1"* (in this order).
❸   Still, both sets are considered equal, when compared using the `assertEquals()`
     method.

Even if the set of TestNG assertions devoted to collections is limited, it might be enough for simple tests. What is important is that in cases of failure a detailed error message is presented – as when, for example, in comparing two sets with different content, the following information is printed by TestNG:

Listing 6.31. Detailed error message printed by TestNG

```
Sets differ: expected [s2] but got [s1, s2]
```

6.9.3. Using External Assertions

Sometimes you will need more for collections testing than TestNG can offer. In such cases, you may refer to other frameworks, which can be combined with TestNG tests. Below you will find examples of **Unitils**[19], **Hamcrest**[20] and **FEST Fluent Assertions**[21] usage for collections testing. However, please make sure that you read the documentation for each of these projects, as this book does not set out to comprehensively describe all of their features.

 The use of matchers libraries (like Hamcrest and FEST) is described in detail in Section 6.5.

Unitils

The test shown in Listing 6.32 gives an example of testing collections content using **Unitils**. With Unitils, it is up to the programmer to decide what it means for two collections to be considered "equal". For the sake of brevity, this test uses the same sets (setA and setB) as shown in Listing 6.30.

Listing 6.32. Collection content testing with Unitils

```
import org.unitils.reflectionassert.ReflectionComparatorMode; ❶
import static org.unitils.reflectionassert
                .ReflectionAssert.assertReflectionEquals; ❷

public class SetEqualityTest {

    // same setA and setB created as in the previous TestNG example

    ...

    @Test
    public void twoSetsAreEqualsIfTheyHaveSameContentAndSameOrder() {
        assertReflectionEquals(setA, setB); ❸
    }

    @Test
    public void twoSetsAreEqualsIfTheyHaveSameContentAndAnyOrder() {
        assertReflectionEquals(setA, setB,
            ReflectionComparatorMode.LENIENT_ORDER); ❹
    }
}
```

---

[19]http://www.unitils.org/
[20]http://code.google.com/p/hamcrest/
[21]http://fest.codehaus.org/Fluent+Assertions+Module

❶❷ Unitils library classes are imported.

❸ This will **fail** because `assertReflectionEquals()` verifies both the content and the order of collections elements by default.

❹ By setting `ReflectionComparatorMode` to `LENIENT_ORDER` we can alter the `assertionReflectionEquals()` so that it only verifies the content and is indifferent to the ordering of elements.

 Unitils offers some other assertions that are helpful for collections testing too. For example, you can use it to verify that elements of a collection have certain values of a specific property. Please refer to Unitils documentation for more information.

In cases of test failure, some very detailed information about the collections subject to comparison will be printed. Below, an exemplary error message is shown. It was caused by a failed test, which asserted the equality of two collections that were not exactly equal.

Listing 6.33. Detailed error message of Unitils assertions

```
Expected: ["s1", "s2"], actual: ["s2", "s1"]

--- Found following differences ---
[0]: expected: "s1", actual: "s2"
[1]: expected: "s2", actual: "s1"
```

Testing Collections Using Matchers

Matcher libraries offer some interesting features that are helpful for collections testing. As discussed in Section 6.5, they furnish two main benefits:

- very readable code,

- very detailed error messages (in case of test failure).

Both of the above can be observed in the examples given in this section.

FEST Fluent Assertions, which is a part of **FEST** library, offers many assertions which can simplify collections testing. Listing 6.34 shows some of them. It provides a fluent interface[22], which allows for the chaining together of assertions.

---

[22]See http://martinfowler.com/bliki/FluentInterface.html

Listing 6.34. Testing collections with FEST Fluent Assertions

```
import static org.fest.assertions.Assertions.assertThat; ❶
import static org.fest.assertions.MapAssert.entry; ❷

public class FestCollectionTest {

    // same setA and setB created as in the previous TestNG example

    ...

    public void collectionsUtilityMethods() {
        assertThat(setA).isNotEmpty()
            .hasSize(2).doesNotHaveDuplicates(); ❸
        assertThat(setA).containsOnly(s1, s2); ❹
    }

    public void mapUtilityMethods() {
        HashMap<String, Integer> map
            = new LinkedHashMap<String, Integer>();
        map.put("a", 2);
        map.put("b", 3);

        assertThat(map).isNotNull().isNotEmpty()
                .includes(entry("a", 2), entry("b", 3))
                .excludes(entry("c", 1)); ❺
    }
}
```

❶❷   A few imports of FEST methods.

❸   As mentioned previously FEST provides a fluent interface, which allows for the chaining together of assertions. In this the case verification of emptiness, size and the absence of duplicates all gets fitted into a single line of code, but the code is still readable.

❹   A specialized method, `containsOnly()`, verifies that the given collection contains nothing other than the elements specified.

❺   Similarly, in the case of maps specialized assertions allow for a very readable and concise test.

A different set of assertions is provided by the **Hamcrest** library. Some of these are shown below:

Listing 6.35. Testing collections with Hamcrest assertions

```
import static org.hamcrest.MatcherAssert.assertThat; ❶
import static org.hamcrest.collection.IsCollectionContaining.hasItem;
import static org.hamcrest.collection.IsCollectionContaining.hasItems;
import static org.hamcrest.collection.IsMapContaining.hasEntry;
import static org.hamcrest.collection.IsMapContaining.hasKey;

public class HamcrestCollectionTest {

    // same setA and setB created as in previous TestNG example

    ...

    public void collectionsUtilityMethods() { ❷
        assertThat(setA, hasItem(s1));
        assertThat(setA, hasItem(s2));
        assertThat(setA, hasItems(s1, s2, "xyz"));
    }

    public void mapsUtilityMethods() { ❸
        assertThat(map, hasEntry("a", (Object) 2));
        assertThat(map, hasKey("b"));
    }
}
```

❶   The required Hamcrest classes and methods are imported.

❷   Hamcrest allows us to test whether or not a given collection contains specific values.

❸   In the case of maps, Hamcrest provides assertions for entries (key and value) or keys only.

Both libraries also offer an interesting feature – namely, that of searching objects within collections based on their properties. The example below has been written with FEST Fluent Assertions:

Listing 6.36. Testing collections objects by properties

```
import static org.fest.assertions.Assertions.assertThat;

@Test
public class FestTest {

    public void lookingIntoProperties() {
        Collection<Book> books = new HashSet<Book>();
        books.add(new Book("Homer", "Odyssey"));         ❶
        books.add(new Book("J.R.R. Tolkien", "Hobbit"));

        assertThat(books).onProperty("title").contains("Hobbit");           ❷
        assertThat(books).onProperty("author").contains("J.R.R. Tolkien");  ❸
        assertThat(books).onProperty("author").contains("Bill Clinton");    ❹
    }
}
```

❶   A constructor of the `Book` class sets its two fields - `author` and `title`.

❷❸   These two assertions will pass.

❹   This one will fail - my books collection does not include any work by "Bill Clinton".

Both Hamcrest and FEST offer very detailed and readable error messages. For example, when looking for the String `"xyz"` in a set of two Strings comprising `"s1"` and `"s2"`, the following message is printed by Hamcrest:

Listing 6.37. Detailed error message of Hamcrest collections assertions

```
java.lang.AssertionError:
Expected: a collection containing "xyz"
    got: <[s1, s2]>
```

6.9.4. Custom Solution

If your needs with regard to collection testing are so specific that neither TestNG nor the libraries shown here can satisfy them, then you will have no choice but to come up with your own solution. You will have at least two options for how to proceed:

• write utility methods which will do collections verification as you require it to be done,

• create custom matchers - see Section 6.5.

The first option is faster to implement, but it does not add to the readability of tests. Matchers require some additional work, but they offer greater reusability and a nice testing DSL[23], which gives very readable assertions.

6.9.5. Conclusions

In this section various ways of testing collections have been discussed. First, we looked at what TestNG offers in this respect. Then, examples of Unitils, FEST Fluent Assertions and Hamcrest were given, along with brief information about other features of these libraries. Finally, we took a look at custom solutions.

In conclusion, if your tests involve a great deal of collections testing, I would suggest investing time in mastering one of the libraries presented in this section. FEST Fluent Assertions seems to me the best choice (when it comes to collection testing), because it provides a lot of useful assertions and is very extensible, so you can also add your own if required.

6.10. Reading Data From Excel Files

A commonly arising issue concerns the reading of data for tests from some external source – e.g. Excel. This is especially important if the data is provided by someone else (e.g. QA people, or maybe even your client). The likelihood of them using Excel (or its Open/ LibreOffice counterparts) is quite high.

Figure 6.1. Excel data file (created with LibreOffice)

value	discount
$0.00	0
$999.99	0
$1,000.00	0.01
$1,999.99	0.01
$2,000.00	0.02
$2,999.99	0.02
$5,000.00	0.03

[23]DSL - Domain Specific Language, http://en.wikipedia.org/wiki/Domain-specific_language

Let us assume that the Excel file, with some simple financial data in it, looks as shown in Figure 6.1.

Now, we want to test whether the DiscountCalculator class, when given a value from the first column, returns a discount equal to the one in the second column. In order to do this, we could retype the values from the Excel file into the test code, but this is obviously no more than a short-term solution. Much better would be to read them from the original file. That way, if some new values are added, or some changes are introduced into the file, our test will pick up on them instantly. The test will inform us whether the DiscountCalculator class is still working properly with the new test data. No human intervention needed. Good.

Listing 6.38 shows one of the possible solutions. It imports the data from an Excel file within a data provider method. Next, we can use normal data provider syntax to pass the values read from that Excel file to a test method.

Listing 6.38. Test reading data from an Excel file

```
@DataProvider
public Iterator<Object[]> discountData()
            throws IOException, BiffException { ❶
    ArrayList<Object[]> myEntries = new ArrayList<Object[]>();
    File inputWorkbook = new File("src/test/resources/financial.xls");
    String value, discount;
    Workbook w = Workbook.getWorkbook(inputWorkbook); ❷
    Sheet sheet = w.getSheet(0); ❸
    for (int row = 1; row < sheet.getRows(); row++) { ❹
        value= sheet.getCell(0, row).getContents(); ❺
        discount = sheet.getCell(1, row).getContents(); ❻
        myEntries.add(new Object [] {value,discount});
    }
    return myEntries.iterator(); ❼
}

@Test(dataProvider = "discountData") ❽
public void shouldCalculateDiscount(String value, String discount) { ❾
    assertEquals(DiscountCalculator.calculateDiscount(
        Double.parseDouble(value)), Double.parseDouble(discount)); ❿
}
```

❶   This data provider returns an iterator (see Section 3.6.4) and throws some exceptions, which may occur when reading and parsing an Excel file.

[24]See http://jexcelapi.sourceforge.net/.

❷❸ The principal objects are created using Java Excel API[24].

❹ The first row contains column names, so we skip it.

❺❻ The data is read from the Excel file.

❼ An iterator containing all of the required data is returned.

❽❾ The test method gets data from the `discountData` provider.

❿ A normal TestNG assertion ensues, to make sure that `DiscountCalculator` returns reasonable results.

6.11. Conclusions

We started this section by discussing a few techniques that should definitely be in your testing toolbox. In particular, we took a detailed look at expected exceptions testing, and learned what matchers are good for.

In the earlier parts of this book we were discussing some artificial situations in order to demonstrate the basics of unit testing. This part has been different. We have tackled some real-life problems: *"how to test collections?"* or *"how to triumph over time in time-dependent methods?"* We have learned how to deal with each of them, so they are no longer scary, but just another thing we have to deal with in order to achieve our ultimate goal of high-quality, flawless code.

6.12. Exercises

In this section we have been discussing a number of aspects of advanced unit testing. Now it is time to practice some of these freshly acquired skills.

6.12.1. Design Test Cases: State Testing

A `StringUtils` class contains a `reverse()` method, with a signature as presented on Listing 6.39. List test cases, which would verify that this method really reverses the input String!

Listing 6.39. Signature of reverse Method

```
public String reverse(String s) { ... }
```

6.12.2. Design Test Cases: Interactions Testing

`UserServiceImpl` class contains the `assignPass()` method, as presented on Listing 6.40. The method uses two collaborators to successfully perform its task: `userDAO` and `securityService`.

Listing 6.40. updateUser() method

```
private UserDAO userDAO;
private SecurityService securityService;

@Override
public void assignPass(User user) throws Exception {
    String passwordMd5 = securityService.md5(user.getPassword());
    user.setPassword(passwordMd5);
    userDao.updateUser(user);
}
```

Design the test cases for this method! Please note that this time you will have to think not only about the input parameters (`user`), but also about the values returned (or exceptions thrown!) by `securityService` and `userDAO`.

6.12.3. Test Collections

Write a test for the trivial `UserList` class (shown in Listing 6.41), which will verify that:

- an empty list of users is returned if no users have been added,

- exactly one user is returned if only one has been added,

- two users are returned if two have been added.

To complete this task write the assertions using some tool or other that you have not made use of yet. See Section 6.9 for inspiration.

Listing 6.41. Testing collections - exercise

```
public class UserList {

    private List<User> users = new ArrayList<User>();

    public List<User> getUsers() {
        return users;
    }

    public void addUser(User user) {
        users.add(user);
    }
}
```

6.12.4. Time Testing

Listing 6.42 presents a single test-dependent method. Use the method described in Section 6.8 to test its business logic.

Listing 6.42. Time-dependent method - exercise

```java
public class HelpDesk {

    public final static int EOB_HOUR = 17;

    public boolean willHandleIssue(Issue issue) {
        Calendar cal = Calendar.getInstance();
        int dayOfWeek = cal.get(Calendar.DAY_OF_WEEK);
        if (Calendar.SUNDAY == dayOfWeek || Calendar.SATURDAY == dayOfWeek) {
            return false;
        }
        if (Calendar.FRIDAY == dayOfWeek) {
            int hour = cal.get(Calendar.HOUR_OF_DAY);
            if (hour > EOB_HOUR) {
                return false;
            }
        }
        return true;
    }
}
```

6.12.5. Write a Custom Matcher

Write a custom matcher - using the library of your choice - so that you are then in a position to write nicely readable assertions for the given OperatingSystem class, should you wish to:

Listing 6.43. The OperatingSystem class

```java
public class OperatingSystem {

    private int nbOfBits;

    private String name;

    private String version;

    private int releaseYear;

    // getters and setters omitted
}
```

An example of what you should achieve is presented below (written with FEST, but you can use Hamcrest to achieve a similar effect, if it suits you better):

Listing 6.44. Test of the OperatingSystem class

```
@Test
public class OperatingSystemTest {

    private OperatingSystem os;

    public void testUsingMatcher() {
        OperatingSystem min9 = new Mindows9();
        assertThat(min9).is128bit().wasReleasedIn(2013).hasVersion(9);
    }
}
```

Make sure you take care of any failed assertion messages in such a way that the cause of a failure is explicitly given.

Write some tests using your matcher, and decide whether it was worth the trouble of implementing it.

6.12.6. Make an ID Generator Bulletproof

As an additional exercise, please provide the implementation for an ID generator like that discussed in Section 6.7, that will pass the tests shown in Listing 6.22.

Chapter 7. Points of Controversy

> Discussion is an exchange of knowledge; an argument an exchange of ignorance.
>
> — Robert Quillen

There are many topics related to writing tests that are still up for debate within the developer community. In this section we will discuss some of these. Sometimes a definite answer will be given, sometimes a variety of options will be presented – for you, dear reader, to decide about.

7.1. Random Values in Tests

At first, testing and random values seem to fit together nicely. Some people apparently think that running tests each time with different values can better prove the robustness of their code than running it with some selected values. In my experience, this is a fallacy, and using random values in tests causes more harm than good. In fact, I can recall instances of randomness being used in tests where it proved futile, but none where it turned out to be worthwhile! This section shows some typical cases that are to be avoided.

Before we start discussing code, however, let me just say that there are many ways to generate random values, including:

- custom "utility methods",

- using libraries for general use; e.g. Apache Commons Lang library[1] provides a RandomStringUtils class, which contains a plethora of methods for generating random Strings of the requested length and consisting of different character sets (e.g. only letters, only numbers, a combination of both, etc.),

- using specialized test-focused frameworks like Quickcheck[2] or Feed4TestNG[3].

The issues that I would like to discuss here are not really related to any particular way of generating random values, but rather to the idea of using randomness in your tests.

---

[1] http://commons.apache.org/lang/
[2] http://java.net/projects/quickcheck
[3] http://databene.org/feed4testng.html

7.1.1. Random Object Properties

Let us assume that an SUT (of the `UserToPersonConverter` class) can translate an object of the User class into objects of the `Person` class by turning the user's `name` and `surname` into a person's `nickname`. The implementation of the SUT is shown below:

Let us assume that SUT (class `UserToPersonConverter`) can translate object of `User` class into objects of `Person` class by turning user's `name` and `surname` into person's `nick`. The implementation of SUT is presented below:

Listing 7.1. The UserToPersonConverter class

```
public class UserToPersonConverter {

    public static Person convert(User user) {
        return new Person(user.getName() + " " + user.getSurname());
    }
}
```

A test of this class can take advantage of random values. Such an attempt is shown in Listing 7.2.

Listing 7.2. Test of the UserToPersonConverter class

```
public class UserToPersonConverterTest {

    @Test
    public void shouldConvertUserNamesIntoPersonNick() {
        String name = RandomStringUtils.randomAlphabetic(8);
        String surname = RandomStringUtils.randomAlphabetic(12);
        User user = new User(name, surname);

        Person person = UserToPersonConverter.convert(user);

        assertEquals(person.getNick(), name + " " + surname);
    }
}
```

As far as I understand the idea behind the implementation shown in Listing 7.2, random values are to be used because they (supposedly) highlight the robustness of a given test. It is as if the test were to shout *"Hey look, every time I execute the test it uses a different user's name and still passes! Amazing, isn't it?"*.

7.1.2. Generating Multiple Test Cases

A natural next step in the direction of making the test even more impressive would be to test the same functionality with more random values, within a single execution of a test method. This can be achieved using data providers, for example:

Listing 7.3. Creation of multiple random test cases

```
public class UserToPersonConverterDataProvidersTest {

    @DataProvider
    private static Object[][] getRandomNames() {
        Object[][] values = new Object[100][];
        for (int i = 0; i < values.length; i++) {
            values[i] = new Object[] {RandomStringUtils.randomAlphabetic(8),
                RandomStringUtils.randomAlphabetic(12)};
        }
        return values;
    }

    @Test(dataProvider = "getRandomNames")
    public void shouldConvertUserNamesIntoPersonNick(
            String name, String surname) { ❶
        User user = new User(name, surname);

        Person person = UserToPersonConverter.convert(user);

        assertEquals(person.getNick(), name + " " + surname);
    }
}
```

❶   This test method is executed 100 times with different random values.

Even if the test in Listing 7.3 looks much more serious than the previous one, it is not really much stronger. It only tricks us into thinking that UserToPersonConverter has now been thoroughly tested. Unfortunately it hasn't been.

Let us take another look at the implementation of the UserToPersonConverter class (shown in Listing 7.1). Has it been tested more effectively, just because we have passed 100 nonsensical, unpronounceable names (each time of the same length, namely 8 and 12)? I do not think so. The probability that tests 2 to 100 will reveal some bugs not discovered by the first test is minimal. The diversity of test parameters is very limited, and so is the value added by each of the tests. It would not increase, even if we were to up the number of randomly generated values from 100 to 1000.

When it comes to testing, I would rather prioritize the quality of test cases over the quantity. A good quality test case can expose some holes within the production code. I suggest thinking carefully about the possible scenarios (as discussed in Section 6.1) and then making a deliberate choice of some values. My test of the `UserToPersonConverter` class would definitely contain cases of names and surnames of varied length (including empty strings), with varied capitalization. I might even use some randomness to avoid putting so many names directly in the test code; however, I would make sure that some borderline cases (e.g. empty or extremely long strings) are verified. The variety of my test parameters would definitely be far greater than that generated by the data provider in Listing 7.3.

7.1.3. Conclusions

As you will have observed for yourself, generating multiple tests with random values does not automatically make the test suite stronger. Instead, it can complicate your tests and give rise to a number of issues. However, if randomness is really appropriate within the context of your testing domain, then at least try to do it right. Table 7.1 offers some hints and discusses issues relating to the use of random values in your tests.

Table 7.1. Issues with the random values of parameters

(possible) issue	comment
Why should I test with nonsensical values (e.g. `"(*&KLNHF_98234"` passed as String `name` parameter)?	You should not. "Random" does not have to mean "any". Take control over how parameters values are generated, e.g. use `RandomStringUtils.randomAlphabetic()` method from the Apache Commons Lang library in cases of the `name` parameter.
I do not have control over random values, so how can I guarantee that some values (e.g. boundary values) will always be checked?	Do not rely solely on random values! Apart from random values, you also **have to** make sure boundary values (and any other values which are important to your code) are being used. Probably you need two sources of parameters - one controlled by you, and one random.
Hard to repeat. How can I repeat something which is random?	Repeatability is an important thing. If you do not have it, then you might know there is a bug in your code, but you will not be able to nail it down - which will surely

(possible) issue	comment
	cost you a few gray hairs. However, it is possible to repeat your tests, even when random values are being used. First of all, `testng-results.xml` file contains comprehensive information on parameters passed to test methods, so you can see what values were used there. You can also control the way the random values are generated by choosing the seed, remembering it (e.g. by writing to some test report), and using it later to repeat the tests[a].
"Flickering tests" - every execution of the test suite could end with a different result.	Every time the test fails, add the values which made it fail to your test. And of course, make it pass with these values.
Weird error messages.	Using random test values can result in obscure failure messages. For example, you can learn that the test failed because of some issue with user "IkldlDFg yw,cKxH.zDIF". This might be very confusing, especially if the test case has nothing to do with the user's name. I would suggest using much simpler values, which reveal the intention much better - e.g. "ANY_NAME ANY_SURNAME" would be much more clear.

[a]If you are interested in details, please refer to Jaroslav Tulach's article at http://wiki.apidesign.org/wiki/RandomizedTest

 Some specialized tools, e.g. Quickcheck, provide solutions for some of the issues described above.

I have to admit I am not a big fan of using random values in tests. I do not see many cases where using them would improve the test. In general, I would rather suggest:

- spending more time pondering over important values which should be verified (see the discussion in Section 6.1) instead of generating thousands of random cases.

- using meaningful names instead of random garbage strings.

7.2. Test Dependencies

> A test should be able to stand on its own. It should not rely on any other
> test, nor should it depend on tests being run in a specific order.
>
> — Roy Osherove

For a long time it was believed that **test dependencies are evil**. The ability to run tests independently was considered to be one of the most important features of unit tests. JUnit never supported any form of test dependency and still does not help with achieving that. This generally accepted idea was challenged by TestNG author Cédric Beust, who made it possible to express dependencies between tests written using TestNG[4].

In this section we shall meet with some examples which will enable us to discuss various aspects of test dependencies. But before we start, let us note that there are a variety of things we can have in mind when discussing them.

- Tests can depend on each other at the "data level". For example, one test may use data put into the database by another test. Tests with such dependencies are usually hard to manage, because the connections between them are not obvious (if not stated explicitly).

- A test can rely on behaviour verified by some other test(s). For example, a test which verifies the removal of user accounts from a system may rely on the fact of those user accounts having been properly created.

- Test dependencies can be expressed explicitly (e.g. using annotations provided by the testing framework) or implicitly. The latter situation is much more cumbersome, because it makes test managing much harder.

 Test dependencies play a secondary role in unit tests. Their true power and usefulness is revealed when they are used for integration and end-to-end tests. Then they help immensely by cutting down the execution time (in cases of test failures) and adding to the tests' maintainability by honouring the DRY principle. It is certainly no accident that TestNG (which aims at different types of tests), and not JUnit, was responsible for introducing them.

In general, there are two main reasons for having test dependencies. The first relates to the **DRY principle**, the second to the **fail fast** approach.

---

[4]See Beust's original blog post: http://beust.com/weblog/2005/03/17/are-dependent-test-methods-really-evil/

7.2.1. Test Dependencies and the DRY Principle

The DRY principle says, basically, that everything within the system should be expressed once – and only once. It recognizes the pain caused by information replication: the fact that over the course of time it leads (inevitably, as experience shows) to discrepancies between versions of the same information. So having a piece of data in one place, as the DRY principle encourages us to do, protects us from this serious problem. With tests, this means you should avoid repetition between different test methods. An example will prove that it is possible to make a test respect this principle; however, there is an inevitable price to pay for this.

For example, let us imagine a web console for a system administrator which makes it possible to manage users. One can imagine a test which creates a new user account, and another which removes it from the system. To keep the tests independent, we might come up with two quite separate tests, as shown in Listing 7.4.

Listing 7.4. Independent tests violating the DRY principle

```
@Test
public void testAddition() {
    // adds user X to the system ❶
    // verifies it exists, by issuing SQL query against the database
}

@Test
public void testDeletion() {
    // adds user Y to the system ❷
    // verify that it exists (so later we know that it was actually removed)
    // removes user Y
    // makes sure it does not exist, by issuing SQL query against the database
}
```

❶❷   The same functionality and assertions are present in both tests.

The tests in Listing 7.4 share some common code which creates a new user account, and verifies its existence. Thus the DRY principle has been violated here. If the semantics of user addition were to be changed, then this would make it necessary to rewrite parts of both test methods. Such a maintenance burden could easily be reduced by *"extract method"* refactoring[5] of the code fragment responsible for adding new users into a helper/ utility method - e.g. an `addUser(User user)` method. Then, both `testAddition()` and `testDeletion()` would invoke the `createUser()` method, and the details on how to add a user to the system would be encapsulated in one place.

This would be a positive step forward, but making such a change does not resolve the entire issue. The point is that `testDeletion()` can still fail if the creation of new accounts does not work properly. For example, if the `addUser()` method throws exceptions, then `testDeletion()` will be marked as failed, even though the mechanism of deletion may be working perfectly well. This is misleading. Ideally, `testDeletion()` should only fail if the deletion mechanism is not working.

Even though the test in Listing 7.4 has some issues with code redundancy, there are also some good things about it:

- Both test methods are independent.

    - They can be run in any order, and there is no common test fixture used by both.

    - They can be independently changed, which helps with maintaining them.

- You can understand each of them without looking at any other test method. This enhances their readability.

One can see that verification of the user's existence in `testDeletion()` is superfluous, as this is tested by `testAddition()`. That is indeed true; however, if we remove it, we introduce some kind of dependency between the two tests. When running `testDeletion()` we assume that the addition of user accounts is working, which means we are relying on `testAddition()`. Thus we create an implicit dependency between `testAddition()` and `testDeletion()`.

Another approach to the implementation of these two test cases is shown in Listing 7.5.

---

[5]See http://sourcemaking.com/refactoring/extract-method

Listing 7.5. Dependent tests honouring thc DRY principle

```
@Test
public void testAddition() {
    // adds user X to the system
    // verifies it exists, by issuing SQL query against the database
}

@Test(dependsOnMethods = "testAddition") ❶
public void testDeletion() {
    // removes user X
    // makes sure it does not exist, by issuing SQL query against the database
}
```

❶ Here we have a case of explicit dependency involving the dependsOnMethods attribute of the @Test annotation.

This time, an explicit dependency is established between the tests. It brings with it the following properties:

- It is guaranteed that testDeletion() will be executed after testAddition().

- If testAddition() fails then testDeletion() will be skipped. This seems right: why bother with testing of "delete" if "add" does not work?

- The **DRY** principle is honoured. There is no repetition of code at all. No need to refactor in order to extract any helper methods.

- The dependency of both tests is expressed explicitly (with the dependsOnMethods attribute of the @Test annotation). The testDeletion() test expects certain data stored in a database by testAddition() to be there.

- To understand testDeletion() one must also understand what testAddition() does. This means browsing through the code base, which is an additional effort.

- If there are test dependencies, the manageability of tests is greatly reduced.

As this example demonstrates, test dependencies can help make our tests adhere to the DRY principle. However, this comes at a certain price – namely, the maintenance of such tests.

 Dependency sets the order of execution, but not the immediate sequence! In our example, assuming that we have some more test methods, that would mean that the order of execution might be the following: 1) testAddition(), 2) testMethodA(), 3) testMethodB(), 4) testDeletion().

7.2.2. Fail Fast

Another reason to use test dependencies is that doing so can shorten the execution time. This fits well with the **fail fast**[6] approach, which can be summarized as *"if it has to fail, better make it fail immediately"*. This feature is very important for longer-running tests; however, it is also of some use with unit tests.

Even if the performance gain is minimal, in some cases using test dependencies would be recommended, as they allow relations between tests to be expressed explicitly.

Let us consider an example that shows tests of a constructor and some methods of an object (SUT). This is shown in Listing 7.6.

Listing 7.6. Test dependencies - always running all tests

```
@Test ❶
public void testConstructor() {
    // make sure SUT is properly constructed
}

@Test
public void testBehaviourA() {
    // test some behaviour of SUT
}

@Test
public void testBehaviourB() {
    // test some behaviour of SUT
}

@Test
public void testBehaviourC() {
    // test some behaviour of SUT
}
```

❶   No test depends on the testConstructor() method.

When all tests pass, then everything is fine. But what if testConstructor() fails? It is very probable that all other tests will fail as well (because, for example, the SUT is null). This

---

[6]See http://en.wikipedia.org/wiki/Fail-fast

creates confusion, because the test report will present 4 failed tests, instead of just the one which caused the problem.

And if the SUT has not been properly constructed, then what is the point in verifying its proper behaviour? It might behave properly or it might not, but either way the results are meaningless. For example, you will not know whether it is behaving well because its implementation is good or thanks to a constructor error!

If you fail fast – that is, if you stop the testing of the SUT after `testContructor()` has failed – you will not have any difficulties discovering the root cause of the problems: namely, poor implementation of the SUT's constructor. The test report won't include any other failed tests such as might trick you into thinking some other code was wrong[7]. This is exactly how TestNG works: by skipping (i.e. not running) tests that depend on a failed test.

Listing 7.7 shows the same testing code, enhanced with dependencies amongst the test methods that will allow the test to fail fast. Now if `testConstructor()` fails, all other tests will be marked as skipped. The culprit will be clear.

Listing 7.7. Test dependencies - failing fast

```
@Test
public void testConstructor() {
    // make sure SUT is properly constructed
}

@Test(dependsOnMethods = "testConstructor") ❶
public void testBehaviourA() {
    // test some behaviour of SUT
}

@Test(dependsOnMethods = "testConstructor") ❷
public void testBehaviourB() {
    // test some behaviour of SUT
}

@Test(dependsOnMethods = "testConstructor") ❸
public void testBehaviourC() {
    // test some behaviour of SUT
}
```

❶❷❸ All three behaviour tests will be skipped if `testConstructor()` fails.

---

[7]Of course, after you have fixed the constructor, you might find out that other methods of the SUT are also flawed. But you will be able to discover the problems one at a time, which makes them far easier to fix.

This is an example of tests that rely on behaviour verified by some other test. Another classic example of such tests comes from integration tests: one test verifies that you can connect to some external resource (e.g. a database or web service) and the other tests rely on this in order to test communication with this resource.

 In the case of integration and end-to-end tests it is quite common to have groups of tests that depend on each other (or groups that depend on single tests). For example, a small, selected portion of the tests (e.g. smoke tests) can be run before any other tests, which will be run only if the smoke test succeeds. Group dependencies are rarely useful for unit tests. Please consult the TestNG documentation for more information on the concept of a group in TestNG.

7.2.3. Make It Explicit

Test dependencies may be very useful, but they can certainly also be misused. Probably the worst thing you can do is rely on some test dependencies without expressing them explicitly. The code in Listing 7.8 presents a snippet of test code which does exactly this.

Listing 7.8. Evil hidden dependencies

```
private NotificationServer server = ...; ❶

@Test
public void shouldRegister() { ❷
    server.register(someObject);
    // some assertions here
}

@Test
public void shouldUnregister() { ❸
    server.unregister(someObject);
    // some assertions here
}
```

❶   The SUT is initiated only once and is not cleaned before each test.
❷   This test changes the state of the SUT.
❸   This test relies on the change introduced in `shouldRegister()`. It assumes that `someObject` is registered. However, this expectation is not stated explicitly.

Surprisingly, the tests on Listing 7.8 might work pretty well! As long as the testing framework selects a "proper" (e.g. alphabetical) order of executing them, they will pass.

However, if even the slightest change is introduced, they might fail at some point. This can be induced by a change in the tests (e.g. addition of a new test method, or some innocent-seeming refactoring), but also by a change of environment (e.g. an upgrading of your JDK). Fixing this bug might not be an easy task, and will surely be preceded with head-scratching and repeating things like *"it has to work, it always did!"*. Neither will help, as the tests passed thousands of times accidentally. Now they do not, and you need to investigate the case.

 If you have dependencies in your tests, then better name them explicitly.

7.2.4. Remove Unnecessary Test Dependencies

Sometimes test dependencies are simply there, and the only thing we can do is express them explicitly, so that those responsible in the future for the maintenance of our tests are not taken by surprise. However, I have often observed test dependencies being created for no good reason, thus lowering the quality of our tests and raising the maintenance costs.

An example of such test dependencies is shown in Listing 7.9. This test aims to verify whether the `Account` class allows basic `deposit()` and `withdraw()` operations to be performed. In the real world we would have created many more tests, but such an incomplete test allows us to concentrate on the issue at hand – namely, unnecessary test dependencies.

Listing 7.9. Unnecessary test dependencies

```
@Test
public class AccountDependenciesTest {
    private Account account;
    private static final int INITIAL_AMOUNT = 0;

    @BeforeClass ❶
    public void setUp() {
        account = new Account(INITIAL_AMOUNT);
    }

    public void shouldAllowToDepositMoney() { ❷
        account.deposit(30);

        assertEquals(30, account.getBalance());
    }

    @Test(dependsOnMethods = "shouldAllowToDepositMoney") ❸
    public void shouldAllowToWithdrawMoney() {
        account.withdraw(10);

        assertEquals(20, account.getBalance()); ❹
    }
}
```

❶   The SUT – an object of the `Account` class - is created only once for all tests of this class (as dictated by the `@BeforeClass` annotation). Any changes introduced into it by a test method will be visible to any subsequently executed test method.

❷   This method changes the state of the `account` object (the SUT) by depositing some money there.

❸   The second test method explicitly defines its dependency on the first test method.

❹   The assertion of the second test method takes advantage of the modifications made to the SUT in the previous test: it assumes the balance at the beginning of the test is equal to `30`.

First of all, this is a valid test. It tests some important features of the `Account` class. It is rather easy to read and understand. However, it has a test method which depends on another method, which makes it cumbersome to work with.

For example, suppose we enhance the functionality of the `Account` class with another feature, and add a test method for it, as shown in Listing 7.10.

Listing 7.10. Test for an additional method

```
public void shouldAllowToCloseAccount() {
    account.close();
    assertEquals(0, account.getBalance());
}
```

Now, if we execute our test class with this new test method, two things can happen, depending on the order of execution (which is not guaranteed by default):

- If we are lucky, the new test method gets executed at the very end of the test suite, and nothing bad will happen.

- If the new test method gets executed between `shouldAllowToDepositMoney()` and `shouldAllowToWithdrawMoney()`, then the latter will fail.

A careful programmer will spot this danger at once and take precautionary measures. In particular, adding another test dependency will guarantee that the methods are executed in the desired order. The resulting test might take the form shown in Listing 7.11.

Listing 7.11. More dependencies to the rescue

```
@Test
public class AccountDependenciesMoreTest {
    private Account account;
    private static final int INITIAL_AMOUNT = 0;

    @BeforeClass
    public void setUp() { ... }

    public void shouldAllowToDepositMoney() { ... }

    @Test(dependsOnMethods = "shouldAllowToDepositMoney")
    public void shouldAllowToWithdrawMoney() { ... }

    @Test(dependsOnMethods = "shouldAllowToWithdrawMoney") ❶
    public void shouldAllowToCloseAccount() { ... }
}
```

❶ A new test dependency is introduced to make sure that we do not zero the account's balance before attempting to withdraw from it.

Okay, we have managed to do it this time, but... is what we have done right? Does the test for the account `close()` method have anything to do with the test for `withdraw()` ? Is this dependency semantically correct? I feel as if we had just been guilty of a misuse of test dependencies.

But it is not the philosophical issue that we should be worrying about right now. The problem is that:

- we had to do some additional work to add a test method,

- and we have made our test class harder to maintain.

The "additional work" consists of having to understand which test depends on which, and how to introduce a new test method so as not to break the existing ones. The maintenance cost gets increased, because we need to do this additional work every time we add a new test method. And it will get worse and worse with every added test method, as the complexity of our test class goes up. At some point this could hurt us a lot – especially if we need to modify tests long after they were initially created.

 Even if the dangers of such an approach are not fully and clearly demonstrated by such a limited example, this is something we really should be concerned about. I have witnessed some tests written using a similar approach, with tens of methods. Adding a new method to this test suite turned out to be a real nightmare: each time I had to track down the path of the test dependencies, which was highly frustrating. It felt like searching for needles in a haystack – but there was no alternative, if I wanted to be able to write new tests. I ended up having to substantially refactor the tests, as introducing changes was simply to costly (in terms of both time and energy).

To conclude, adding test dependencies is an important decision. Looking at our original test, and recalling the additional issues connected with it, we can assume that this has something to do with the SUT being shared amongst many test methods (and not being created before each of them). Such sharing of the SUT is a very common pattern for integration tests, and there are some valid reasons for this (e.g. it is not always feasible to generate a clean database scheme before each test method). However, in the case of unit tests it can usually be avoided with ease.

The next code sample - shown in Listing 7.12 - shows a different, dependency-free approach. This time the SUT does not outlive any particular test method; instead, it gets created anew before each of them.

Listing 7.12. Unnecessary test dependencies removed

```
@Test
public class AccountNoDependenciesTest {
    private Account account;
    private static final int INITIAL_AMOUNT = 100;

    @BeforeMethod ❶
    public void setUp() {
        account = new Account(INITIAL_AMOUNT);
    }

    public void shouldAllowToDepositMoney() {
        account.deposit(30);

        assertEquals(INITIAL_AMOUNT + 30, account.getBalance()); ❷
    }

    public void shouldAllowToWithdrawMoney() {
        account.withdraw(10);

        assertEquals(INITIAL_AMOUNT - 10, account.getBalance()); ❸
    }

    public void shouldAllowToCloseAccount() { ❹
        account.close();

        assertEquals(0, account.getBalance());
    }
}
```

❶ The creation of the `account` object is guaranteed to happen before each test method.

❷❸ The state of the `account` object is known, and we can verify the results of methods that have been executed by performing comparisons with this initial state.

❹ New test methods are added "just like that" - no additional effort is required.

This simple change – having the SUT created before each method – ensures that its state will be well known to each of them. This simplifies things greatly and renders test dependencies obsolete. Adding a new test method will now be completely painless.

As this example demonstrates, sometimes our design decisions (i.c. the way we go about the process of test fixture creation) force us to use test dependencies. With unit tests we have a lot of freedom to decide about how the SUT is to be created. My advice is to take full advantage of this and aim at having independent tests, which are much simpler to understand and cheaper to maintain.

7.2.5. Conclusions

The examples presented in this section demonstrate that test dependencies can take various forms. If we use them, there is always some trade-off involved. We can opt for **test independence**, or we can concentrate on the **DRY principle** and the **fail fast approach**. Once again, there is no easy answer as to which way to go. It depends on which of these test code features you value more.

I have witnessed (and have even participated in creating) some test code which was completely impossible to maintain, owing to the number of dependencies between test methods. These dependencies made any changes to the test code virtually impossible, at the same time as adding very little in return. What made it even harder was that some dependencies were not expressed explicitly.

In my experience, test dependencies are very helpful and dangerous at the same time. I use them mainly for integration and end-to-end tests. When it comes to unit tests, I use them less frequently. One thing I am certainly never prepared to accept is the creating of hidden dependencies involving tests.

 The idea of independent tests has been around right from the start of unit testing, and not without good reason!

7.3. How Many Assertions per Test Method?

> Chuck Norris can unit test an entire application with a single assert.
> — Wisdom of the Internet ;)

The idea of having only **One Assertion Per Test Method** (I will use the acronym OAPTM for this from here on) is quite popular among developers. Some of its popularity may be attributed to the misuse of multi-assertion test methods, which tend to grow into many lines of code (in the hands of inexperienced or incompetent developers). It has also been discussed on popular forums and promoted by a number of prominent TDD and testing proponents, including Dave Astel and Roy Osherove.

All of the code examples presented so far in this book make it quite obvious that I myself do not subscribe to this idea and do not follow it. And even though I understand and share some of the motivations behind it, I will try to persuade you **not** to subscribe to it either – at least, not in its dogmatic version.

7.3.1. Code Example

Let us take a look at an example, to make sure we understand the problem in hand. I will use an example taken from the "One Assertion per Test" post by Dave Astels[8]. It relates to the problem of parsing some information passed as a `String` argument and creating a reasonable domain class out of it. In Listing 7.13 I use original test method names, but have replaced JUnit with TestNG.

Listing 7.13. Address parsing – one assert per test method

```
@Test
public class AddressParsingOneAssertTest {

    private Address anAddress;

    @BeforeMethod
    public void setUp(){ ❶
        anAddress = new Address("ADDR1$CITY IL 60563$COUNTRY");
    }

    public void testAddr1() { ❷
        assertEquals("ADDR1",  anAddress.getAddr1());
    }

    public void testCsp() { ❸
        assertEquals("CITY IL 60563",  anAddress.getCsp());
    }

    public void testCountry() { ❹
        assertEquals("COUNTRY",  anAddress.getCountry());
    }
}
```

❶   `setUp` sets the test fixture for every test method,

❷❸❹ each test method contains only one assert.

---

[8]See http://www.artima.com/weblogs/viewpost.jsp?thread=35578

As you can see, OAPTM in us having a lot of very focused, tiny, often even just one-line, test methods. To get a broader understanding of "what address parsing looks like", you need to scan at least a few of them. What you get in return is that if a constructor of the `Address` class does not work properly, you will know all about it - i.e. failing test cases will tell you exactly what works and what doesn't.

A counterpart test – i.e. a test which uses several assertions per test method – is shown in Listing 7.14.

Listing 7.14. Address parsing – several assertions per test method

```
@Test
public class AddressParsingManyAssertsTest {

    @Test
    public void shouldParseAddress() { ❶
        anAddress = new Address("ADDR1$CITY IL 60563$COUNTRY"); ❷

        assertEquals("ADDR1",  anAddress.getAddr1());
        assertEquals("CITY IL 60563",  anAddress.getCsp());
        assertEquals("COUNTRY",  anAddress.getCountry());
    }
}
```

❶   Only one test method - with three assertions.
❷   No need for `setUp` method.

This time the number of test methods is significantly smaller, but they themselves are slightly larger (though still reasonably short). It is very easy to understand what "address parsing" means, since all parsing assertions are grouped together. On the downside, though, it might happen that any bugs introduced into the `Address` class constructor only reveal themselves gradually – one by one, in consecutive runs of the `AddressParsingManyAssertsTest` test class.

   A   matcher-based   solution   would   be   even   better.   For example: `assertThat(anAddress).hasCountry("COUNTRY").hasCsp("CITY  IL  60563").hasAddr1("ADDR1")`.

One important thing to notice is that even though in the second version of the test there is more than one assert per test method, each test method tests only one thing - the ability of the `Address` constructor to parse addresses properly.

7.3.2. Pros and Cons

Allow me now to take up the commonly cited reasons for following the OAPTM rule (as put forward by its proponents) and comment on them as they relate to the code present in the Listing 7.13 and Listing 7.14.

Table 7.2. Arguments for using only one assert per test

argument	comment
Using more than one assertion per test method leads to testing more than one thing - which violates the SRP.	Use of many assertions per test method **may potentially lead** to testing too much, this is true. However, it does not have to be so. The question is, what granularity of this *'one thing'* you are testing makes you feel comfortable. For me, testing the ability of `Address` class constructor to parse address passed as a `String`, is just the right size of a thing (of a functionality) to be tested in single test method.
Tests written this way are easier to maintain (thanks to smaller, focused methods).	This is a very subjective statement. The number of test methods created with OAPTM rule can be really high. Maintaining them might be a nightmare, especially that you need to browse through many of them to get a clear picture of tested functionality.
When a test fails it is dead simply to deduce what went wrong.	If you write good test with many asserts you can achieve the same effect. Current IDEs are capable of telling you exactly which assertion failed, so I do not see any gain from using OAPTM in this aspect.
If more than one asserts are about to fail, they will - in case of multiple asserts per test, only the first one will fail, so you need to rerun your tests to see the next one failing.	This is true, but not something you should worry about. From my experience, such situations (where one assertion failure "hides" another failures), is more than rare - in fact I can not recall it ever happened to me. I shield myself from such effect, writing assertions one by one, and following the TDD rhythm. Of course, this does not defend me against such effect, when I introduce some changes

argument	comment
	to an existing class. However, as stated previously, I believe this threat to be more of theoretical, than practical meaning.
It is easier to create intention-revealing method names for one-assertion tests.	Maybe so, but as proved by original code on Listing 7.13, it is still pretty easy to come with lousy names (e.g. `testCsp()`) even if using one assert per test! I am confident that finding good intention-revealing names for many-assertions is possible, and that OATPM does not have any advantages here.

7.3.3. Conclusions

Even as a firm believer in small, focused, easy-to-understand methods, I think that OAPTM goes too far, and does more harm than good. It results in too many lines of code being scattered amongst a multitude of tiny methods – something which is much harder to understand and maintain. It saves me from one problem (having too many assertions per test method), only to inflict on me another (having too many test methods). No. Sorry, OAPTM! I can judge on my own when a test method is getting too large, without needing to follow such dogmatic rules. And as long as I stick to the TDD approach, I will rarely, if ever, be stricken by the downside of the multiple asserts approach. My test methods are very concise and readable, and I can easily find intention-revealing names for them. My IDE will guide me straight to the fallen assertion every time a test fails.

My advice would be not to take the "one assert per test" recommendation too literally. Get clear about the reasons behind it, but follow another, similar rule, which says that **each test method should concentrate on a single feature of the SUT**. Sometimes numerous assertions will be required to test a certain feature, sometimes one will suffice. But in my opinion, the number of assertions should not be your main concern. What really matters is the scope of the SUT features covered by each test method.

 The only thing that would get me writing so many tiny test methods would be if I was being paid by LOCs. :)

7.4. Private Methods Testing

Everyone agrees that we should test publicly available methods. They provide the functionality used by clients, so it would be unreasonable to leave them untested. However, when it comes to testing `private` methods, two different voices can be heard. Let us hear them.

7.4.1. Verification vs. Design - Revisited

Some people say this is something you simply should not do. They point out that it is a bad idea to make assumptions about the internal implementation of an object: all we should care about is its public API. They will point to the weak design of a class as the culprit, and will tend to fix it in order to have a more testable solution. They perceive private methods, which cry out to be tested, as being indicative of hidden classes, which should be extracted and tested properly via their public API[9]. A practical argument against testing private methods is that they are prone to alteration during refactorings, so their tests are endangered.

Others will have no such objections. They say we should test everything that might possibly break (see Section 10.5), no matter if it be a publicly available part of a class or not. They want to have their code covered with tests, and do not feel inclined to perform complicated refactorings or redesigns of code that seems "good enough".

 If you are experiencing a sense of déjà vu right now, then rest assured - you are not in an altered matrix[10]. No - it is a perfectly reliable indicator of your brain's working as it should! We were indeed discussing two similar points of view in Section 1.3.

7.4.2. Options We Have

So, what to do, when faced with such a dilemma? Several things.

The first thing you could, and probably should, do is to avoid such a situation. How? By **following the TDD approach**. Think about how `private` methods come to life when you

---

[9]As extreme programmers put it, *"you should listen to your code"* and follow its advices.
[10]http://en.wikipedia.org/wiki/Deja_vu

code test first. The answer is, that they are created during the refactoring phase, which means their content is fully covered by tests (assuming that you really follow the TDD rules, and write code only when there is a failing test). In such cases there is no problem of an "untested `private` method which should somehow be tested", because such methods simply do not exist.

Alas, this is not the ultimate answer to our problem! It is the right answer when writing software from scratch, but will not help you when working with legacy code. What is more irritating is that when faced with legacy code, we often run up against the "chicken and egg" dilemma:

- a class requires a refactoring, but you cannot perform this, because you lack the tests to tell you whether or not it will break things along the way,

- tests should be written for the class, but this is not easily achieved without it having been refactored first.

And so we have a closed circle. Definitely, then, we will have to explore further options to find a way out of this situation.

Another approach you can take, even with the most vicious legacy code, is to **refactor a little, test a little**, and then refactor again, and test, and refactor, etc. moving in baby steps. You will probably need to start with integration tests (which are sometimes easier to write for legacy applications, which consists of many tightly coupled classes and external resources like databases) and then gradually make your tests more focused. Step by step… This is a tedious task, and by no means a short one. The benefit is that you end up with a loosely coupled, testable application. However, it is a potentially dangerous approach and, given the complexity of the code and its legacy nature, will not guarantee success.

Because of the difficulties involved with this, some people opt to take the "easy" path. They use techniques (and/or tools) which will allow them to **test private methods as they are**, without any additional work on the code structure (or with only a minimal amount of this).

To sum things up, let us make the following observations:

- No one wants to promote private methods testing - but some of us believe that sometimes this is the only way.

- Some developers demand that their code be tested and 100% object-oriented, while others believe that testing is enough and do not struggle to achieve clean design.

- When writing new code, we are conveniently positioned to write it so that it is fully tested via its public API. TDD might help to achieve this.

- When working with legacy code we compromise on private method testing. Since the code plays unfair, we also forget about fair-play.

7.4.3. Private Methods Testing - Techniques

Keeping in mind all the arguments against private methods testing, we should at least be prepared to test them. Sometimes it might just save our lives! Now we shall discuss the two most popular techniques for testing private methods. We will use the following class to demonstrate them:

Listing 7.15. Class with a private method

```
public class SomeClass {

    private boolean privateMethod(Long param) { ❶
        return true;
    }
}
```

❶   This is the method we would like to test.

Reflection

This technique uses a `Method` class from the `java.lang.reflect` package[11], which allows one to gather information on methods, but also to tweak them – e.g. introducing changes to their access modifiers. An application of this class in test code is shown in Listing 7.16.

---

[11]See http://docs.oracle.com/javase/7/docs/api/java/lang/reflect/package-summary.html

Listing 7.16. Testing private methods using reflection

```java
public class PrivateMethodReflectionTest {

    @Test
    public void testingPrivateMethodWithReflection()
            throws NoSuchMethodException, InvocationTargetException,
                    IllegalAccessException {
        SomeClass sut = new SomeClass(); ❶

        Class[] parameterTypes = new Class[1];
        parameterTypes[0] = java.lang.Long.class;
        Method m = sut.getClass()
            .getDeclaredMethod("privateMethod", parameterTypes); ❷
        m.setAccessible(true); ❸

        Object[] parameters = new Object[1];
        parameters[0] = 5569L;

        Boolean result = (Boolean) m.invoke(sut, parameters); ❹

        assertTrue(result); ❺
    }
}
```

❶　　The SUT only contains a single private method, which is to be tested.
❷❸　Reflection is employed to set `privateMethod()` as accessible.
❹　　`invoke()` returns `Object`, so we need to cast it to the expected type.
❺　　Asserting that `privateMethod()` works as expected.

Obviously, this is not the sort of code we should be writing everyday! It is ugly, it uses magic (disguised as reflection), and it will break if you refactor `privateMethod()` to anything else. We could dispose of some of its weaknesses using a tool that will hide all this nasty code behind some nice API. This can be done, for example, using PowerMock's `org.powermock.reflect.Whitebox` class. Listing 7.17 shows this.

Listing 7.17. Testing private methods using PowerMock

```
public class PrivateMethodPowermockTest {

    @Test
    public void testingPrivateMethodWithReflection()
            throws Exception, IllegalAccessException {
        SomeClass sut = new SomeClass();

        Boolean result = Whitebox
            .invokeMethod(sut, "privateMethod", 302483L); ❶

        assertTrue(result);
    }
}
```

❶ All reflection calls are hidden behind a convenient API. You do not even have to cast the result to an appropriate type.

Even though this code looks much nicer than that of the previous attempt, it still cannot be refactored safely. Calling methods using their name (`String`) as the parameter is not a healthy approach.

One more thing to note is that neither the approach involving direct use of reflection, nor that which makes use of Powermock, require us to modify the production code. This is a good thing.

Access Modifiers

Another option we have is to weaken the access modifier of a private method – something which will make it more easily accessible by test code. However, we do not usually want to make such a method `public`. Adding new methods to the API of a class, just because we want to test it, would be too much. Fortunately, we can achieve our goal by relaxing the access modifier just a little. This is shown in Listing 7.18.

Listing 7.18. Testing private methods by relaxing access modifiers

```
public class SomeClass {

    boolean privateMethod(Long param) { ❶
        return true;
    }
}

public class PrivateMethodModifierTest {

    @Test
    public void testingPrivateMethodWithReflection() {
        SomeClass sut = new SomeClass();
        assertTrue(sut.privateMethod(9238423L)); ❷
    }
}
```

❶   `privateMethod()` is no longer `private` - it has a "default" access modifier,
❷   which means it can be called directly from classes within the same package.

This solution requires a serious change in the production code, which might not be possible. On the other hand, the test code is "normal" - that is, free from any unexpected constructs. It is also immune to name changes of tested methods, as refactoring tools will easily update the new method name within the test code.

7.4.4. Conclusions

When writing the section on private methods testing, I must confess I was in two minds as to whether I should describe this at all. One part of me argued that it is evil and anti-OO, and that I should not include it in a book that sets out to promote good practice, and that puts a lot of pressure on one with respect to the quality of one's code. The other part of me argued that I should have faith in my readers. My role will be to present and describe the different options so that you, dear reader, can decide by yourself which way to go. So it looks as though, in the end, this second part of me must have prevailed!

I have tried very hard to discourage you from testing private methods. I still think that with good design, you will never need to test them directly. However, I do think that **sometimes** (very rarely, but still...) you might need to use the techniques described in this section. This is why I have decided to include them in the book.

A note on tools. The authors of some tools - e.g. TestNG or JUnit - have never got around to enhancing their tools in order to make them capable of testing private methods - even though there have been some expectations on the part of community members that they would do so. This is probably because they view private methods testing as something that does not deserve to be facilitated.

7.5. New Operator

A seam is a place where you can alter behavior in your program without editing in that place.

— Michael Feathers *Working Effectively With Legacy Code (2004)*

When introducing test doubles (in Chapter 5, *Mocks, Stubs, Test Spies*), we assumed that the collaborators of the SUT could be replaced easily. This is the case if they are "injected" into the SUT - as constructor parameters, method parameters or using setters. However, this is not always the case. This section explains what can be done if there is no straightforward way of replacing the SUT's collaborators.

Listing 7.19 presents some very simple code. The `myMethod()` method of the `MySut` class creates another object (of the `MyCollaborator` class) using the `new` operator. Then it uses this newly created object (calls its methods, uses values it returns, etc.).

Listing 7.19. Typical use of the Java new operator within the method body

```java
public class MySut {

    public void myMethod() {
        MyCollaborator collaborator = new MyCollaborator();
        // some behaviour worth testing here which uses collaborator
    }
}
```

The code in Listing 7.19 is perfectly valid Java code and, frankly, not complicated either. However, testing interactions between the SUT and its collaborator requires some additional effort. A test skeleton for such a method would look as shown below:

Listing 7.20. Testing new - a test skeleton

```
public class MySutTest {

    @Test
    public void testMyMethod() {
        MySut sut = new MySut(); ❶
        MyCollaborator collaborator = mock(MyCollaborator.class); ❷
        // make sut use collaborator ❸

        // set expectations regarding collaborator's behaviour
        // execute sut's method(s)
        // verify results and/or collaborator's behaviour
    }
}
```

❶   Creation of the SUT.
❷   Creation of a test double for the SUT's collaborator.
❸   "Make sut use collaborator" - but how?!

When writing a test for the MySut class, we very quickly encounter a problem. There is no direct way to force sut to use a test double of the MyCollaborator class. This means that we cannot easily control the SUT's environment. One option we have is to forget about testing in isolation, and test both classes (MySut and MyCollaborator) together. While this might work out pretty well in the short run (see the discussion in Section 5.5), it makes it hard to test all of the scenarios we should test. We don't need to relive the whole debate about this: isolation in tests is usually worth fighting for, so let us fight for it!

Even though myMethod() uses the new operator to create its collaborator, the discussion in this section also covers other similar situations. In particular, if myMethod() had used a factory pattern (e.g. MyCollaborator collaborator = MyFactory.getCollaborator(...)), instead of the new operator, or had used a lookup service (e.g. MyCollaborator collaborator = LookupService.findCollaborator(...)), that would have caused exactly the same problem when testing. The solutions discussed in the following sections would also apply to these similar scenarios.

Now that we understand the problem, let us discuss possible solutions to it. Each of them has its own pros and cons, which will be discussed in the sections below. But before we take a closer look at them, let us get clear about exactly what kind of a dilemma we are faced with here.

As was stated in Section 1.3, tools for testing can be divided into two types. Some of them only deal with verification, while others are more concerned with design. Mockito belongs to the second group: it works perfectly with well-written, loosely coupled code, but "refuses" to test code that is tightly-coupled. The problem we are facing right now – the use of either the `new` operator or static methods - is precisely a representation of what happens when the code is not loosely coupled. The ties between objects (in this case between `sut` and `collaborator`) are so tight that it is hard to loosen them for testing purposes.

Having read this, one might well expect the solutions called for to come from using both types of tool. And this is exactly the case. Either we can use a tool that allows us to test tightly coupled code, or we will find it necessary to introduce some changes to the original code (hopefully making it better), and then use a tool from the second group.

7.5.1. PowerMock to the Rescue

We shall start with a tool which can simply ignore the nuisance that is the `new` operator, and create a test double, as if that were no issue at all. Such "magic" is possible with PowerMock.

Listing 7.21 presents a test class which uses PowerMock. It does not differ substantially from what we have encountered so far, but uses some annotations and classes which we have not yet come across.

 PowerMock acts as a kind of wrapper around different mocking frameworks. It enhances their functionality with some new features. I will not go deeply into the details of the PowerMock syntax, nor will I discuss all of its capabilities. Please refer to PowerMock's documentation for the full list of features, and detailed instructions on how to use it with Mockito and TestNG.

Listing 7.21. Using PowerMock to test the new operator

```java
import org.powermock.api.mockito.PowerMockito;
import org.powermock.core.classloader.annotations.PrepareForTest;
import org.testng.IObjectFactory;
import org.testng.annotations.ObjectFactory;

@PrepareForTest(MySut.class) ❶
public class MySutTest {

    @ObjectFactory ❷
    public IObjectFactory getObjectFactory() {
        return new org.powermock.modules.testng.PowerMockObjectFactory(); ❸
    }

    @Test
    public void testMyMethod() throws Exception {
        MySut sut = new MySut();
        MyCollaborator collaborator = mock(MyCollaborator.class); ❹

        PowerMockito.whenNew(MyCollaborator.class)
            .withNoArguments().thenReturn(collaborator); ❺

        // normal test using Mockito's syntax
        // e.g. Mockito.when(collaborator.someMethod()).thenReturn(...) ❻
    }
}
```

❶   In this case, the `@PrepareForTest` annotation informs PowerMock that the `MySut` class will create a new instance of some other class. In general, this is how PowerMock learns, about which classes it should perform some bytecode manipulation.

❷❸   In order to use PowerMock with TestNG, we need to make PowerMock responsible for the creation of all of the test instances.

❹   The test double is created as usual - with the static `mock()` method of Mockito.

❺   This is where the magic happens: whenever a new object of the `MyCollaborator` class gets created, our test double object (`collaborator`) will be used instead. Two of PowerMock's methods - `whenNew()` and `withNoArguments()` - are used to control the execution of a no-arguments constructor of the `MyCollaborator` class.

❻   There is nothing special in the test method itself - we can use normal Mockito syntax to verify the behaviour, to stub or to spy.

And that is it. Except for some boilerplate code required in order to use PowerMock and TestNG together, there is not much new here: only that in some places the `PowerMockito` class is used instead of the Mockito class. Apart from this, the code looks very similar to what we have come across so far.

Let us conclude by summing up what this example has showed us:

- there are tools (i.e. PowerMock) capable of dealing with the new operator, static method calls, and other language constructs, which are commonly recognized as being "untestable",

- it is possible to test classes like the MySut class without changing (refactoring or redesigning) them at all,

- PowerMock works nicely with TestNG and Mockito (and also with JUnit and EasyMock),

- tests written with PowerMock do not differ much from what we have become used to.

After seeing what PowerMock can do for us, we should answer one question, which is surely shouting in our heads: *"Why bother with anything else if I can do it so easily using PowerMock?!"*

There is a serious reason for avoiding using such tools. It is all about the quality of your code - in particular, about its maintainability. By using PowerMock as shown in Listing 7.21, you reproduce in your test code the tight-coupling which exists in the production code. Now, every time you change your production code, your tests will fail. By including implementation details in your tests (as PowerMock requires you to do) you have created an additional force which will make it harder to introduce changes to your production code. This is not good.

Additionally, PowerMock lets you get away with suboptimal design. For example, a class can have way too much responsibility and still be capable of being tested with PowerMock. Testing it with other tools would be very cumbersome, but with PowerMock you will not feel the pain. In short, using PowerMock deprives you of valuable feedback about the quality of your code, which other tools will give you.

 However, there are situations where having PowerMock in your toolbox is a real blessing. That is why I have decided to present this tool, even though I myself do not use it on a daily basis.

7.5.2. Redesign and Inject

Now we will be going in a direction quite opposite to that which we went in with PowerMock: we shall be working on the production code, to make it more testable. After this goal has been accomplished, we will be able to use a common Mockito approach, without using any reflection or class loading tricks.

Basically, there are two ways in which a collaborator object can be replaced easily with a test double:

- create a new field in a MySut class of the MyCollaborator type, and

  - either pass an object of the MyCollaborator class as the constructor's argument, or via a setter method,

  - or redesign myMethod() so it takes an object of the MyCollaborator class as one of it arguments.

No matter which option we choose, writing test code will then be a piece of cake. Listing 7.22 shows a refactored MySut class (with a constructor-injected collaborator), and Listing 7.23 shows a test written for this class.

Listing 7.22. MySut class with constructor-injected collaborator

```
public class MySut {

    private final MyCollaborator collab; ❶

    public MySut(MyCollaborator collab) { ❷
        this.collab = collab;
    }

    public void myMethod() {
        // some behaviour worth testing here which uses collaborator ❸
    }
}
```

❶❷ An object of the MyCollaborator class is provided by MySut's clients when they create objects of the MySut class.

❸ No new operator is used within myMethod(). The collaborator object has been created outside of the MySut class and passed as a constructor parameter.

The `myMethod()` method does not deal with the creation of collaborators anymore. It uses a `collab` object of the `MyCollaborator` class, which is already available when `myMethod()` is executed.

Listing 7.23. Testing of the redesigned MySut class

```
public class MySutTest {

    @Test
    public void testMyMethod() {
        MyCollaborator collaborator = mock(MyCollaborator.class);
        MySut sut = new MySut(collaborator); ❶

        // normal Mockito stubbing/test spying test
    }
}
```

❶　The updated constructor of the `MySut` class allows for straightforward injection of a `collaborator` test double.

The test in Listing 7.23 holds no surprises for us. Replacing the collaborator of `sut` is simply a matter of passing the appropriate test double to its constructor.

As this example demonstrates, a complicated case can be turned into something far simpler (from a testing point of view) by the redesign of the SUT. If it is possible to replace the cumbersome creation of objects (involving either the `new` operator or static factory methods) with a dependency injection, then testing becomes a trivial task.

Even so, there are some downsides – or, at least, some issues we should be aware of:

• production code gets altered to meet the requirements of the tests themselves (isn't this a casc of thc tail wagging thc dog?),

• such a redesign breaks existing clients (it truly is a **redesign**, not a refactoring),

• you need to write some additional code.

On the "plus" side, there are two important things:

• the design of production code is improved (`myMethod()` can take care of its business task, and need not occupy itself with objects creation),

- tests are very simple to write (which also means they are easy to understand and maintain).

After we have discussed all of the possible options, some conclusions will be drawn, but even now, I would like to encourage you to use this technique, because it addresses the real cause of the pain, not merely its symptoms. By redesigning your production code you make it better, and you get "testability" as a side effect.

7.5.3. Refactor and Subclass

In some cases the redesign discussed in the previous section is not feasible. For example, it might be the case that we cannot afford to break a client that uses the old API. In such a case, we need to find another way to make the class more testable. This can be done by a certain refactoring.

 The pattern presented in this section is known by many names. [meszaros2007] calls this pattern a *Test-Specific Subclass*, while [feathers2004] uses the name *subclass and override*.

Listing 7.24 shows a slightly changed version of the original MySut class.

Listing 7.24. Refactored version of the MySut class

```
public class MyRefactoredSut {

    public void myMethod() {
        MyCollaborator collab = createCollaborator(); ❶
        // some behaviour worth testing here which uses collaborator
    }

    // method extracted to facilitate testing ❷
    MyCollaborator createCollaborator() { ❸
        return new MyCollaborator();
    }
}
```

❶ Instead of invoking the new operator directly there is a call to a new method.

❷ I strongly recommend adding a short comment to the extracted method, so it is clear that it has been created for the purpose of conducting unit tests.

❸ The extracted method has a default access modifier, …and not very impressive content.

As for the access modifier of the extracted `createCollaborator()` method, we can choose between making it `protected` or using default access protection (so-called "package-private"). This has some impact on our test classes. If we keep them in the same package as the production code, then the default access will be good enough. If they reside in different packages, then we will need to make the access less restrictive (`protected`). Some information on the organization of test packages is given in Section 9.1.

The change introduced to the original class is minimal. All we did is a simple "extract method" refactoring. At first it might seem useless, but in fact it opens up a new testing possibility. Listing 7.25 shows a test which takes advantage of this minor refactoring.

Listing 7.25. Test of the refactored version of the MySut class

```java
public class MySutRefactoredTest {

    private MyCollaborator collaborator;

    class MyRefactoredSutSubclassed extends MyRefactoredSut { ❶
        @Override
        protected MyCollaborator createCollaborator() { ❷
            return collaborator;
        }
    }

    @Test
    public void testMyMethod() {
        MyRefactoredSut sut = new MyRefactoredSutSubclassed(); ❸
        collaborator= mock(MyCollaborator.class); ❹

        // normal Mockito stubbing/test spying test
    }
}
```

❶❸ A new class is introduced - a subclass of the original class (the one we intend to test). An object of this newly introduced class - `MyRefactoredSutSubclassed` - will be tested.

❷ The new class overrides the `createCollaborator()` method. The new implementation returns a test double of the `MyCollaborator` class.

❹ There is no need to inject `collaborator` to `sut` - this is done by a `myMethod()` of SUT's parent class (see Listing 7.24).

This simple technique, as presented in this section, can be really handy. Let us conclude by now listing some of its pros and cons:

- It does not break the clients (the SUT's API has not been changed) and it lets you write tests at the same time.

- Changes are limited to the SUT class.

- The design of production code is somewhat worse than it was before the refactoring. The newly introduced method is awkward, and poses a potential encapsulation issue. (I must remark that I have never seen any harm being done because of this slight reduction in the SUT's integrity.)

- The SUT's `myMethod()` still creates collaborators (instead of focusing on its business tasks), which means its design has not been improved.

- Some people feel bad about testing a subclass instead of a real SUT. Personally, I would be very happy to test the real thing, but just having a test of a strictly controlled subclass has proved more than adequate for my purposes.

7.5.4. Partial Mocking

The technique demonstrated in this section is very similar to the previously presented *subclass and override* technique. The difference lies in the implementation, which requires less coding and relies on some Mockito features.

The first step is almost identical to the one previously discussed. You must extract a method which will deal solely with the creation of a new object. Listing 7.26 shows this.

Listing 7.26. Refactored version of the MySut class

```
public class MyPartialSut {

    public boolean myMethod() {
        MyCollaborator collaborator = createCollaborator();
        // some behaviour worth testing here which uses collaborator
    }

    MyCollaborator createCollaborator() { ❶
        return new MyCollaborator();
    }
}
```

❶   Extracted method.

So far, nothing new here. The difference is only visible when it comes to the tests class. But before we inspect any new code, we need to learn something new about Mockito. Mockito allows us to "spy" on real objects. That means we can decide which methods of a real object are invoked, and which are being intercepted (and stubbed). The Javadoc of the `spy()` method explains this in the following way: *"Creates a spy of the real object. The spy calls real methods unless they are stubbed."*

This feature is deployed in Listing 7.27, which illustrates the use of a *partial mocking* technique. Additionally, it presents a new static Mockito method - `doReturn()`. We use

```
doReturn(collaborator).when(sut).createCollaborator();
```

instead of

```
when(collaborator.someMethod()).thenReturn(true);
```

to avoid execution of the real method (`someMethod()`), because:

- the real method might throw some exceptions,

- if we are to verify it, then the number of invocations would grow.

Listing 7.27. Partial mocking test of the refactored MySut class

```
public class MySutPartialTest {

    @Test
    public void testMyMethod() {
        MyPartialSut sut = spy(new MyPartialSut());  ❶
        MyCollaborator collaborator = mock(MyCollaborator.class);

        doReturn(collaborator).when(sut).createCollaborator();  ❷
        // normal Mockito stubbing/test spying test
    }
}
```

❶   Surprise! The SUT has **not** been created using the `new` operator. Instead, another static method of Mockito has been used.

❷   Another unusual situation. We request that our SUT returns some canned values for a given method invocation.

As was mentioned before, when created with the `spy()` method `sut` behaves like a normal object of its class, until some of its methods are stubbed. In the case of our example, all the SUT's methods, except for `createCollaborator()`, would be executed as if `sut` had been created with the `new` keyword. However, this one method - `createCollaborator()` - is different. When `createCollaborator()` is executed, it is intercepted by Mockito, which returns some canned values without touching the real `sut` object at all.

Well, this is confusing! Our SUT is performing two roles here: first of all, it is being tested (which is not shown in the above listing, for reasons of brevity), and secondly, it is being used as a test stub, to provide some canned values.

 Partial mocking using the `spy()` method has its quirks. Make sure you read the Mockito documentation before using it!

As for *pros and cons*, this technique is very similar to the one discussed previously, with the following differences:

- There is no need to create a subclass. This is done "under the hood" by Mockito.

- The test code is more concise.

- The SUT is even more confusing than before …are we testing the real thing, or some strange artifact created by Mockito?

In conclusion, we may say that this technique is very similar to the one discussed previously (Section 7.5.3). The idea is the same: introduce changes to the SUT, and replace a part of it with some canned behaviour. With the previously presented technique, this was done by hand. In this section, we have learned how to do it with Mockito. There is no semantic difference between these two approaches. Some people feel that the first technique is better (probably because they have visible control over the subclassing of the SUT), while others will argue that the use of a framework makes things simpler by automating things which were done by hand. It is really hard to choose a winner here.

The thing to remember is that this technique allows for the testing of some cumbersome code, but **does not make this code any better**. If your aim is to verify things, this might be enough for you. If you want cleaner code, you should rather think about redesigning your classes, as discussed previously.

7.5.5. Conclusions

In this section, we have discussed various options for testing code which uses the `new` operator to create collaborators. Four different approaches have been discussed. Each of them had some pros and cons, which have been discussed in the sections above. Table 7.3 summarizes the salient features of each of the options on offer.

Table 7.3. Comparison of new operator testing approaches

	PowerMock	redesign	refactor & subclass	partial mocking
required SUT change	no change	API change, DI introduced (breaking clients)	refactoring - method extracted	refactoring - method extracted
SUT's design	no change	improved - business logic separated from collaborators creation	slightly worse than before (method extracted to facilitate testing)	slightly worse than before (method extracted to facilitate testing)
test code	different than usual	simple	complicated, testing subclass of SUT	complicated, SUT is tested and also stubbed
amount of work	minimal	might be significant	medium	medium (but less than Refactor & Subclass)
SUT is a `final` class	not a problem	not a problem	can not use this technique	can not use this technique

- The **PowerMock** option is especially attractive when working with **legacy code**, which is something we cannot modify (or are too scared to modify…). Its selling point is its ability to test nasty code without any struggle.

- **Redesign** is probably **the right way to go**, but it requires more work than other techniques, and breaks clients (because of API change). Its main benefit is **improved design of production code**.

- Both **Refactor & Subclass** and **Partial Mocking** offer similar benefits: the **ability to test classes without API change**. However, they require some effort, cannot be used with final classes, and do not make production code better (they rather make it slightly worse).

To conclude, I would strongly recommend that you always aim at making the design better, thus leaving PowerMock as a tool of "last resort" – one that may save your life when battling with especially vicious legacy code.

7.6. Capturing Arguments to Collaborators

Sometimes there is a need to verify whether arguments passed to collaborators are exactly as they should be. This might be tricky, especially if they are created within the SUT's method. In this section we will discuss possible solutions which allow us to test such code.

First, let us meet the classes which will be used to demonstrate this issue. There are three of them:

- `PIM` - which represents a Personal Information Manager[12]. This is the SUT.

- `Calendar` - a collaborator of PIM.

- `Meeting` - argument to `Calendar`'s method call.

All three types are shown in the listings below:

Listing 7.28. Calendar interface

```
public interface Calendar {

    public void addEvent(Event event);
}
```

---

[12]http://en.wikipedia.org/wiki/Personal_information_manager

Listing 7.29. Meeting class

```
public class Meeting implements Event {

    private final Date startDate;
    private final Date endDate;

    public Meeting(Date startDate, Date endDate) {
        this.startDate = new Date(startDate.getTime());
        this.endDate = new Date(endDate.getTime());
    }

    public Date getStartDate() {
        return startDate;
    }

    public Date getEndDate() {
        return endDate;
    }
}
```

Listing 7.30. PIM - the sut

```
public class PIM {

    private final static int MILLIS_IN_MINUTE = 60 * 1000;

    private Calendar calendar;

    public PIM(Calendar calendar) { ❶
        this.calendar = calendar;
    }

    public void addMeeting(Date startDate, int durationInMinutes) { ❷
        Date endDate = new Date(startDate.getTime()
                + MILLIS_IN_MINUTE * durationInMinutes);
        Meeting meeting = new Meeting(startDate, endDate);
        calendar.addEvent(meeting);
    }
}
```

❶ The collaborator is passed as a constructor argument - there will be no problem with injecting its test double into the SUT within the test code.

❷ A new object of the Meeting type is created, and is then used as a parameter to the collaborator's addEvent() method.

The problem we face when testing the PIM class is the following: how to make sure that the addMeeting() method constructs a proper Meeting object? We need to somehow intercept the parameter passed to calendar.addEvent(). There are two ways we can do it.

 The problem with addMeeting() method testing comes from its poor design. It is responsible for too many things - it deals with the creation of the Meeting object, and interacts with the calendar collaborator. If we were to split its functionality and, for example, introduce another collaborator responsible for the creation of proper Meeting objects, than there would be no issue with testing arguments of the addEvent() method!

7.6.1. Capturing Arguments - Creating Identical Objects

How about creating an object of Meeting class identical to the one which we expected would be created by the addMeeting() method of SUT? Then we can verify whether the addEvent() method of the calendar test double has been called with an identical Meeting object. Sounds good, so let us try it!

Listing 7.31. Creating objects identical to expected arguments

```java
public class PIMTest {

    private static final int ONE_HOUR = 60;
    private static final Date START_DATE = new Date();
    private static final int MILLIS_IN_MINUTE = 1000 * 60;
    private static final Date END_DATE
        = new Date(START_DATE.getTime() + ONE_HOUR * MILLIS_IN_MINUTE);

    @Test
    public void shouldAddNewEventToCalendar() {
        Calendar calendar = mock(Calendar.class);
        PIM pim = new PIM(calendar);
        Meeting expectedMeeting = new Meeting(START_DATE, END_DATE); ❶

        pim.addMeeting(START_DATE, ONE_HOUR); ❷

        verify(calendar).addEvent(expectedMeeting); ❸
    }
}
```

❶   An object of the Meeting class is created, identical to the one which we expect to be created by SUT's addMeeting() method.

❷   Execution of the method of the SUT being tested.

❸   Verification of whether the calendar.addEvent() method has been called with exactly the same Meeting object.

Looks good? Yes, but unfortunately it does not work. The test fails with the following failure message (stacktrace lines have been omitted for greater readability):

Listing 7.32. The test fails - objects are not identical

```
Argument(s) are different! Wanted:
calendar.addEvent(
    com.practicalunittesting.Meeting@1242b11
);
Actual invocation has different arguments:
calendar.addEvent(
    com.practicalunittesting.Meeting@1878144
);
```

Hmm, strange! I could have sworn that the addMeeting() method constructs a proper Meeting object... And in fact it does! The problem lies elsewhere. The Meeting class does not override the equals() method, so the objects' equality is verified by reference, and thus fails. We can fix it by adding appropriate methods[13] to the Meeting class. Below you can see an implementation of the equals() method generated by IntelliJ IDEA:

---

[13]Remember, if you override equals() you should also override hashCode()!

Listing 7.33. Implementation of the equals() method

```
@Override
public boolean equals(Object o) {
    if (this == o) return true;
    if (o == null || getClass() != o.getClass()) return false;

    Meeting meeting = (Meeting) o;

    if (endDate != null ? !endDate.equals(meeting.endDate)
        : meeting.endDate != null) return false;
    if (startDate != null ? !startDate.equals(meeting.startDate)
        : meeting.startDate != null) return false;

    return true;
}

@Override
public int hashCode() { ... } ❶
```

❶ The `hashCode()` method implementation is not important right now, but remember: it should also be overridden!

Now, if we rerun the test, it passes. Good, we have the first solution to the problem of verifying whether the arguments passed to the collaborator are as expected.

However, this is not an ideal solution. On the **plus** side, we may say that:

- it works!

- it is quite straightforward and easy to understand.

Unfortunately, there are more things to say on the **minus** side:

- A domain object in question might not have the `equals()` method implemented.

- In worse cases, a domain object's `equals()` might already be implemented, and might behave differently than as required by our test.

- The verification is "total" - it checks everything that our `equals()` method checks. This might lead to overspecified tests.

- There is no direct assertion on the properties of the collaborator's method argument.

Because of these downsides, we need to find some better solution.

7.6.2. Capturing Arguments - Using Mockito's Features

Listing 7.34 shows another approach to writing a test for arguments of the collaborator's method. It uses the Mockito `ArgumentCaptor` class.

Listing 7.34. Use of the ArgumentCaptor class

```
public class PIMTest {

    private static final int ONE_HOUR = 60;
    private static final Date START_DATE = new Date();
    private static final int MILLIS_IN_MINUTE = 1000 * 60;
    private static final Date END_DATE
        = new Date(START_DATE.getTime() + ONE_HOUR * MILLIS_IN_MINUTE);

    @Test
    public void shouldAddNewEventToCalendar() {
        Calendar calendar = mock(Calendar.class);
        PIM pim = new PIM(calendar);
        ArgumentCaptor<Meeting> argument
            = ArgumentCaptor.forClass(Meeting.class);    ❶

        pim.addMeeting(START_DATE, ONE_HOUR);

        verify(calendar).addEvent(argument.capture());    ❷
        Meeting meeting = argument.getValue();    ❸
        assertEquals(meeting.getStartDate(), START_DATE);    ❹
        assertEquals(meeting.getEndDate(), END_DATE);    ❺
    }
}
```

❶ An object of the `ArgumentCaptor` class is created, which will gather information on arguments of the type `Meeting`.

❷ The `addEvent()` method's having been called is verified, and Mockito is instructed to capture arguments of this method call.

❸ The actual argument to the `addEvent()` method is extracted from the `ArgumentCaptor` object.

❹❺ What we have here are classic assertions which verify that the right object has been passed as an argument to the `addEvent()` method.

As shown in Listing 7.34, we can use `ArgumentCaptor` to verify arguments passed to collaborators. This solution has some positive features:

- it does not rely on the `equals()` method of the domain object (in our case, of the `Meeting` class),

- it can be used to test arbitrary properties of arguments,

- "normal" assertions are used to specify our expectations regarding the arguments.

In general, Mockito does a good job of facilitating the task of verifying a collaborator's arguments. However, as the Mockito documentation warns, having to use `ArgumentCaptor` might be indicative that the code is not well-designed:

> Over reliance on capturing arguments would be a code smell in my opinion as most well abstracted code should not need to do this. However for testing legacy code and interactions with outside systems ArgumentCaptors can be very useful.
>
> — Mockito Documentation

7.7. Conclusions

The issues discussed in this chapter are nothing short of real-life problems. You will encounter them mostly when working with legacy code, but also when making decisions about how to design the application you are working on right now. And you will have to make your choices. In this section we have discussed some important dilemmas, in the hope that when the time comes, you will have enough knowledge to choose the right solution to the problem you are faced with. Maybe you will redesign your application and avoid the problem of private methods testing, or maybe you will use the sort of brute-force techniques that will enable you to do that. This depends on the context of the problem in hand, and on your own personal experience and preferences.

7.8. Exercises

Let us recap what we have learned in this chapter by doing some exercises.

7.8.1. Testing Legacy Code

So that you can fully understand the obstacles involved in testing legacy code, please write tests for the code presented below. Try to repeat this exercise using the different techniques described in Section 7.5 and Section 7.6. Make sure that you follow the "redesign" approach at least once, changing the code so it is easily testable using standard techniques.

Listing 7.35. Sending emails is not hard, is it?

```
public class MailClient {

    public void sendEmail(String address, String title, String body) {
        Email email = new Email(address, title, body); ❶
        EmailServer.sendEmail(email); ❷
    }
}
```

❶   `Email` has no functionality apart from keeping all this data.

❷   `sendEmail()` is a static method.

Please note that `static` methods can be tested with the same approaches as the `new` operator, which was discussed in Section 7.5.

Part IV. Listen and Organize

You should listen carefully to your tests. They might be telling you something.

— Wisdom of the TDD Folks

Organizing is what you do before you do something, so that when you do it, it is not all mixed up.

— A. A. Milne

Chapter 8. Getting Feedback

> This report, by its very length, defends itself against the risk of being read.
> — Winston Churchill

Writing tests, especially in a test-first manner, is all about getting rapid and precise feedback. We have already tackled this subject. We have discussed the green/red colors which indicate the success or failure of tests, and mentioned the importance of error messages. In this section we will learn what (detailed) information about the tests is available, and how to customize it to our liking.

When reading about the ways of getting feedback from test tools (usually in the form of various reports), please bear in mind that there are two common uses for them. First of all, they are here to help a developer learn about the issues with his tests. Secondly, they help the whole team (or even some stakeholders) to get a good understanding of the situation. While your IDE can help you with the former, your colleagues and superiors may require something more. This section covers both requirements

Is Customization Worth the Trouble?   This section gives a lot of information about the customization of existing test reports and about writing custom ones. The question is, whether such activities are worth the trouble. Well, I cannot answer this question for you. It is up to you to decide. If, like me, you like tools to behave exactly as you want them to, if you set your own keyboard shortcuts in MS Word, Thunderbird or your IDE, if you believe that a one-off effort can bring everyday benefits for a long time to come, then you should probably read this carefully and think about how you would like your reports to be. But if you are usually happy with default settings (even to the extent of never touching the gear-system on your bike *"cos it's good the way it is right now"*) then simply read about the default reports, and do not bother with customization.

 When talking about feedback information we must mention Javadocs. In contrast to what we have discussed so far, they do not give us information about the execution of tests, but help us instead to understand their purpose and business value. Some hints about writing Javadocs have already been given in Section 4.2.3.

8.1. IDE Feedback

If you usually run your tests via an IDE (see Appendix B, *Running Unit Tests* for some hints) then it is crucial that you know how to make the best of it. This section explains what information you can acquire from IntelliJ IDEA and Eclipse about the tests being executed. As both IDEs are subject to ongoing development, you should also check their original documentation. It is possible that some new helpful features will have been added after this book has been written.

8.1.1. Eclipse Test Reports

No matter if you use JUnit or TestNG, Eclipse prints information about the executed tests in a unified manner.

In the event that **all your tests have passed**, all you will usually want to know is which tests were run. Eclipse provides this information as shown below:

Figure 8.1. Eclipse: passed tests

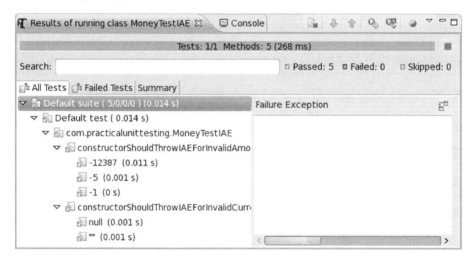

The green bar on top makes it clear there are no failed tests. The pane on the left provides the list of executed tests (in the form of a tree, so you can see which class and package they belong to). Information on execution time is also provided, even though this is usually not so important with unit tests. As Figure 8.1 shows, in cases of tests which use data providers, detailed information on arguments is printed as well. Moreover, there is a console pane, which shows the output of each test and any other messages printed by the testing framework. (Even so, there are not many occasions when we would have a reason to want to check its content, if all of the tests have passed).

In the event of failure, Eclipse will warn you about the problem by changing the bar color from green to red. As Figure 8.2 shows, Eclipse also provides the following information:

- which test method failed and, in the case of data providers, what the arguments were (in our case -7 and BLA),

- a failure exception message which is "clickable", so you can easily move to the test code and start fixing things.

Figure 8.2. Eclipse: failed tests

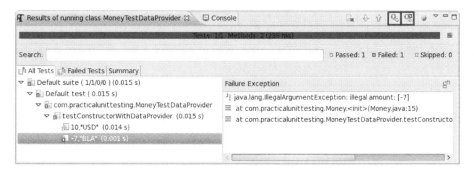

Eclipse also makes it possible to rerun all recently executed tests, or to run only the failed ones (these two options are marked with red rectangles in the picture above).

8.1.2. IntelliJ IDEA Test Reports

IntelliJ IDEA supports both JUnit and TestNG frameworks. It offers common commands and a common user interface (called Test Runner Tab) for running tests for each of them. In this section we shall be discussing what sort of information you can gain from IntelliJ IDEA after running your tests.

In the event that **all of your tests have passed**, you will in general be interested in two things: what tests were run and how long it took (this is especially important if you run integration or end-to-end tests). Both kinds of information are provided by IntelliJ IDEA, but you will need to configure it a little bit to get to see them. By default, when all tests pass, you see only the basic status information - a green bar and a printed summary message. This is shown in Figure 8.3.

Figure 8.3. IntelliJ IDEA: passed tests

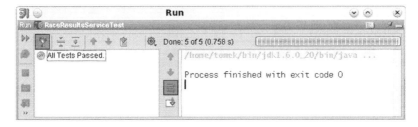

If you want to know more you need to customize the view. IntelliJ IDEA will use the latest settings of the Test Runner Tab, so configuring it will be a one-off action. In order to see what tests have been run, switch off the Hide Passed button and select the Expand All button. In addition, to get the test execution statistics (i.e. execution time) select the Show Statistics option from the cog button menu. The resulting view is shown in Figure 8.4 (red rectangles mark the aforementioned options).

You can adjust the size of each pane to your liking (when preparing illustrations for this book, I was obliged to shrink this slightly, so unfortunately some parts may not be fully visible).

Figure 8.4. IntelliJ IDEA: passed tests - customized view

This time much more information is available. The left pane lists all the test methods executed during the last run in the form of a tree (with each package and class as a node, and each test method as a tree leaf). The pane in the middle shows the console output of each of the tests (in this case the tests have not printed any messages, so it is almost empty).

Clicking on test names (in the left panel) results in the middle pane showing the test output for a selected test case.

The pane on the right shows the test execution statistics. They are not very useful for unit tests, because the execution time of such tests is negligible, so you may as well switch statistics off.

In the event of failure, IntelliJ IDEA will warn you about the problem by changing the bar color from green to red. Obviously, when some test fails, you will want to fix the bug right away, so your expectations of support from IDE are going to be much higher than if all of the tests passed. First of all, you will want to know which test has failed, and which assertion has not been met. Secondly, you will want to be able to navigate with ease directly to the test code which failed. Thirdly, you will want to rerun tests (all of them, or maybe only the failed ones), after having introduced some changes to the code. All of this is supported by IntelliJ IDEA.

Figure 8.5. IntelliJ IDEA: failed tests

It is possible to configure the Test Runner Tab so that after having executed the tests it focuses on the first failed test. Figure 8.5 shows such a scenario. The assertion error is printed along with the precise lines of test code where the verification failed. They are clickable, so you can easily move to the test code and start fixing things.

8.1.3. Conclusion

As we have observed in the course this section, both IntelliJ IDEA and Eclipse provide highly readable test execution reports. The overall result is clearly visible in the form of a green or red bar. The results of each test are also shown. In cases of passed tests, only a minimal amount of information is printed, so the screen does not become clogged up with unimportant data. However, in the event of failure, both IDEs show more of the data, and this helps you to fix the bug right away. They offer quick navigation from assertion error to test code.

8.2. The Default Reports of TestNG

TestNG gives you a full report on its actions by default, including information on failed tests (which is probably the most important reason for bothering to look at test reports). If you make a lot of use of command line, you will often find yourself using the reports provided by TestNG to learn about the issues with your tests.

Although the same reports will be generated, they will be placed in different directories depending on what build tool you use. In the case of Gradle, you will find them in the `build/reports/tests` directory, while Maven puts them in the `target/surefire-reports` directory (in both cases you can configure the output folder - please consult the documentation of your build tool).

Listing 8.1 shows the typical content of the reports directory after the tests have finished (some elements have been omitted for the sake of readability). Should you happen to be running your tests with Maven, the test suite will be named differently: some files would then be prefixed with `Command Line` instead of `Gradle`.

Listing 8.1. Content of build/reports/tests directory

```
|-- Gradle suite ❶
|    |-- Gradle test.html
|    |-- Gradle test.properties
|    |-- Gradle test.xml
|    |-- classes.html
|    |-- groups.html
|    |-- index.html ❷
|    |-- main.html
|    |-- methods-alphabetical.html
|    |-- methods-not-run.html
|    |-- methods.html
|    |-- reporter-output.html
|    |-- testng-failed.xml
|    |-- testng.xml.html
|    `-- toc.html
|-- emailable-report.html ❸
|-- index.html ❹
|-- testng-failed.xml ❺
|-- testng-results.xml ❻
|-- testng.css
```

❶❷ A set of comprehensive reports on tests that have been run. Check it, if you want detailed information, or when you are looking for some bug or weird behaviour of your tests. You will find a lot of data here: information on groups, classes, test methods which have not been executed, etc.

❸ A concise HTML report, well-suited to being sent by email to the team (or anyone interested in the results of the tests).

❹ A summary of the execution of the tests, in HTML format. Not really helpful, but it does link to the full report.

❺ An XML file with the names of any failed tests. Not useful for debugging, as it contains only the names of the tests - no stacktrace or error messages of failed assertions are available here. But its purpose is to help with the rerunning of failed tests.

❻ Comprehensive information on all tests that have been run (in XML format).

When working with command line I would suggest you check the `testng-results.xml` file and look for a `FAIL` message within the file. You can also create some bash aliases or scripts to retrieve interesting information from these files with a single command. In the event that you need a more sectional view, I suggest using the HTML reports.

8.2.1. Adding More Information to the HTML Reports

We will start the customization of reports with a simple task. Let us add (log) some information from the test class into the report. This task is facilitated by TestNG, so all you have to do is use the `log()` method of the `org.testng.Reporter` class, as shown below:

Listing 8.2. Adding more information to the HTML report

```
import org.testng.Reporter;
import org.testng.annotations.Test;

@Test
public class ReporterTest{

    void shouldAddSomethingToReport() {
        Reporter.log("Very Important Log Message");
    }
}
```

Now, if you visit the HTML report, you will find this message printed. It is visible next to the test results (as shown in Figure 8.6) and also on a separate report page, which groups all output logged with the `Reporter.log()` method. You can even put some HTML tags into your log message.

Figure 8.6. Additional information included within the HTML report

```
Reporter output for
Gradle suite

shouldAddSomethingToReport
  Very Important Log Message.
```

 Logs of the `Reporter` class can be adjusted using log levels (see TestNG Javadocs).

8.3. Writing Custom Reporters and Listeners

There are two different options when it comes to tweaking TestNG to output some information about the tests:

1. If you are interested in **post test execution reports** then implementations of the `org.testng.IReporter` interface will be what you are after. Section 8.3.1 provides an example of such a custom reporter.

2. If you are interested in **real-time reporting** (that is, you want to see some information as the tests are progressing), then you need to use listeners implementing the `org.testng.ITestListener` interface. Listeners are discussed in Section 8.3.2.

There are many reasons to implement custom reporters and listeners. You might be interested in, for example:

- getting more detailed information printed to the console,

- implementing a GUI progress-bar widget, which would show how the execution of tests is progressing,

- taking a screenshot after each failed Selenium test executed with the TestNG framework,

- writing test results to the database.

Apart from writing your custom reporters and/or listeners, which is discussed in this section, you must also register them to TestNG, so that TestNG can inform them about the progress and/or results of the execution of the tests. Appendix B, *Running Unit Tests* explains how to achieve this using Maven and Gradle.

8.3.1. Writing Your Own Test Reporter

It is possible that none of the reports provided with TestNG will meet your expectations. Maybe you need some other data to be included in the report, or maybe you need another file format. Whatever the case, TestNG makes it possible to write your own implementation of test reporters. This section provides an example of this.

Let us say that you require a report of the execution of your tests in the form of an Excel file. Your non-technical boss needs it to have some feeling of being in control of the situation (poor guy… ;). An example of the result is shown in Figure 8.7.

Figure 8.7. Sample output of the ExcelReporter

Class	Method	Result
AllResultsTest	shouldBeError	FAILURE
AllResultsTest	shouldFail	FAILURE
AllResultsCopyTest	shouldFailCopy	FAILURE
AllResultsCopyTest	shouldBeErrorCopy	FAILURE
AllResultsCopyTest	shouldBeSkippedCopy	SKIPPED
AllResultsTest	shouldBeSkipped	SKIPPED
AllResultsTest	shouldPass	SUCCESS
AllResultsCopyTest	shouldPassCopy	SUCCESS

Writing your own reporter is not very complicated, but does require some knowledge of the internal data structures of TestNG. Fortunately, the existence of numerous sample reporters (see the TestNG source code, `org.testng.reporters` package) will furnish you with a lot of examples to learn from.

In order to develop such a report, you should implement an `IReporter` interface containing only one method: `generateReport()`. Then you must do the following:

1. extract the required information from the objects passed to the `generateReport()` method of the `IReporter` interface, and

2. write them to a file of your choice.

In our example, the Apache POI library[1] has been used to create the Excel file. One possible implementation is shown in the listings below. The whole class is quite long (the creation of Excel spreadsheets requires some coding), so I have decided to concentrate on those parts which relate to the reporting capabilities of TestNG (the complete version of `ExcelReporter` is included in the book's source code).

---

[1]See http://poi.apache.org/.

The code we must implement in order to create an Excel report contains concepts from both Apache POI and TestNG. However, the "TestNG part" of this task is not very demanding. An `ISuite` object, which is passed to the `generateReport()` method (this is the method of the `IReporter` interface, which we have to implement) contains objects of the `ITestContext` type, which happen to provide you with all of the information about the executed tests. All we need to do is to iterate through these objects and pass the interesting data to the Apache POI library, which will then take care of creating the Excel spreadsheet.

Listing 8.3. Implementation of generateReport() method

```
public class ExcelReporter implements IReporter { ❶

    @Override ❷
    public void generateReport(List<XmlSuite> xmlSuites,
            List<ISuite> iSuites, String outdir) {
        createHeaderRow(); ❸
        addResults(iSuites);❹
        autosizeColumns(); ❺
        writeReportFile(outdir); ❻
    }
...
```

❶❷ The `ExcelReporter` class implements the `org.testng.IReporter` interface and overrides the `generateReport()` method. TestNG will invoke this method and feed it with data, after all the tests have been completed.

❸❺ These two methods - `createHeaderRow()` and `autosizeColumns()` - make our report a good deal prettier, while their implementation is specific to the Apache POI library. Please see the source code to learn about them.

❹ The `addResults()` method contains the core functionality of retrieving data from the objects provided by TestNG. The next listing shows this.

❻ The writing of the output file is handled by Apache POI. Please see the source code for the implementation.

Listing 8.4. Retrieving data from what TestNG offers

```
private int rowNb = 1;

private void addResults(List<ISuite> iSuites) {
    ISuite suite = iSuites.get(0);
    Map<String, ISuiteResult> r = suite.getResults();
    for (ISuiteResult suiteResult : r.values()) { ❶
        ITestContext testContext = suiteResult.getTestContext();
        writeTestMethodResult(testContext.getFailedConfigurations());
        writeTestMethodResult(testContext.getFailedTests());
        writeTestMethodResult(testContext.getSkippedConfigurations());
        writeTestMethodResult(testContext.getSkippedTests());
        writeTestMethodResult(testContext.getPassedTests());
    }
}
```

❶   Iterating through the results of each test suite. Objects of the `ISuiteResult` type
hold information on test methods that have failed, passed or been skipped. There
are also separate objects which track the skipped and failed configuration methods
- for example, methods annotated with the `@BeforeClass` annotation). Each time the
`writeTestMethodResult()` method is invoked, where this actually writes the final data
to the cells of the Excel spreadsheet (see the next listing).

Listing 8.5. Creating spreadsheet cells with data

```
private void writeTestMethodResult(IResultMap results) { ❶
    for (ITestResult result : results.getAllResults()) {
        HSSFRow row = sheet.createRow(rowNb++);
        createCell(row, 0, result.getTestClass().getName()
            .substring(result.getTestClass()
            .getName().lastIndexOf('.') + 1)); ❷
        createCell(row, 1, result.getName());

        switch (result.getStatus()) {
            case 1: createCell(row, 2, successStyle, "SUCCESS");
                break;
            case 2: createCell(row, 2, failureStyle, "FAILURE");
                break;
            case 3: createCell(row, 2, skippedStyle, "SKIPPED");
                break;
            default: createCell(row, 2, failureStyle, "UNKNOWN");
        }
    }
}
```

❶ The `writeTestMethodResults()` method iterates through method results (of the `ITestResult` type) and creates Excel cells with the test class name, test method name, and the execution result (as shown in Figure 8.7).

❷ The details of the creation of the spreadsheet cells (enclosed within the `createCell()` method) are specific to Apache POI, and have been omitted for the sake of brevity - you will find them in the book's source code.

The example presented in this section proves that TestNG offers enough information to create a detailed report of the test execution. The output format can be whatever is required: pure text, an Excel spreadsheet or some graphic representation of passed and failed tests (e.g. a bar chart).

 Appendix B, *Running Unit Tests* explains how to make TestNG use your custom reporter.

8.3.2. Writing Your Own Test Listeners

If you are unhappy with the default output of TestNG tests as they are executed (in a runtime), you can easily change it by writing your own test listeners. In this section we will analyze two simple examples of custom test listeners. Writing custom test listeners mainly benefits those who make a lot of use of command line.

TestNG provides a specialized interface - `ITestListener` - precisely for the purpose of getting runtime information about the tests that are executing. This is exactly what we are looking for, if our goal is to provide rapid feedback for developers, e.g. by implementing some GUI widgets like progress bars. The `ITestListener` interface provides the following methods:

Table 8.1. Methods of the ITestListener class

method	description
`onStart(ITestContext context)`	Invoked before any test or configuration method is called.
`onFinish(ITestContext context)`	Invoked after all the tests have finished.
`onTestStart(ITestResult result)`	Invoked before each test is executed.
`onTestFailure(ITestResult result)`	Invoked when a test has failed.

method	description
`onTestSkipped(ITestResult result)`	Invoked in the event of a test having been skipped.
`onTestSuccess(ITestResult result)`	Invoked when a test has passed.
`onTestFailedButWithinSuccessPercentage (ITestResult result)`	This method refers to the special case of a test annotated with the `successPercentage` annotation. We have not discussed this feature, because it is only used in some rare situations - for example when performing some integration tests with an unreliable third-party system[a].

[a]See http://beust.com/weblog/2005/02/01/testing-asynchronous-code/ for an example.

As shown in Table 8.1, you can get information regarding all of the tests that have been executed (analyzing objects of the `ITestContext` type that have been passed to the `onFinish()` method), or inspect the results of each single test by analyzing objects of the `ITestResult` type that have been passed to methods which are invoked before and after the execution of each test. This way you can immediately print information on progress (e.g. the result of the last test to be executed, its execution time, etc.), but also provide some summary information (e.g. the number of passed and failed tests).

When writing a custom listener, we could implement the `ITestListener` interface or extend a `TestListenerAdapter` class. The second option is preferable, because this class provides a default (empty) implementation of all methods of the `ITestListener` interface, so we only need to override the ones specifically required for our particular use case.

DotTestListener

The first listener - `DotTestListener` - is copied directly from the TestNG documentation. It prints a character for each executed test: **.** (a dot) for passed test, **F** for failed, and **S** for skipped. Its usage brings two benefits:

- it lets you watch the progress of the test (which is quite important if you switched off all test logs, as advised in Section 8.5),

- it makes it very clear whether some tests have failed or been skipped (the letters **F** and **S** stand out clearly from amidst the lines of dots).

Sample output with some failed and skipped tests is shown in Listing 8.6.

Listing 8.6. Sample output of the DotTestListener

```
Running TestSuite
.....FFFS...............................................
........................................................
......
Tests run: 112, Failures: 3, Errors: 0, Skipped: 1,
    Time elapsed: 0.783 sec <<< FAILURE!

Results :

Failed tests:
shouldCreateUriThatContainsOriginalId(com.practicalunittesting.SomeTest)
shouldCreateUriThatContainsOriginalId(com.practicalunittesting.SomeTest)
shouldCreateUriThatContainsOriginalId(com.practicalunittesting.SomeTest)

Tests run: 112, Failures: 3, Errors: 0, Skipped: 1

[INFO] ----------------------------------------------------------------
[ERROR] BUILD FAILURE
```

The implementation, which uses `TestListenerAdapter` as a parent class, is trivial. It is shown in Listing 8.7.

Listing 8.7. Implementation of the DotTestListener class

```
import org.testng.ITestResult;
import org.testng.TestListenerAdapter;

public class DotTestListener extends TestListenerAdapter {  ❶
    private int m_count = 0;  ❷

    public void onTestFailure(ITestResult tr) {  ❸
        log("F");
    }

    public void onTestSkipped(ITestResult tr) {  ❹
        log("S");
    }

    public void onTestSuccess(ITestResult tr) {  ❺
        log(".");
    }

    private void log(String message) {  ❻
        System.out.print(message);
        if (m_count++ % 40 == 0) {
            System.out.println("");
        }
    }
}
```

❶   `TestListenerAdapter` is used as a parent class.
❷❻ There is some simple logic, which makes the output a good deal nicer (line length set to 40 characters).
❸❹❺ `TestListenerAdapter` methods have been overridden.

`DotTestListener` overrides three methods of the `TestListenerAdapter` class. As shown in Listing 8.7, each of them receives an `ITestResult` object, which contains a wealth of information about the test. In this simple case we do not make any use of them.

SkippedTestListener

By default, TestNG does not print detailed information on skipped tests. It only prints out the number of such tests. Because this information is not very easily visible, it has led to my team experiencing some difficulties. There have been several occasions when we missed information on skipped tests and proceeded with a false sense of *"everything being just fine"*.

Tests are skipped sometimes for some trivial reasons – such as having `DataProvider` return a different number of arguments than was expected by the test method. I have noticed that people (me included) tend to only look at the number of failed tests. Somehow, the information that some were skipped gets ignored.

The `SkippedTestListener` listener prints information about skipped tests in the same way that TestNG informs about failed tests. This way it is hard to overlook them. A sample result is shown in Listing 8.8.

Listing 8.8. Sample output of the SkippedTestListener

```
Running TestSuite

SKIPPED SomeTest        someTestMethod
SKIPPED SomeTest        otherTestMethod

Tests run: 112, Failures: 0, Errors: 0, Skipped: 2, Time elapsed: 0.236 sec
```

The implementation is very concise thanks to `TestAdapterListener`, which does the whole job gathering information on the execution of tests. This is shown in Listing 8.9.

Listing 8.9. Implementation of the SkippedTestListener class

```
public class SkippedTestListener extends TestListenerAdapter { ❶

    @Override
    public void onFinish(ITestContext testContext) {
        for (ITestResult result : getSkippedTests()) { ❷
            System.out.println(String.format("SKIPPED\t%1$-40s%2$-40s",
                getTestClassName(result), result.getName()));
        }
    }

    public static String getTestClassName(ITestResult result) {
        return result.getTestClass().getName().substring(
            result.getTestClass().getName().lastIndexOf(".") + 1);
    }
}
```

❶   Once again, the `TestListenerAdapter` class gets extended.

❷   All we have to do is iterate through the skipped test methods. This is possible thanks to the `getSkippedTests()` method, which has been inherited from the `TestListenerAdapter` class.

I use this listener, together with the previously presented `DotTestListener`. This is a truly powerful combo - you simply cannot miss the warnings about failed or skipped tests.

 Appendix B, *Running Unit Tests* explains how to make TestNG use your custom listener.

8.4. Readable Assertion Messages

An assertion message has just one purpose: to make the developer understand instantly what has gone wrong: no guessing, no head-scratching. You just look at the assertion message and you are sure about what it is that is not working. This does not mean that you know where the bug is, but it is the first step on the way to revealing and fixing it.

 When looking at the examples in this book you may reach the conclusion that working on assertion messages is a waste of time. Well, yes, sometimes it is. However, bear in mind that you are now in "training mode". The examples are simple and you are focusing on them to the exclusion of all else. In real life it will be different. You will be surprised by a not-so-clear error message when you least expect it, when your mind is focused on some completely different part of the system (and also, probably, when the deadline is near…). Doesn't it make more sense to lose 15 seconds now, and maybe save a lot of grey hairs later? It is up to you to decide.

Assertion messages provide feedback every time a test fails. Sometimes, in fact quite often, the default information printed by TestNG is good enough. In other cases you will have to do some additional work to make them really helpful. In general, you can do two things to improve the situation:

- add an additional message parameter to the `assertXYZ()` methods of TestNG (for example, `assertEquals(a, b, "some message here");`,

- override the `toString()` method of some domain objects.

8.4.1. Add a Custom Assertion Message

From time to time, you may benefit from adding a custom message to the assertion method. For example (going back to the `Money` class that we discussed earlier), consider these two messages, each printed by a failing test. The first one is printed by the following assertion: `assertEquals(money.getAmount(), 10)`:

Listing 8.10. No assertion message

```
java.lang.AssertionError:
Expected :10
Actual   :15
```

The second output is printed by the following assertion: `assertEquals(money.getAmount(), 10, "wrong amount of money");`:

Listing 8.11. Custom assertion message

```
java.lang.AssertionError: wrong amount of money
Expected :10
Actual   :15
```

While the first version (without any message) leaves us in doubt about the nature of the problem, the second version states explicitly that the problem was with money[2]. The gain is rather minimal: usually all you have to do is look at the test method name (which is always included in the stack trace) to understand the context.

In fact, the additional message is rarely required. Instead of working on that, you would be better off improving the name of the test method (see Section 9.3) so that when it fails, you know exactly why - just by reading its name.

8.4.2. Implement the toString() Method

A good example of when I would recommend doing some more work on an assertion message is the following: let us assume that there is a `Client` class and a test which creates two clients with different properties. If an assertion on clients' equality fails (`assertEquals(clientA, clientB)`), we will encounter the following error message:

---

[2]You could call this a 'real-life example', couldn't you? ;)

Listing 8.12. Cryptic assertion error message

```
java.lang.AssertionError:
Expected :com.practicalunittesting.Client@64ea66
Actual   :com.practicalunittesting.Client@158f9d3
```

Hmm, not really much help, is it? In order to improve the message it is enough to override the `toString()` method of the `Client` class, e.g. like this:

Listing 8.13. Implementation of the toString() method

```
@Override
public String toString() {
    return "Client{" +
        "name='" + name + '\'}';
}
```

Now the error message will be much more informative:

Listing 8.14. Fixed assertion error message

```
java.lang.AssertionError:
Expected :Client{name='Mary Hopkins'}
Actual   :Client{name='John Brown'}
```

8.4.3. Use the Right Assertion Method

And while we are discussing the informativeness of failure messages, please consider the following comparison of different assertions.

Table 8.2. Comparison of assertion failure messages

assertion	failure message

`assertTrue(2 * 2 == 5)`	`java.lang.AssertionError:`
	`Expected :true`
	`Actual   :false`

`assertEquals(2 * 2, 5)`	`java.lang.AssertionError:` `Expected :5`
`assertThat(2 * 2).isEqualTo(5)`	`Actual   :4`

Table 8.2 shows clearly how the misuse of `assertTrue()` leads to a weak assertion message, leaving the developer with no information as to the cause.

8.5. Logging in Tests

The Loudmouth: A unit test (or test suite) that clutters up the console with diagnostic messages, logging messages, and other miscellaneous chatter, even when tests are passing. Sometimes during test creation there was a desire to manually see output, but even though it's no longer needed, it was left behind.

— James Carr *2006*

Let's make it absolutely clear: **you do not need logs for unit tests**. They are only there because we are so used to the fact that we do verify our software by reading through billions of logs. This is unnecessary with unit tests. It may even lead to some problems, especially if you run your tests from the command line.

 This section is aimed mainly at developers who use the command line for running tests. IDEs are quite good at only presenting users with the results of tests, so even thousands of log lines will not be a problem for them.

Watching screens showing logs rolling for a few seconds at the speed of light will not give you anything. You cannot read it, and if the test fails, it should give you exact information on what happened, right? I understand that for integration tests it might be worthwhile to watch Spring or JBoss logs getting printed and see there are no warnings there, but what is the point for unit tests?

And the worst thing of all is when you test for expected exceptions and they are printed within the logs which roll over your screen at such a rapid pace. The first time you see it, you shiver, and check it immediately, and then you sigh with relief. And later, after n-th execution of the tests, you get used to exception stack traces being printed, and you start ignoring them. And then comes a day, when some other exception happens, and you do not react at all. You simply do not care, because *"these exceptions were always there"*, and you do not try to investigate it. In fact, you are so used to the idea of a build's being successful even if some exceptions have been logged, that you do not bother to get to see the final result of a build. You assume it passes, when in reality it has just failed. And then you commit the code and your information radiator goes red, and your team starts yelling at you. Uh, no good...

Personally, I am perfectly happy coding with my logs turned off (by having a separate configuration of logging frameworks) and a custom test listener which prints single letters for each test - **.** (a dot) if it has passed, **F** if it has failed, and **S** if the test has been skipped (exactly as described previously in Section 8.3.2). In the event of test failures, I rely solely on the assertion messages.

Even if you do not want to switch your logs off, the thing to remember is that you should **stop relying on your logs**. The tests should be automated – they should be precise in pointing out the problem, which means that no logs-hunting should be necessary to understand the cause of failure.

8.6. Debugging Tests

Debugging? Haven't we already mentioned that by testing we can save hours spent on debugging sessions? Well, yes. Still, sometimes you run your tests and you do not understand why they are not working. You stare at the screen and cannot figure out what is going on. Do not stare any longer. Fire up a debugger and look inside.

With unit tests you get direct support from your IDE. Debugging test code does not differ from normal debugging sessions. If you are already familiar with debugging, there will not be much that is new to learn. The same rules apply as when debugging a running application. This should not be a surprise, because tests **run** your application (even though they do it in some specific, strictly controlled way).

Appendix B, *Running Unit Tests* covers running a debugging session with Eclipse and IntelliJ IDEA.

8.7. Notifying The Team

A common request is that you notify the team (or some superiors) about the results of your tests. The reason is quite sensible: there are some people who ought to know whether all the tests have passed or not. Perhaps because they will be able to fix it, or maybe because they need to know the status of the project. No matter what the reason is, such functionality can be implemented at the level of TestNG (or almost any other testing framework). For example, one could write a custom test listener which, after all tests had finished, would send an email notification using the Java Mail API[3]. TestNG developers have even made this task easier by generating a separate report precisely for the purpose of sending it by

---

[3]See http://www.oracle.com/technetwork/java/javamail/index.html

mail (see Section 8.2). In short, custom implementation of notifications is possible, but I would argue that this is not the right approach.

There are two main reasons for saying this. First, you should let your testing framework take care of executing tests and creating reports. This is what testing frameworks are for. TestNG is quite extensible, which means you can enhance it with almost any functionality you wish, but this does not mean you should do so.

The second reason is that there are already solutions for the notifications sending issue. I would hope that your team makes use of a continuous integration server, which runs all tests continually. Any popular CI solution will offer a notifications service, and usually much more besides. For example, in the case of Jenkins[4], a very popular open-source CI server, there are more than 30 notification plugins[5] which allow the sending of information about build results (including test results) by email, Jabber, Skype, Twitter and many more.

To conclude, first you should *"use the right tool for the job"*, and second, in the presence of such a wealth of freely available options, why bother with implementing your own solution?

8.8. Conclusions

In this section we have concentrated on ways of getting feedback information about the execution of tests. First, we covered feedback generated by the IDE. Then we moved to the output generated by TestNG. We learned about the default for this, and explored options for customization. We also did some coding and created our own listeners and reporters. In so doing we made TestNG print information that was of value to us, both during the execution of the tests and after they had finished. As the few straightforward examples given here demonstrate, TestNG will furnish us with comprehensive information about the tests that have been executed, and it is up to us how we use it.

To gather even more data on the execution of tests, we also plunged into the world of assertion messages, logging and debugging.

Well, quite a lot of information. Now that you know all of this, how do you plan to use it? Will you rely on the default information returned by your IDE and testing framework, or

---

[4]See http://jenkins-ci.org
[5]See https://wiki.jenkins-ci.org/display/JENKINS/Plugins

do you perhaps feel that some customization is required? Remember, you will be running unit tests frequently and checking their results multiple times, so make sure you feel comfortable with the feedback you are getting.

8.9. Exercises

The exercises presented in this section should make you familiar with the default output of tests. They should also give you some practical experience with the customization of elements responsible for the content and format of various test execution reports.

8.9.1. Study Test Output

Simply run some tests and study the output. Make sure you know where to find information on the cause of a failed test. Remember, there are usually several ways to obtain the required information. Spend some time getting to know them all, so you can choose the one which suits you best.

8.9.2. Read Test Data from a CSV File

Given a simple CSV file with test data:

```
name,surname,age
John,Doe,33
Mary,Doe,32
... etc.
```

implement the following functionality:

- a data provider should read the data from this file and pass it to the test method (see Section 6.10 for an example),

- headers from the CSV file should be used to write the following values to the report (using the `Reporter.log()` method, as shown in Section 8.2.1):

  - name: John, surname: Doe, age: 33

  - name: Mary, surname: Doe, age: 32

  - etc.

8.9.3. Custom Test Listener

Your task is to write a custom test listener which prints out the following information about each test method that is executed:

- the test result,

- the name of the test class,

- the name of the test method,

- the time of execution of this test method.

An example of output is presented below:

Listing 8.15. Sample output of the TimeTestLoggingListener class

```
OK        FirstTest        fifthTestMethod        1944
OK        FirstTest        firstTestMethod        3799
OK        FirstTest        fourthTestMethod       1920
OK        FirstTest        secondTestMethod       4891
OK        FirstTest        thirdTestMethod        2963
OK        SecondTest       methodA                3525
OK        SecondTest       methodB                1390
OK        SecondTest       methodC                 117
OK        SecondTest       methodD                4571
OK        SecondTest       methodE                4552
```

This information should be printed to the console (System.out) in runtime.

8.9.4. Debugging Session

Make yourself comfortable with the debugging of tests. Using your favorite IDE, set some breakpoints (in test code and in the source code of the tested classes) and execute some tests. Practise working through all the typical scenarios of a debugging session:

- setting breakpoints,

- getting information on the values of variables,

- various types of moving forward (step into, step over, etc.).

Chapter 9. Organization Of Tests

> Good order is the foundation of all good things.
>
> — Edmund Burke

> Rules are mostly made to be broken and are too often for the lazy to hide behind.
>
> — Dougleas MacArthur

When the number of your tests grows, the way they are written and stored becomes more and more important. This section discusses some decisions relating to various "organizational" aspects of your tests. Even though parts of this section do not contribute directly to your testing abilities, it will surely make you aware of the broader context for your tests. This is because writing a single class is just the beginning: sooner or later your test suite will become huge, and then it will really matter how it is organized.

 How your tests are organized is something that will affect not only your work but also that of your teammates. Before you deviate from the most common paths (for example by changing project layout to something non-standard), please make sure that your colleagues also think it is a good idea!

9.1. Package for Test Classes

We have already discussed where source code and test code should be kept. The general consensus is that they should reside in different directories (as shown in Listing 9.1). Such a separation is respected by all currently used tools, and helps us to steer clear of the peril of releasing production code with which some test classes have come to be mingled.

Listing 9.1. Production code and test code in different directories

```
.
`-- src
    |-- main
    |   `-- java ❶
    `-- test
        `-- java ❷
```

❶   The subdirectory where production code is kept.

❷ The subdirectory for test code.

However, agreeing on the separate directories does not end the discussion. Another question is about the packages used for test classes.

Basically, there are two possible options:

1. test classes should use the same packages that are used by the production code being tested (e.g. a test for a `my.project.User` class should also be kept in a `my.project` package),

2. test classes should use different packages - usually prefixed or suffixed with `tests`, e.g. `my.project.tests`.

 The first option still assumes that the test code resides in a different directory from the production code!

Why does this matter? To be perfectly frank, usually it does not matter so much. Having tests in the same package gives you the following:

- there is no need to import some classes (e.g. the SUT class) into your tests, making your imports list shorter,

- it is possible to test some cumbersome cases by relaxing the access modifiers of some methods to "default" (see Section 7.4 and Section 7.5).

On the other hand, keeping test classes in different packages results in the following:

- you **can not** use the "default" access modifier to test private methods

  - ...however, you can still use a `protected` access modifier.

- it is very clear which classes belong to production code and which to test code; while it is usually not a problem for test classes (as they are pre/suffixed with `Test`), it might be important for various utility classes of test code.

I would encourage you to use a different package for tests, as it makes it harder to do things which, under normal circumstances, should be avoided (once again - private method testing, as well as certain other dubious techniques). However, this decision is not so very important, and can easily be changed if required (changing the package of tests will not break any clients, as usually no other code depends on test classes).

9.2. @Test Annotations

TestNG offers two styles of `@Test` annotation - on classes and on methods. They can be used alternately to some extent. A single @Test annotation on a test class has the consequence that all public methods of this class will be considered test methods. If you want more fine-grained control - i.e. if you only want some methods to be treated as test methods - you can use method-level annotations. Using method-level annotations is required if it is a part of some more specific scenario - e.g. if the method uses a data provider to get parameters.

 Remember that if both annotations are present, then the method-level annotation attributes will override values specified at class-level.

One good thing about class-level annotations is that you do not have to remember to put them on every method. I have seen test classes that lacked `@Test` annotations on some methods (for unknown, or forgotten reasons), where this resulted in tests not being run. Having `@Test` annotations on class level makes you immune to such issues. In the event of there being some public non-test methods, you must mark them with an `@Test(enabled = false)` annotation. This way TestNG will not try to execute them as tests.

Whichever style of annotation your team chooses, make sure that it is used consistently. My team once "lost" some tests during refactoring, simply by moving some test methods from one class (which used class-level annotations) to another (which used method-level annotations). Be consistent: it pays off.

9.3. Name Your Tests Consistently

The naming schema of test classes and test methods can make a real difference. If consistent and well thought out, it will help you go to the right place in your code - exactly where you want to be. If chaotic, with no obvious patterns, it will slow down your development by forcing you to browse through your codebase class by class instead of jumping instantly to this one important place. Another important thing about naming is that it helps us to understand the role and purpose of each test. This is very important when adding new tests or when looking to identify the reason for a particular test failure.

In this section we will take a look at two main factors which impact on how hassle-free or problematic your experience of working with test code is likely to be: names of test classes and names of test methods. Additionally we will also consider naming schemas for test-doubles.

9.3.1. Test Class Names

The most popular pattern for naming test classes is to append a `Test` suffix to the name of the class being tested. This results in test classes like `UserDAOTest`, `PasswordValidatorTest` and `BankAccountTest`, which test production classes named `UserDAO`, `PasswordValidator` and `BankAccount` respectively. The benefits of this pattern are the following:

* it is dead simple,

* it is honored by a number of tools which:

    * streamline the process of configuring the testing plugins of build tools (e.g. Maven, Gradle), as classes with the `Test` suffix are recognized by default as test classes,

* allow you to move quickly between test and production code with your IDE (so, for example, you can jump from `BankAccount` to `BankAccountTest` with one keyboard shortcut),

* there is a one-to-one mapping between production class and test class, so you know that:

    * all tests of the given class are in this one place,

    * and, vice-versa, that this test class contains nothing but tests for a single class,

* it is commonly used (so everyone feels at home when your code follows this schema).

There are not many counterproposals for test class naming schemes[1]. The overwhelming majority of code that I have seen follows the simple schema presented above. And there are not many reasons, if any, for you not to follow it as well. I follow this pattern 99% of the time (and would encourage you to do the same), but there are also some cases where I renounce it. Two of them are described below.

---

[1]One that I am aware of, derived from the BDD approach, makes the test class name part of a "when" element of a BDD convention - see http://www.slideshare.net/wakaleo/junit-kung-fu-getting-more-out-of-your-unit-tests

Splitting Up Long Test Classes

When a test class starts to grow beyond the "safety limit" I have established for myself, I start to wonder whether splitting it up would not perhaps be a good idea. A common scenario, when I do split a test class up, is that there is a lot of arguments checking and numerous tests for expected exceptions. I usually move these tests to a separate class and use a different suffix - `WrongValuesTest` - to distinguish it. In the case of an exemplary `MyClass`, I would end up with the following test classes:

1. `MyClassTest` - all tests that puts the "valid" behaviour of the class through its paces. This test class shows the right way to use `MyClass`.

2. `MyClassWrongValuesTest` - all tests that put the SUT through its paces and fail (fast!) with an expected exception. This test class shows what happens when `MyClass` is used in an incorrect way.

The second test class - `MyClassWrongValuesTest` - is usually much simpler (but sometimes longer) than `MyClassTest`. Often it will contain some data providers, whose role is to provide various illegal values for different test methods. Test doubles are rarely required there (except, maybe, for dummies); this is because no methods are really called on them, as arguments checking is usually the first thing you do.

 The necessity of splitting up a test class might by indicative that what you should really be splitting up is the class being tested itself! If it cannot be tested with one test class, maybe it is too big - maybe it has too much responsibility? If so, then fix this problem, and the test class will automatically shrink to an appropriate length.

Test Class Per Feature

Another way to go with test class naming is to base their name not only on a tested class, but also on a tested feature. The following story illustrates the usability of such an approach.

One day I was asked to introduce a change to a certain legacy code class called `DataProvider`. This class was responsible for some computations and offered some methods which returned the mean values of some calculated numbers. The then current implementation was to return `null` if some data required for calculations was missing. At some point our client introduced a new monitoring tool, which was consuming data returned by the `DataProvider` class in order to draw some charts. It transpired that this new tool did not like `null` values at all, so a change was requested – so that it would return zeros instead of `null` values.

I took a look at the existing code, and found no tests for the class. It was not possible to test the class thoroughly (because it would have taken too much time), so I decided to only introduce tests which would cover the functionality in question. Because I did not intend to test the whole class, I decided to abandon the `ClassNameTest` pattern. Instead, I created a new test class and called it `DataProviderMeanValuesZerosInsteadOfNullsTest`. Even though it went against the norms of my working practice, I felt it was the right thing to do. The test class name indicated clearly that it was meant to test the `DataProvider` class, the suffix informed people that it was a test class, and the rest served to indicate what part of the class functionality was being tested.

 If it ever should come about that we decide to cover the whole class with tests (not very likely, though…), then the `DataProviderMeanValuesZerosInsteadOfNullsTest` will probably be merged into it.

9.3.2. Test Method Names

TestNG, like all current testing frameworks, give you complete freedom when it comes to naming test methods. This is because identification of test methods is based on annotations and not on method names. With freedom, though, comes a need to make choices, and many different options to choose from. Let's discuss this issue and see if we can get to choose the best one.

 Please refer to Section 10.1 for additional discussion about why some naming schemas are more appropriate than others.

Historically, method names were prefixed with the word `test` - e.g. `testConstructor()`, `testReturnsNonNullArray()`, etc. This naming schema was popularized (or rather enforced) by JUnit, which treated all methods that followed this pattern as test methods, and executed them during tests execution (ignoring any methods with different names). And for a long time everyone was happy with it.

However, the limitations of this naming schema started to show up. First of all, it was not obvious what a particular test method was all about, just by looking at its name. It was quite common to find lengthy test methods which, under a common name such as, for example, `testUserAdd()`, verified many features of a class being tested. This was especially painful when dealing with failed tests, as there was not much one could learn from the information that *"testUserAdd() has failed"*. Such an error message does not inform us about exactly what has failed: i.e. which feature of the class tested is not working properly. Because of this, method names started to grow and contain much more information. For example `testConstructor()` was split into several more focused test methods with names like `testConstructorThrowsExceptionForInvalidArguments()`, for example.

This was definitely a step in the right direction, but still not quite good enough. Developers at this time were fascinated by the expressiveness of new dynamic languages (e.g. Ruby[2]) and fluent interfaces[3], and this meant they were really irritated by the presence of this obligatory `test` prefix. Many of us demanded that failed test messages should be readable as proper English sentences (or, at least, be as close to this ideal as possible). The rescue came with a new wave of testing frameworks (TestNG in particular) which used annotations instead of method names patterns to recognize test methods. This made it possible to come up with a more readable naming pattern.

This new pattern was based on the idea that the test method name should convey information about the following:

- preconditions of the test - the state of the SUT and the environment before the test,

- triggering actions - what makes the SUT act in the expected way,

- expected results of the test - what should be returned by the SUT, or what state the SUT should be in after the test is finished, or what actions should be performed by the SUT during the test,

- optionally, the name or role of the SUT,

- in addition, the `test` prefix was replaced with `should`, which allows one to create specification-like method names.

Of course, it is usually not possible to include a full description of all these kinds of information in the method name itself. What is possible, though, is to include just enough

---

[2] http://ruby-lang.org
[3] http://en.wikipedia.org/wiki/Fluent_interface

details to convey the main purpose of the test. Also, each of the elements can be omitted, if its presence does not enhance the readability of the test method. Table 9.1 provides some examples of test method names which follow the guidelines described above.

Table 9.1. Examples of test method names

class name	test methods
`OrderTest`	`constructorShouldThrowExceptionForNullUser()`
	`constructorShouldCreateValidOrderForValidUser()`
`PasswordValidatorTest`	`shouldNotAcceptDictionaryBasedPasswords()`
	`shouldNotAcceptPasswordWithoutDigits()`
	`shouldNotAcceptShortPasswords()`
	`shouldAcceptLongComplicatedPassword()`
`BookingSystem`	`shouldAllowToBookTableForOneHourAndMore()`
	`shouldDisallowToBookForLessThanHour()`
	`shouldAllowToCreateRecurrentReservation()`
	`shouldAllowToCancelExistingReservation()`

In the case of the examples presented in Table 9.1, all test method names specify exactly what is expected of the SUT (e.g. `shouldThrow…()`, `shouldNotAccept…()`, `shouldAllow…()`), and under what conditions or with what arguments (e.g. `…ForNullUser()`, `…PasswordsWithoutDigits()`, `…ExistingReservation()`). When a test fails, the first line of the message already furnishes us with enough information to understand what it is that is not working properly.

What is attractive about this naming schema is that it leaves some room for customization. Some of the examples shown in Table 9.1 do not start with `should`, but with the `constructor` prefix, which makes it clearer which part of the SUT is being tested by a particular method.

 Test method names are of secondary importance compared to their content, but they can push your thinking in the right direction - or, for that matter, the wrong one. The use of the "should" prefix helps (some people would say forces) us to focus on the expected behaviour of the SUT, and leads to "testing behaviour and not methods" (see Section 10.1). Thinking in terms of the responsibilities of the SUT will make you test at the right level of abstraction. This is especially important when coding code-first, because it is then so very easy to test implementation details instead of the behaviour of an external SUT.

9.3.3. Naming of Test-Double Variables

Let us take a look at the variable names we have used so far when working with test doubles. An example is given in the listing below.

Listing 9.2. Original variables' names

```
Messenger messenger;
TemplateEngine templateEngine;
MailServer mailServer;
```

The names of variables, as shown in Listing 9.2, inform us about the types of objects (e.g. it is obvious that `mailServer` is of the `MailServer` type). However, they do not convey any information concerning the role which these objects play in our tests. One of them is an **SUT**, another one a **test spy**, another a **stub**. Yet this difference is not expressed by the names of the variables in test code, and can only be discovered on closer inspection.

Some people suggest giving more intention-revealing names to all variables. For example:

Listing 9.3. Intention-revealing names of variables

```
Messenger sut;
TemplateEngine stubTemplateEngine;
MailServer spyMailServer;
```

This version of the names of the variables gives much more insight into their purpose in test class. A single glance is sufficient to let us know that the real testing is to be done using `sut` and `spyMailServer`, while `stubTemplateEngineReq` is only assisting in this process. Another variation of this idea is to reverse the order and put the type of test double as a suffix, e.g. `mailServerSpy`, `templateEngineStub`. This way the information concerning the type of the object is more easily visible – something which some people consider more valuable.

It is up to you to decide whether you find this worthwile. With short tests, with a very limited number of DOCs (as they should be), these additional hints, embedded within the variable names, are rather unnecessary. If you have more DOCs and more complex tests than it may help you to understand the tests. On the other hand, short, simple, focused tests are what we should be striving for, so instead of renaming variables, maybe it would be better just to write better tests.

 Whatever naming scheme you decide to follow, please make sure you feel comfortable with it (and that so do your colleagues).

9.4. Comments in Tests

> Good code is its own best documentation. As you're about to add a comment, ask yourself, "How can I improve the code so that this comment isn't needed?"
>
> — Steve McConnell *Code Complete (1993)*

When it comes to comments, the same rules apply as with production code. In general, it is better to have clean code with no comments than perfectly commented-upon spaghetti-code. In general:

• do not comment on the obvious,

• comment on everything that might surprise your fellow developers (explain why you have chosen such a strange, non-standard way of doing something…),

• give information about any important things which cannot be read off directly from the code (e.g. the business purpose of some test or other).

If you stick to these simple guidelines, your code will have a minimal number of comments, and only valuable ones at that. The old truth about good code not needing comments is even more true with test code. Here are several reasons why comments in test code are rarely required:

• Test code should be (and hopefully is) very simple. It is all about arrange/act/assert – the creation of objects, execution of methods and verification of results. If you keep it simple (see Section 10.2), then there should be nothing complex which requires comments.

- By giving descriptive names to variables, test classes and test methods (see Section 9.3), you ensure that there will be no need to include any comments. All important information can be read off from the code itself.

Personally, my test code is almost free of comments. There are only three situations where I (sometimes) put comments in code. First, when adding a test because of a **reported bug**. In such a case, I usually add a link to the issue on bug tracker, and (optionally) write a short explanation of what the problem was. Sometime, I also add a comment on the reasons for selecting a **particular set of test data**. This often has something to do with business requirements, and cannot be read from the code. It also happens that some tests of legacy code which use **non-standard techniques** (like the ones described in Section 7.5) require a comment. Apart from these rare occasions, I do not comment on my test code at all.

9.5. BDD: 'Given', 'When', 'Then'

> BDD is a second-generation, outside–in, pull-based, multiple-stakeholder, multiple-scale, high-automation, agile methodology. It describes a cycle of interactions with well-defined outputs, resulting in the delivery of working, tested software that matters.
>
> — Dan North

In this section I would like to present a slightly different style of writing unit tests. This style comes from the Behaviour-Driven Development (BDD) approach.

Because BDD is more applicable to higher-level tests (i.e. end-to-end tests) than unit testing, I will not explain it in detail. There are numerous good sources on the Internet explaining BDD, and I would encourage you to spend some time reading about it. What I would suggest is that we concentrate on the technical aspects of writing unit tests BDD-style. Before doing this, let me quickly introduce BDD in a few sentences:

- BDD was introduced by Dan North in 2003.

- BDD is more customer-oriented than TDD, mainly because its primary use is in higher level tests. Some BDD ideas are applicable to unit tests (and with very good results).

- BDD pays a great deal of attention to the readability of tests. Many BDD frameworks allow tests to be written in almost natural language.

- Some people say that BDD is a *"TDD done right"* – one more reason to put some effort into learning it.

In fact, some elements presented in this book - for example the test methods naming schema in Section 9.3 - are very compatible with what BDD suggests, so we could even say that we have already had a taste of doing things BDD-style. However, most developers link BDD to the famous **'given/when/then'** pattern, which is a trademark of BDD. And that is exactly what I would like to discuss in this section.

The idea of given/when/then comes from scenarios[4] being written in the following manner:

> Given some initial context (the givens), When an event occurs, then ensure some outcomes.
>
> — Dan North *Introducing BDD (2006)*

An exemplary scenario written in such a manner could be the following:

- **Given** that a user *John* is logged in,

- **When** he clicks a *profile* button,

- **Then** a page profile filled with his data is displayed.

9.5.1. Testing BDD-Style

TestNG does not provide any syntactic sugar to support BDD. The usual way of mimicking the style of BDD is by putting the 'given/when/then' words in comments, as shown in Listing 9.4[5]. This code is an equivalent of a test we have already discussed in Section 10.1.

---

[4]A BDD scenario is a rough equivalent of requirements and/or test cases
[5]Some people suggest that adding empty lines instead of given/when/then words is good enough. I agree.

Listing 9.4. Testing a BankAccount class - BDD style

```
@Test
public class BankAccountBDDTest {

    public void shouldBeEmptyAfterCreation() {
        // given
        BankAccount account = new BankAccount();

        // when
        int balance = account.getBalance();

        // then
        assertEquals(balance, 0);
    }

    public void shouldAllowToCreditAccount() {
        // given
        BankAccount account = new BankAccount();

        // when
        account.deposit(100);

        // then
        int balance = account.getBalance();
        assertEquals(balance, 100);
    }

    public void shouldAllowToDebitAccount() {
        // given
        BankAccount account = new BankAccount();

        // when
        account.deposit(100);
        account.withdraw(40);

        // then
        int balance = account.getBalance();
        assertEquals(balance, 60);
    }
}
```

Anything shocking in the above listing? I do not think so. It only differs from what we have been discussing so far in respect of a few details:

- slightly longer test methods, which contain everything that is required to test a certain story (including setting up of objects),

- a clear structure for each of the test methods,

- clear separation of action (e.g. `account.getBalance()`) and assertion (e.g. `assertEquals(balance, 60)`).

 When it comes to unit tests, there is no such thing as an instance of "pure" BDD. Listing 9.4 shows one possible way to write this test BDD-style, but this is probably not the only valid way to do it.

As Listing 9.4 shows, in BDD the structure of the test method is really important. Some test methods are (slightly) longer than necessary, just to satisfy the clear separation between the `when` and `given` phases (e.g. there is no need for a `balance` variable to exist - `assertEquals(account.getBalance(), 60)` would suffice). This approach brings a lot of clarity, and a little bit of redundancy, to every test method.

Another thing to notice is the single assertion within each test method. This is something I criticized in Section 7.3; however, it starts to make sense with the BDD approach.

9.5.2. Mockito BDD-Style

In contrast to TestNG, Mockito facilitates writing tests BDD-style. It provides a `BDDMockito` class, which allows you to use a `given()` method in the same way as we have been using the `Mockito.when()` method up to now (i.e. to set expectations on test doubles). This makes Mockito tests more BDD-like. Listing 9.5 shows this.

Listing 9.5. Mockito test - BDD style

```
import static org.mockito.BDDMockito.given; ❶

public class BddMockitoTest {

    private static final int ID_USER = 329847;

    @Test
    public void shouldReturnClient() {
        // given
        User USER = new User();
        UserDAO dao = mock(UserDAO.class); ❷
        UserService service = new UserService(dao); ❸
        given(dao.getUser(ID_USER)).willReturn(USER); ❹

        // when
        User user = service.loadUser(ID_USER);

        // then
        assertEquals(user, USER);
    }
}
```

❶   Importing of a `given()` method of the `BDDMockito` class.
❷❸ Setting up the SUT (`service`) and injecting a test double (`dao`).
❹   Use of a `given()` method helps to keep the BDD given/when/then rhythm. It is equivalent to `when(dao.getUser(ID_USER)).thenReturn(USER);`, but does not use a `when()` method, which would be confusing as we are still in the "given" part of the test code.

As shown in the listing above, this amounts to a nice piece of syntactic sugar, but nothing groundbreaking. However, it does help to express the rhythm of a BDD test, which is a good thing.

9.6. Reducing Boilerplate Code

If you work with Mockito a lot, you might be interested in cutting down the boilerplate code of test doubles creation. All those instances of `myMock = mock(SomeClass.class)`, which seem to show up in every test method, are really annoying, right? The good news is that Mockito makes it possible to get rid of the boilerplate code. In this section we will take a look at Mockito's annotations and its one-liner stubbing feature.

Consistency is good. Whether you decide to use the features presented in this section or choose not to do so, be consistent about this.

Listing 9.6 shows two simple classes which will be used to demonstrate these new Mockito features. Their names - SUT and Collaborator - reveal their purpose clearly, in both cases.

Listing 9.6. SUT and Collaborator classes

```
public class Collaborator {
    public String doSth() {
            return "xyz"; ❶
    }
}

public class SUT {
    private Collaborator collaborator;

    public void setCollaborator(Collaborator collaborator) {
        this.collaborator = collaborator;
    }

    public String useCollaborator() {
        return collaborator.doSth(); ❷
    }
}
```

❶ The default value returned by the doSth() method is *"xyz"*,

❷ Here we have a simple delegating method which is supposed to return what collaborator returns.

A typical test for this sort of functionality is shown below. I have decided to use a setUp() method this time (see Section 9.7), because I believe this is a more common scenario.

Listing 9.7. Typical test with a lot of boilerplate code

```
public class BoilerplateCodeTest {

    private Collaborator collaborator;
    private SUT sut;

    @BeforeMethod
    public void setUp() {  ❶
        sut = new SUT();
        collaborator = Mockito.mock(Collaborator.class);
        sut.setCollaborator(collaborator);
        when(collaborator.doSth()).thenReturn("abc");
    }

    @Test
    public void shouldReturnABC() {
        assertEquals(sut.useCollaborator(), "abc");
    }
}
```

❶   This is where the repetitive code occurs – the creation of the SUT, the creation of test doubles, injecting them and stubbing.

The question is whether we can do anything about this.

 Please bear in mind that under "normal" circumstances, the boilerplate code section is much larger than shown in Listing 9.7. Usually there will be more than one test double in your code. Multiply it by the number of tests which use test doubles and the reason for cutting down the size of all of the set up activities becomes evident.

9.6.1. One-Liner Stubs

The first thing we can do is to make the creation and stubbing of collaborator slightly shorter. Mockito allows for one-line stubbing, which is shown in Listing 9.8.

Listing 9.8. Reducing boilerplate code with one-line stubbing

```
public class OneLinerStubbingTest {

    private Collaborator collaborator =
            when(mock(Collaborator.class).doSth())
                .thenReturn("abc").getMock();  ❶
    private SUT sut;

    @BeforeMethod
    public void setup() {  ❷
        sut = new SUT();
        sut.setCollaborator(collaborator);
    }

    @Test
    public void shouldReturnABC() {
        assertEquals(sut.useCollaborator(), "abc");
    }
}
```

❶ In this line, a test double gets created and stubbed. Note the `getMock()` method at the end of the invocation chain.

❷ No test double creation in `setUp()` method.

Personally, I am not a big fan of this feature. Its usage does not bring serious code reduction, and, in my opinion, slightly obscures the view. If you plan to use it, I would recommend putting the actual creation and stubbing code in your `setUp()` method, so all creation code is in one place.

9.6.2. Mockito Annotations

Now let us move on to the main point of boilerplate code reduction. An example of what can be achieved is shown in Listing 9.9.

Listing 9.9. Creating test doubles using Mockito annotations

```
import org.mockito.Mock; ❶
import org.mockito.MockitoAnnotations; ❷

public class AnnotationsTest {

    @Mock private Collaborator collaborator; ❸
    private SUT sut;

    @BeforeMethod
    public void initMocks() {
        MockitoAnnotations.initMocks(this); ❹
    }

    @BeforeMethod
    public void setup() {
        sut = new SUT();
        sut.setCollaborator(collaborator); ❺
        when(collaborator.doSth()).thenReturn("abc"); ❻
    }

    @Test
    public void shouldReturnABC() {
        assertEquals(sut.useCollaborator(), "abc"); ❼
    }
}
}
```

❶❷ Importing of Mockito annotations,

❸ The collaborator, which will be replaced by a test double, is marked with an `@Mock` annotation.

❹ This line instructs Mockito to create test doubles for all fields marked with an `@Mock` annotation.

❺❻ There is nothing surprising here about the way the test double of `collaborator` is used. It gets injected into the SUT (using a setter) and is instructed to return a canned value.

❼ This test proves that the test double behaves as instructed: it returns *"abc"* instead of the default *"xyz"*.

Now, that was interesting. There was no explicit line creating a test double, and yet it behaved as if it had been created in the usual way.

In the case shown in Listing 9.9, not much has been gained. In fact, for a single test with one test double, the number of lines grows. However, if you use this technique for a whole suite, with many test methods and many test doubles, then the decrease in the number of code lines might be visible.

 In (rare) cases where you have more than one collaborator of the same kind, you could use the `name` attribute of an `@Mock` annotation to instruct Mockito about which field of the SUT should be replaced with which test double. Please consult the Mockito documentation for details.

Nice, but we can go even further, and inject test doubles into the SUT using annotations. For example:

Listing 9.10. Injecting test doubles using Mockito annotations

```
public class AnnotationsTest {

    @Mock private Collaborator collaborator;

    @InjectMocks private SUT sut = new SUT(); ❶

    @BeforeMethod
    public void initMocks() {
        MockitoAnnotations.initMocks(this);
    }

    @BeforeMethod
    public void setup() { ❷
        when(collaborator.doSth()).thenReturn("abc");
    }

    @Test
    public void shouldReturnABC() {
        assertEquals(sut.useCollaborator(), "abc");
    }
}
```

❶ `@InjectMocks` tells Mockito to …well, to inject mocks into this particular object. Please note that the SUT is created here and not in `setUp()` method.

❷ In contrast to the previous version of the `setUp()` method, here there is no SUT creation and no setting of collaborator.

Wow! No setting of collaborator, and still the execution of the `useCollaborator()` method does not fail with a `NullPointerException`! In reality the collaborator is injected to sut behind the scenes. Mockito does this by matching available test doubles with the SUT's fields.

You will be even more surprised when you remove the setter (the `setCollaborator()` method) from the SUT class, and watch the test still work. This is because Mockito does not really execute setters to set fields, but uses a reflection mechanism to modify them directly.

Now, let us summarize and discuss what we have just been learning about.

In our pursuit of better, cleaner, more readable test code, we have learned about Mockito annotations - `@Mock` and `@InjectMocks`. Both can be used to cut down the boilerplate code related to the creation and injection of mocks. By using them, we have:

• shortened the setup phase of the test code,

• got rid of repetitive, boilerplate test double creation and code setting.

However, in passing the responsibility for test double creation and injection over to Mockito, we must agree to certain things, namely:

• that the SUT must be created before injection happens (see the example in Listing 9.10),

• that Mockito uses reflection, which can lower code coverage measures (and that it bypasses setters).

Using `@Mock` and `@InjectMocks` annotations might have both good and bad effects on the readability of your code. On the one hand the code becomes more concise, and ceases to be cluttered up with repetitive statements. On the other, with larger tests you can lose track of "what was created where", and achieve the opposite effect – namely, that of diminished readability.

Please make sure you read carefully about the annotations presented in this section, in the Mockito documentation. There are some gotchas which might take you by surprise if and when you use them.

 Mockito offers several more annotations similar to the `@Mock` annotation; however, their use is very limited. Please consult the Mockito documentation to learn about them.

9.7. More on Test Fixture Setting

In the course of performing our tests we have been very meticulous to make sure that the SUT and collaborators are in the "fresh" state, before every test method. We made sure that these objects are clean, without any changes that were introduced by earlier tests. This way, we are taking and important step in the direction of tests that are independent– which is, generally, a valuable thing[6]. This works pretty well in the case of unit tests, provided that the objects are cheap to create (which is usually true, as they have no connection to databases and the like). However, this is only a part of the story.

First, we will take a look at the remaining `@BeforeXYZ` annotations, that we haven't met yet. Than, we will discuss some issues related to the creation of SUT and collaborators.

9.7.1. TestNG BeforeXYZ Annotations

We have already introduced the `@BeforeMethod` annotation, but TestNG offers four other `@Before…` annotations which allow for very detailed control of test fixture creation. Each `@Before` annotation is accompanied by an `@After` annotation, which allows you to clean test fixtures after test(s) have finished. This permits you to maintain full control over the creation of objects (and other test resources), as well as allowing for their removal.

Even so, **when it comes to unit tests, they are rarely used**. In my experience, `@BeforeMethod` and `@BeforeClass` are all you need for 99.99% of your unit tests. `@After` annotations are even less useful for unit tests: in general, you do not touch files, streams or databases which you would want to clean up (close, delete, remove) after the tests.

For the sake of completeness, Table 9.2 shows all the annotations which can be used for setting a test fixture. The descriptions are copied directly from the TestNG documentation.

Table 9.2. @Before and @After annotations

annotation	description
@BeforeSuite	The annotated method will be run before all tests in this suite have run.

---

[6]See Section 7.2 for some discussion.

annotation	description
@AfterSuite	The annotated method will be run after all tests in this suite have run.
@BeforeTest	The annotated method will be run before any test method belonging to the classes inside the `<test>` tag is run[a].
@AfterTest	The annotated method will be run after all the test methods belonging to the classes inside the `<test>` tag have run.
@BeforeGroups	The list of groups that this configuration method will run beforehand. This method is guaranteed to run shortly before the first test method belonging to any of these groups is invoked.
@AfterGroups	The list of groups that this configuration method will run afterwards. This method is guaranteed to run shortly after the last test method belonging to any of these groups is invoked.
@BeforeClass	The annotated method will be run before the first test method in the current class is invoked.
@AfterClass	The annotated method will be run after all the test methods in the current class have been run.
@BeforeMethod	The annotated method will be run before each test method.
@AfterMethod	The annotated method will be run after each test method.

[a] `<test>` tag refers to part of the `testng.xml` file, which plays a role in one of the ways in which TestNG tests can be run. Please refer to the TestNG documentation for detailed information on this topic.

Listing 9.11 shows a simple test which uses some of the aforementioned annotations. Listing 9.12 shows the output of its execution. Please remember that the order of test methods execution is not guaranteed.

Listing 9.11. TestNG annotations for test fixture setting

```
publi class AnnotationsTest {

    @BeforeClass
    void beforeTestClass() {
        System.out.println("before class");
    }

    @BeforeMethod
    void beforeTestMethod() {
        System.out.println("before test method");
    }

    @Test
    public void testA() {
        System.out.println("AAAAA");
    }

    @Test
    public void testB() {
        System.out.println("BBBBB");
    }

    @AfterMethod
    void afterTestMethod() {
        System.out.println("after test method");
    }

    @AfterClass
    void afterTestClass() {
        System.out.println("after class");
    }
}
```

Listing 9.12. Output generated by AnnotationTest

```
before class
before test method
AAAAA
after test method
before test method
BBBBB
after test method
after class
```

As shown above, methods marked with @BeforeClass and @AfterClass annotations are run, respectively, before and after all tests of this class, while @BeforeMethod and @AfterMethod annotations are used, respectively, for methods which are to be run before and after each test method.

In conclusion, let us mention that for purposes of unit testing you will probably only use a subset of the TestNG annotations. However, do make sure you understand their purpose. This way you will be able to take control over the creation of objects in your tests, which can help you avoid some bugs that are hard to track down.

9.7.2. Is Set-up the Right Thing for You?

We already know now that it is usually a good thing to make sure that we test a "fresh" SUT and collaborators before putting them through their paces with our test methods. However, this raises the question of **how** this has been achieved. And this is where some issues arise.

In many cases we have been **setting the test fixture within a set-up method** that is guaranteed to run before every test. By creating the SUT and DOCs within a method annotated using `@BeforeMethod` annotation, we take an important step in the direction of tests that are independent – which is, generally, a worthwhile thing to do. In other cases, in particular in cases of shorter tests, we have been **setting the test fixture directly within test methods**, without using any separated methods annotated with `@BeforeXYZ` annotations. Both approaches are shown in the table below.

Table 9.3. Two approaches to test fixture creation

within set-up method	within test methods
<pre>public class MyTest {

  private SUT sut;
  private Collaborator col;

  @BeforeMethod
  public void setUp() {
    sut = ...;
    col = ...;
    sut.setCollaborator(col);
  }

  public void testA() {
    sut.doA();

    // assertions here
  }</pre> | <pre>public class MyTest {

  public void testA() {
    sut = ...;
    col = ...;
    sut.setCollaborator(col);

    sut.doA();

    // assertions here
  }

  public void testB() {
    sut = ...;
    col = ...;
    sut.setCollaborator(col);</pre> |

within set-up method	within test methods
| ```
public void testB() {
  sut.doB();

  // assertions here

}
}
``` | ```
    sut.doB();

    // assertions here
  }
}
``` |

The use of set-up methods for test fixture creation is heavily criticized by some developers. They point out that by removing test fixture creation from the test methods, we make the test methods less readable: i.e. they cannot be understood in isolation, but the reader also needs to go through the methods annotated with @BeforeXYZ annotations. No doubt this is something we should be worried about!

On the other hand, creating the same SUT objects and collaborators in multiple test methods also has its downsides. Test classes grow in length, and the DRY principle is violated. The readability of test methods is also not perfect: they are often quite long and contain a lot of set-up logic (but everything is in one place, which is a good thing).

And what is the correct answer to this riddle? I would say there are three factors in play here:

- the DRY principle,

  - If the DRY principle is very dear to you, you will probably use the set-up methods approach. After you have got used to the fact that some of the test logic is also included within set-up methods, you will have no problems reading your tests.

- the readability of tests,

  - On the other hand, if you are into BDD, you will rather enjoy your tests' being self-contained.

- consistency,

  - If you like your codebase to be written in the same way throughout, you will probably want to follow one approach in all your tests. If this is not the most important factor, then you will probably do what I did when writing tests for this book: use the set-up approach for test classes with multiple test methods (and multiple collaborators), but put the test-fixture creation within test methods in cases of shorter tests.

If you use the set-up methods approach, feel free to give them more intention-revealing names than `setUp()`!

9.8. Creating Complex Objects

Up till now, all the objects we have created for testing purposes have been dead simple. That may have been handy for demonstrating various different issues involved in unit testing, but it has not been at all realistic. In this section we take a look at issues relating to the creation of complex objects for test purposes.

Writing tests which use rich domain objects can turn out to be tedious work. To test their different functionalities you need to set them with different sets of properties. Unfortunately this results in long and obscure tests, which are hard to understand or maintain. The following features are symptomatic of a weak approach to test fixture creation:

- a lot of test fixture code in every test method,

- duplicated code - usually because multiple tests require similar objects,

- test abstraction polluted by detailed objects creation parts.

A common approach to improving this situation is to create some private methods that will be responsible for the creation of domain objects. Unfortunately, often this does not really cure the illness, but replaces it with another one - an entangled web of small methods calling one another. This might be a real nightmare to understand, debug and maintain.

In this section we will learn about two approaches to dealing with domain objects creation. They are not guaranteed to make our tests perfect in this respect, but their use should at least limit the harm done by test fixture setup code.

 In my "career" as a code reviewer, I have witnessed many tests which have been completely unreadable, owing to the chaotic way in which the domain objects had been created.

For the purposes of our discussion we will be using a simple `Employee` class. Let us assume that this class is immutable[7] - something which, in general, is a good thing. There is no point in showing the code of `Employee`. For the sake of the ensuing discussion it will suffice to say that it has numerous fields (some being primitives and some objects of the `Address`, `Phone` and `Position` types), and that all its fields are initialized via a constructor (no setters).

This time we are not really interested in tests (assertion) as such, but only in that part of them which is responsible for objects creation. An example of `Employee` objects creation within test code is shown below.

Listing 9.13. Utility method to create employees

```
@Test
public class EmployeeTest {

    private static Phone MOBILE_PHONE = new Phone("123-456-789"); ❶
    private static Phone STATIONARY_PHONE = new Phone("123-456-789");
    private static Address HOME_ADDRESS = new Address("any street");

    private Employee createEmployee(
            String name, String surname, Position employee) {
        return new Employee(name, surname, employee,
                HOME_ADDRESS, MOBILE_PHONE , STATIONARY_PHONE); ❷
    }

...
```

❶❷ Some properties of the `Employee` class, not important to the test cases, are reused between tests.

---

[7]See http://en.wikipedia.org/wiki/Immutable_object

Listing 9.14. Creation of employess

```
...
    public void ceoCanDoEverything() { ❶
        Calendar cal = Calendar.getInstance();
        cal.set(2010, 3, 1);
        Date startCeo = cal.getTime();
        cal.add(Calendar.DATE, 1);
        Date endCeo = cal.getTime();
        Position ceo = new Position("ceo", startCeo, endCeo);
        Employee ceoEmpl = createEmployee("ceoName", "ceoSurname", ceo); ❷
        // some methods execution and assertions here
        // which verify that CEO can really do everything
    }

    public void pmCanDoALot() { ❸
        Calendar cal = Calendar.getInstance();
        cal.set(2008, 7, 12);
        Date startPm = cal.getTime();
        cal.add(Calendar.YEAR, 3);
        Date endPm = cal.getTime();
        Position pm = new Position("pm", startPm, endPm);
        Employee pmEmpl = createEmployee("pmName", "pmSurname", pm); ❹
        // some methods execution and assertions here
        // which verify that PM can really do a lot
    }

}
```

❶❸   Both test methods contain similar, yet slightly different, code, responsible for the creation of an employee.

❷❹   Execution of the `createEmployee()` method.

There is nothing special about the code shown above. It is the kind of code that all of us have created more than once. It is not especially nice or readable, but it serves its purpose. A private method `createEmployee()` facilitates, at least to some extent, the creation of similar objects.

The test code shown in Listing 9.14 is aware of the details of the `Employee` class. There is no reasonable abstraction which would make reading the code easier. All we really want to do in the test methods is create a project manager and a CEO. But it is not possible to do this "just like that" - we need to go deep into some properties of the `Employee` class to achieve this simple thing. This lowers the readability of the test code.

Looking at the code in Listing 9.14, we can predict its future evolution. Probably some more static values will be used (e.g. are start and end dates important? - if not they will end up as static values). During the implementation of more sophisticated test scenarios, it will transpire that some properties of employees, e.g. mobile phone, will become important. Then, new private utility methods will be created, to make it possible to create employees with certain fields set with default or custom values. Private methods will start to call one another (code reuse is good, is it not?) and the code will grow. Very soon, working with it will not be a pleasure anymore.

 The immutability of objects, which in general is a good thing, makes creating multiple objects of the same kind rather cumbersome. You cannot reuse an object created in one test method (or in some "setup" section) and change some of its properties using setters. If the `Employee` class had not been immutable, then it would have been easier to reuse it across tests. In the ensuing sections we will learn how to make immutability less difficult to work with.

9.8.1. Mummy Knows Best

It is time to introduce an **Object Mother** pattern. Basically, this is a Factory pattern[8], whose purpose is test fixture creation. Each Object Mother method creates a single aggregate. Object Mother centralizes objects creation and makes tests more readable by providing intention-revealing methods. We can think of Object Mother as a more object-oriented alternative to the private utility methods presented in the previous section. If we were to move the code from both of the test methods shown in Listing 9.14 to a separate class, we could then rewrite the test code, so that it would then look as shown in Listing 9.15.

---

[8]See http://www.oodesign.com/factory-pattern.html

Listing 9.15. Object Mother pattern

```
@Test
public class EmployeeObjectMotherTest {

    public void ceoCanDoEverything() {
        Employee empl = ObjectMotherEmployee.ceoEmployee();
        // some methods execution and assertions here
    }

    public void pmCanDoALot() {
        Employee empl = ObjectMotherEmployee.pmEmployee();
        // some methods execution and assertions here
    }
}
```

The above code is much clearer, and does not delve into the implementation details of the
`Employee` class. All this is enclosed within the `ObjectMotherEmployee` class. This kind of
separation of concerns between test code and objects creation code is definitely a good
thing.

In some implementations, Object Mother goes beyond the standard factory pattern
by providing methods which facilitate changing objects during tests. For example, an
`addAddress()` method can be used to simplify the setting of a new employee's address. It
can even work with an immutable `Employee` class: for example, by copying data from one
`Employee` object into another, via a constructor.

On the downside, let us note that the `ObjectMotherEmployee` class might soon become quite
bloated. Eventually, we may end up with numerous Object Mothers (calling one another),
or with an Object Mother with plenty of methods (making it a God Object[9]) - hard both
to understand and to maintain.

9.8.2. Test Data Builder

Another approach we can adopt is to employ a different creational pattern. This one - called
Test Data Builder - was also created with test code in mind. It requires some additional
coding, but in return it offers a kind of internal DSL - one specializing in objects creation.
This opens up some new possibilities.

---

[9]See http://en.wikipedia.org/wiki/God_object

Let us have a look at the code shown in Listing 9.16. It presents a new class - `EmployeeBuilder` - which will be used to construct very different objects of the `Employee` type. Some of its fields and methods have been omitted for the sake of brevity.

Listing 9.16. Test Data Builder pattern

```
public class EmployeeBuilder {

    private Position position;
    private Address address;

    ... some more fields here

    private Phone stationary;
    private String firstname;
    private String lastname;

    public EmployeeBuilder withFirstname(String firstname) { ❶
        this.firstname = firstname;
        return this;
    }

    public EmployeeBuilder withLastname(String lastname) {
        this.lastname = lastname;
        return this;
    }

    public EmployeeBuilder withAddress(Address address) {
        this.address = address;
        return this;
    }

    ... some more similar methods here

    public EmployeeBuilder withPosition(Position position) {
        this.position = position;
        return this;
    }

    public Employee build() { ❷
        return new Employee(firstname, lastname,
                position, address, mobile, stationary);
    }
}
```

❶   Each field of the `Employee` class is represented by a setter method which returns an instance of `EmployeeBuilder`. This allows us to chain the methods in any order.

❷   The `build()` method calls a constructor of the `Employee` class and returns the result of the creation.

In addition to `EmployeeBuilder`, we also need builders for all of the other domain classes that will be used (by composition) by the `Employee` class. Such builders would be very similar to the `EmployeeBuilder` class we were discussing earlier. Listing 9.17 provides an example of another builder.

Listing 9.17. Test Data Builder used to create Position class

```java
public class PositionBuilder {

    private String title;
    private Date from;
    private Date to;

    public PositionBuilder withTitle(String title) {
        this.title = title;
        return this;
    }

    public PositionBuilder start(int year, int month, int day) {
        Calendar cal = Calendar.getInstance();
        cal.set(year, month, day);
        this.from = cal.getTime();
        return this;
    }

    public PositionBuilder end(int year, int month, int day) {
        Calendar cal = Calendar.getInstance();
        cal.set(year, month, day);
        this.to = cal.getTime();
        return this;
    }

    public Position build() {
        return new Position(title, from, to);
    }
}
```

What is interesting in Listing 9.17 are its `start()` and `end()` methods. They take integers (year, month, day) as parameters, which, as we shall see in a minute, make them easier to use. By using primitives in the API of this builder, we free up its clients from being involved in the cumbersome process of creating `Date` objects.

Let us now take a look at how two such builders might be used in tests. This is shown in Listing 9.18.

Listing 9.18. Test Data Builder pattern used in test code

```
@Test
public class EmployeeTestDataBuilderTest {

    private EmployeeBuilder anEmployee() { ❶
        return new EmployeeBuilder()
            .withFirstname("John").withLastname("Doe")
            .withMobile(
                    new PhoneBuilder().withNumber("123-456-789").build())
            .withStationary(
                    new PhoneBuilder().withNumber("456-789-012").build())
            .withAddress(
                    new AddressBuilder().withStreet("Some Street").build());
    }

    public void pmCanDoALot() {
        Employee pmEmpl = anEmployee() ❷
            .withPosition(
                new PositionBuilder().withTitle("PM") ❸
                    .start(2010, 1, 1).end(2011, 7, 3).build()) ❹
            .build();
        // some methods execution and assertions here
    }

    public void ceoCanDoEverything() {
        Employee ceoEmpl = anEmployee() ❺
            .withPosition(
                new PositionBuilder().withTitle("CEO") ❻
                    .start(2011, 1, 1).end(2011, 5, 5).build()) ❼
            .build();
        // some methods execution and assertions here
    }
}
```

❶ Here we have a utility method which creates a "typical" employee, that will then be modified further. Please note, this method returns an `EmployeeBuilder`.

❷❺ When creating objects, the `anEmployee()` utility method is used. This allows us to express things like *"CEO is an employee but with such and such properties"*, etc.

❸❻ If objects of other types are required, their builders are created and called.

❹❼ The use made here of the `start()` and `end()` methods of `PositionBuilder` is very simple indeed. There is no need to create objects of the `Date` type.

I remember when I first saw this pattern in action: it felt very awkward to me. Back then, I found this kind of code hard to read. But that was only a first impression. After some time spent studying this pattern, I discovered that it confers several benefits:

• In contrast to private methods with multiple parameters, in the case of Test Data Builders the meaning of each value is very clear. There is no confusion about what the name of a person or street, the title of a song, etc., is. Every value can be easily recognized by the method name it is passed to.

• The test code can be read without problems (once you get used to it). It is clear what the properties of each created object are.

• Even though the Employee objects are immutable, EmployeeBuilder objects are not. This means we can reuse and modify them.

• Writing such code is a pleasurable experience, because the IDE will prompt you with auto-complete hints.

On the downside, we have to mention that the creation of builders requires some (maybe even significant) coding. However, let us remember that the implementation of each builder is trivial.

 Have a look at the Make It Easy library[10] by Nat Pryce, which facilitates the creation of Test Data Builders.

9.8.3. Conclusions

In this section we have taken a closer look at how more complex objects could be created within test code.

First, a "natural", unstructured approach was presented. This approach can be recommended only for very simple domain models. If used for the creation of many different complex objects, then the test code will be very hard to understand and maintain.

Then we introduced an **Object Mother** pattern. It encapsulates objects creation code and provides some intention-revealing methods. Thanks to this the test code itself is free of

---

[10]http://code.google.com/p/make-it-easy/

objects creation code. However, it does not remove the real source of the problem: instead it moves it from the area of test code to that of utility classes. Compared to the first approach, this one requires only a minimal additional amount of coding.

The last approach we adopted was that of using **Test Data Builders**. This gave us a lot of flexibility in creating objects, but at the price of maintaining some additional code (much larger than in the case of Object Mother). I would recommend this approach for complex domain objects.

 When creating domain objects for your tests starts to get painful, it might mean that they are too complicated.

9.9. Conclusions

In this chapter you will have learned some things about the organization of tests. We started with basic matters. First, we compared two options for using packages for test classes. Then we looked at the pros and cons of using class-level and method-level `@Test` annotations. After discussing a naming schema for test classes (`ClassNameTest`) and test methods (`should...()`), we also tackled the topic of comments within test code.

Things got harder, then. We discussed a slightly different approach to writing tests, called BDD. In fact, BDD is much more than this - it is a different mindset, which pays a great deal of attention to fulfilling customers' requirements. This topic is huge, but here we have concentrated exclusively on its influence on how unit tests should be written.

After this we went on to discuss ways of removing some redundant code from Mockito-powered tests, and took a look at the creation of a couple objects - both of them capable of saving us from writing some lines of code, and of making our tests easier to maintain.

These last few points are already steering us in the direction of the maintainability and quality of tests, which is very good, because this is exactly what we will be discussing in the next part of the book. But first let us practise a little!

9.10. Exercises

In addition to the exercises presented below, do not forget to read some more about Behaviour Driven Development! Many tools and ideas, especially for integration and end-to-end tests, are based on the BDD approach.

9.10.1. Test Fixture Setting

Enhance the test from Listing 9.19, so some actions are executed:

- before the tests of this class are executed,

- after the tests of this class have been executed,

- before each test method is executed,

- after each test method has been executed.

Add some `System.out.println()` statements (or a logger, if you consider `System.out.println()` to be lame) to the created method. Execute the test, and observe whether the order of execution is as expected.

Listing 9.19. Test fixture setting

```
@Test
public class TestFixtureTest {

    public void testMethodA() {
        System.out.println("method A");
    }

    public void testMethodB() {
        System.out.println("method B");
    }
}
```

9.10.2. Test Data Builder

The listing below shows the `Transaction` class. It is a simple POJO with no logic but only getters and setters methods (which have been omitted in the listing to make it shorter).

Listing 9.20. Transaction class

```
public class Transaction {

    private long id;

    private String state;  ❶

    private boolean retryAllowed;

    private String message;

    private String billingId;

    // getters and setters omitted

    ...
}
```

❶   There are four possible values of the state field - PROCESSING, OK, CANCELLED, ERROR.

Write a test which creates a number of objects of the Transaction class using the Test Data Builder pattern. Compare the result with the "normal" approach of creating objects directly within your test code (using their constructor and setters).

Part V. Make Them Better

There's always room for improvement, you know - it's the biggest room in the house.

— Louise Heath Leber

Chapter 10. Maintainable Tests

Applications maintainability - the holy grail of software development! We write code every day, trying to make it so good it will withstand the test of time. We hope that we, or our colleagues, working with this code sometime in the future, will be able to understand it at a glance. We hope to be able to introduce changes easily without causing chaos throughout the entire application.

We should write our tests with the same attitude, trying to make them maintainable. Why? Because, as we have already discussed, they play a crucial role in supporting and documenting our production code. In this section we will discuss various aspects of the maintainability of tests.

10.1. Test Behaviour, not Methods

The rule we will be discussing in this section is very simple: *"Test behaviour, not methods!"*. This means that when writing tests, we should think about the SUT in terms of its responsibilities - in terms of the contract it has with its client. We should abstract from the SUT's implementation, which is of only secondary importance. What matters is that the SUT should fulfill the requirements for which it was designed. And to make sure it really does, we should write these requirements in the form of test cases. The requirements know nothing about the actual implementation, and neither should our tests.

 This may seem trivial, but unfortunately I frequently see this simple rule being violated, which leads me to be think that it is, after all, worth discussing.

Below, in Listing 10.1, an example of a suboptimal test of the `BankAccount` class is presented. Each test method attempts to test a single method of the public API of `BankAccount`: `getBalance()`, `deposit()` and `withdraw()`.

In order to better present the main issue of this section, I have decided to keep all tests truncated to a very limited number of test cases. In reality, I would use many more test cases, probably employing parametrized tests (see Section 3.6).

Listing 10.1. One test method per one production code method

```
@Test
public class BankAccountTest {

    private BankAccount account;

    @BeforeMethod
    public void setUp() {
        account = new BankAccount();
    }

    public void testBalance() { ❶
        account.deposit(200);
        assertEquals(account.getBalance(), 200);
    }

    public void testDeposit() { ❷
        account.deposit(100);
        assertEquals(account.getBalance(), 100);
        account.deposit(100);
        assertEquals(account.getBalance(), 200);
    }

    public void testWithdraw() { ❸
        account.deposit(100);
        account.withdraw(30);
        assertEquals(account.getBalance(), 70);
        account.withdraw(20);
        assertEquals(account.getBalance(), 50);
    }
}
```

❶   Test for the `getBalance()` method. Note that it also uses a `deposit()` method.
❷   Test for the `deposit()` method. It also calls `getBalance()`.
❸   Test for the `withdraw()` method, which likewise also calls `getBalance()`.

As Listing 10.1 shows, isolation is not possible in unit tests at the level of methods. Each test method calls various methods of the SUT - not only the one they have pretensions to testing. It has to be like that, because you really cannot test the `deposit()` method without checking the account's balance (using the `getBalance()` method).

There are also some other issues with this approach. Let us list them:

• If any of the test methods should fail, then an error message (e.g. *"testDeposit has failed"*) will not be informative enough for us to instantly understand which of the SUT's requirements has not been fulfilled (where this is really important from the client's point of view).

- Each of the SUT's methods is involved in multiple user-stories, so it is very hard to keep a *"one test method per production code method"* pattern. For example, how might we add a test to the existing code, which would verify that after creation an account has a balance of zero? We could enhance the `testBalance()` method with an additional assertion, but that would make it prone to fail for more than one reason. Which is not good, and leads to confusion when the test does fail.

- Test methods tend to grow as the SUT is enhanced to reflect new requirements.

- Sometimes it is hard to decide which of the SUT's methods is really being tested in a certain scenario (because more than one is being used).

- Test methods overlap with each other - e.g. `testBalance()` is a repetition of what will be tested by `testDeposit()` and `testWithdraw()`. In fact, it is hard to say why `testBalance()` is there at all - probably because a developer felt she/he *"needed to have a test for the `getBalance()` method"*.

When I see test code like this, I know for sure that it was written after the SUT had already been implemented. The structure of the test reflects the structure (implementation) of the SUT code, which is a clear sign of this approach. From what I have observed, such tests rarely cover everything required of the SUT. They check what obviously needs to be checked, given the SUT's implementation, but do not try to test anything more (thus avoiding solving some of the dilemmas listed above).

 What is interesting is that this test is good enough to achieve 100% code coverage of a valid implementation of the `BankAccount` class. This is one more reason **not** to trust the code coverage (see also Section 11.3).

Is there a better approach? Yes, and - what is really nice - it does not require any additional work. It only requires us to concentrate on the SUT's behaviour (which reflects its responsibilities) and write it down in the form of tests.

An example of this approach is shown in the two listings below. As can be seen, some of its methods are identical to the previous approach, but the test as a whole has been created with a completely different mindset, and it covers a broader set of the SUT's responsibilities.

Listing 10.2. Testing behaviour, not implementation

```
@Test
public class BankAccountTest {

    private BankAccount account;

    @BeforeMethod
    public void setUp() {
        account = new BankAccount();
    }

    public void shouldBeEmptyAfterCreation() { ❶
        assertEquals(account.getBalance(), 0);
    }

    public void shouldAllowToDepositMoney() { ❷
        account.deposit(100);
        assertEquals(account.getBalance(), 100);
        account.deposit(100);
        assertEquals(account.getBalance(), 200);
    }

    public void shouldAllowToWithdrawMoney() { ❸
        account.deposit(100);
        account.withdraw(30);
        assertEquals(account.getBalance(), 70);
        account.withdraw(20);
        assertEquals(account.getBalance(), 50);
    }
...
```

❶ There is no test for the `getBalance()` method, because its proper functioning is validated by other tests.

❷ This is identical to the previous `testDeposit()` method, with the exception of the method name, which is much more informative.

❸ As above - identical to the `testWithdraw()` method, but better named.

Listing 10.3. Testing behaviour, not implementation

```
...

    @Test(expectedExceptions = NotEnoughMoneyException.class)
    public void shouldNotAllowToWithdrawFromEmptyAccount() { ❶
        // implementation omitted
    }

    @Test(expectedExceptions = InvalidAmountException.class)
    public void shouldNotAllowToUseNegativeAmountForWithdraw() { ❷
        // implementation omitted
    }

    @Test(expectedExceptions = InvalidAmountException.class)
    public void shouldNotAllowToUseNegativeAmountForDeposit() { ❸
        // implementation omitted
    }
}
```

❶❷❸ New methods added. This was possible, because the developer was thinking in terms of the SUT's responsibility.

The two versions of the `BankAccountTest` test class differ substantially when it comes to test methods naming. Good test method names include information about the scenario they verify. This topic is discussed in detail in Section 9.3.2.

Table 10.1 compares what was tested and how, with both approaches.

Table 10.1. Comparison of two approaches to testing

use-case scenario	testing implementation	testing behaviour
when opening a new account, its balance should be zero	oops, forgot about this one!	`shouldBeEmptyAfterCreation()`
it is possible to credit an account	`testDeposit()` and `testBalance()`	`shouldAllowToDepositMoney()`

use-case scenario	testing implementation	testing behaviour
it is possible to debit an account	`testWithdraw()`	`shouldAllowToWithdrawMoney()`
should not allow for accounts misuse	oops, forgot about these too!	`shouldNotAllowToWitrdrawFromEmptyAccount()`, `shouldNotAllowToUseNegativeAmountForDeposit()` and `shouldNotAllowToUseNegativeAmountForWithdraw()`

One might be tempted to claim that this is just a single example, and a biased one at that. Well actually, no. I have witnessed this far too many times to have any doubts about it being how things are: **when testing implementation only a subset of scenarios is being verified**, test methods are overlapping, and are prone to grow to include all possible scenarios for each test method. The key is to think about test methods as about mini user stories: each of them should ensure that some functionality important from the client's point of view is working properly.

So, as a rule of thumb, forget about implementation. Think about requirements. TDD might make it easier for you to code like this.

 Some IDEs offer "a feature" which generates test methods based on production code (so if your class has a `doSomething()` method, the tool will generate a `testDoSomething()` method). This can lead you down the wrong path - that of methods testing rather than class responsibilities testing. Avoid such solutions. Stay on the safe side by following the test-first approach.

10.2. Complexity Leads to Bugs

> Controlling complexity is the essence of computer programming.
> — Brian Kernighan

Do not put any complexity into your tests! No `if` structure, no `switch` statements, no decision making. Otherwise you risk finding yourself in a situation where the results of tests are influenced by two factors at the same time: the quality of the logic of production code and the quality of the logic of test code. This is one too many.

If any test fails, you need to discover where the bug is - in the production code or the test code. A worse thing can also happen - it is possible that tests pass thanks to errors in test code unintentionally rectifying errors in production code. (Yes, two wrongs sometimes make a right!) This is a serious danger.

Another thing you lose out on by putting logic inside your test code is that it can no longer serve as documentation. Who wants to read documentation that requires the solving of logical puzzles?

Remember, what you are supposed to be doing is testing the correctness of production code. Do not make it any harder than necessary.

10.3. Follow the Rules or Suffer

> Procedural code gets information, then makes decisions. Object-oriented code tells objects to do things.
>
> — Alec Sharp

> Daughter, do not talk with strangers!
>
> — Demeter *Ancient Greece (700 BC)*

The two quotes which open this section refer to two famous principles of good design, both of them notorious for being breached: *"Tell, Don't Ask!"*[1] and *"Law of Demeter"*[2]. The first one states that the object should ask others to do whatever it wants, rather than doing the job based on the data they are willing to provide. The second principle dictates with whom the object is allowed to talk.

This section gives an example of what happens when you break these two rules.

10.3.1. Real Life is Object-Oriented

Imagine you get in a taxi. *"To the airport, please!"*, you say, and the driver nods his head. Now, you want to know how long it will take to get there. What question would you rather ask:

---

[1] See http://pragprog.com/articles/tell-dont-ask for details.
[2] See http://en.wikipedia.org/wiki/Law_of_Demeter for a more detailed description.

1. How long will it take?

2. Please tell me (so I can do the maths myself):

   a. How far is the airport?

   b. What is your average speed travelling to the airport from here?

I have never heard of anyone who used the second approach. In real life we act quite smartly, asking people who know (or at least should do) and only caring about the result (i.e. leaving the boring details to them). So why on earth do we write code that follows the second approach? And we really do! I see this happening all the time.

Let us have a look at an example from the domain of finance[3] in order to illustrate the difference between these two approaches. The example is as follows. There is a function that calculates the value of all assets of a client. It takes a collection of funds as a parameter and returns a single number as an output. Each fund consists of two registers. A client has a number of entities within each register.

10.3.2. The Non-Object-Oriented Approach

A possible implementation of a `Client` class is shown in Listing 10.4. Some details have been omitted, so we can concentrate on the crucial part: calculating the value of a client's assets.

---

[3]The example is only a slightly modified version of a real business domain problem and real code that once got implemented as part of some long-forgotten project.

Listing 10.4. Client class written using a non-object-oriented approach

```
public class Client {

    private final List<IFund> funds;

    ...

    public BigDecimal getValueOfAllFunds() {
        BigDecimal value = BigDecimal.ZERO;
        for (IFund f : funds) {
            value = value.add(f.getCurrentValue().getValue().multiply(
                new BigDecimal(
                    f.getRegisterX().getNbOfUnits()
                    + f.getRegisterY().getNbOfUnits()
                )
            ));
        }
        return value;
    }
}
```

As shown in Listing 10.4, a client has to do some complex calculations in order to obtain the result. For each fund it needs to:

- get the current fund value (`f.getCurrentValue().getValue()`), which is a two-step process, because `IFund` returns `ICurrentValue` object, which contains the real value,

- multiply this value by the number of units in both registers.

Then, the results for all funds must be added together to obtain the final amount.

If you are seriously into object-oriented programming, you will surely have noticed that the code in Listing 10.4 breaches both of the principles mentioned at the beginning of this section:

- *"Tell, Don't Ask!"* has been broken, because `Client` asks for data instead of telling others to give him results,

- *"Law of Demeter"* has been broken, because `Client` talks with friends of his friends (i.e. with registers and current value, both of which are accessed as friends of funds).

This makes it obvious that we are in trouble. The client seems to know everything about everything, when in fact all they should be interested in is the value of each fund they own.

The details of the internal structure of funds should be completely hidden from them, but are not. Based on this observation, we can say that the types used in this example have a serious problem with information hiding[4]: they reveal their internal design. This goes against the norms of good practice in programming, and will cause problems when the code needs to be changed.

 …but the **main problem** with such code is… that it works! The results obtained are correct. This code really calculates what it should. This leads people to conclude that the code itself is also correct. The widespread *"If it works, don't fix it!"* approach[5] results in such code being left as it is. The problems come later - usually when the code should be changed. This is when the troubles begin.

So, right now we will attempt to test it. There are many test cases that should be verified (with different combinations of number of funds and values), but for our purposes it will suffice to choose just one: a client having two funds. This does not sound like a difficult task, does it? Well, let us take a closer look.

Okay, so here is what I will need for my test: two test doubles of the IFund type, each of them having a value; so two ICurrentValue test doubles will also be required. Each fund also has two registers, so another four test doubles will be required (of the IRegister type). And it seems like all of these test doubles will be stubs. I only need them because I want them to return some canned values. Anything else? No, these are the main points. So let us get started.
— Tomek *Thinking Aloud about How to Test Non-Object-Oriented Code*

The listing is divided into two parts, so it renders better.

---

[4]See http://en.wikipedia.org/wiki/Information_hiding
[5]Please consult [martin2008] for a different approach - the **Boy Scout Rule** rule: *"Leave the campground cleaner than you found it."*.

Listing 10.5. Test of the non-object-oriented Client class - setup

```
public class ClientTest {

    private int NB_OF_UNITS_AX = 5; ❶
    private int NB_OF_UNITS_AY = 1;
    private int NB_OF_UNITS_BX = 4;
    private int NB_OF_UNITS_BY = 1;
    private BigDecimal FUND_A_VALUE = new BigDecimal(3);
    private BigDecimal FUND_B_VALUE = new BigDecimal(2);

    @Test
    public void totalValueShouldBeEqualToSumOfAllFundsValues() {
        Client client = new Client(); ❷
        IFund fundA = mock(IFund.class); ❸
        IFund fundB = mock(IFund.class);
        IRegister regAX = mock(IRegister.class);
        IRegister regAY = mock(IRegister.class);
        IRegister regBX = mock(IRegister.class);
        IRegister regBY = mock(IRegister.class);
        ICurrentValue currentValueA = mock(ICurrentValue.class);
        ICurrentValue currentValueB = mock(ICurrentValue.class);

        ...
```

❶   Some primitive values that are also required for this test.

❷   A client: our SUT.

❸   The SUT's collaborators - direct and indirect.

Listing 10.6. Test of the non-object-oriented Client class - actual tests

```
        . . .

        when(fundA.getRegisterX()).thenReturn(regAX); ❶
        when(fundA.getRegisterY()).thenReturn(regAY);
        when(fundB.getRegisterX()).thenReturn(regBX);
        when(fundB.getRegisterY()).thenReturn(regBY);
        when(regAX.getNbOfUnits()).thenReturn(NB_OF_UNITS_AX);
        when(regAY.getNbOfUnits()).thenReturn(NB_OF_UNITS_AY);
        when(regBX.getNbOfUnits()).thenReturn(NB_OF_UNITS_BX);
        when(regBY.getNbOfUnits()).thenReturn(NB_OF_UNITS_BY);

        when(fundA.getCurrentValue()).thenReturn(currentValueA); ❷
        when(fundB.getCurrentValue()).thenReturn(currentValueB);
        when(currentValueA.getValue()).thenReturn(FUND_A_VALUE);
        when(currentValueB.getValue()).thenReturn(FUND_B_VALUE);

        client.addFund(fundA); ❸
        client.addFund(fundB);

        assertEquals(client.getValueOfAllFunds(),
            BigDecimal.valueOf((5 + 1) * 3 + (4 + 1) * 2)); ❹
    }
}
```

❶   Instructing stubs on what they should return.
❷   Hmm, interesting - instructing a stub to return a stub…
❸   Setting the SUT in the desired state - it should own two funds.
❹   Verification.

This test is very long, and there are some really disturbing and confusing features to it:

- the test class knows all about the internalities of funds and registers,

  - the algorithm of calculation,

  - the internalities of all types involved in calculations (e.g. that a register has units),

- a number of test doubles are required for this test,

- the test methods consist mostly of instructions for stubs concerning the values they should return,

- stubs are returning stubs.

All this makes our test **hard to understand and maintain**, and also **fragile** (it needs to be rewritten every time we change anything in the funds value calculation algorithm).

And now some really **bad news**: we would need more than one test like this. We need a test for 0 funds, for 1 fund, and for 7 funds (when the marketing guys come up with a brilliant idea of some extra bonus for people who have invested in more than 6 funds), and all this multiplied by various values of funds. Uh, that would hurt really bad.

Do We Need Mocks?

In the example as presented so far, we have used test doubles for all collaborators of the `Client` class. In fact, a few lines of test code could have been spared, if we had used real objects instead of classes. True, but on the other hand:

- as discussed in Section 5.5, this would be no more than a short-term solution,

- in real life, the values of funds might be fetched from some external source (e.g. a web service), which would make it much harder to test.

Because of this, replacing all collaborators with test doubles seems a valid choice.

10.3.3. The Object-Oriented Approach

Mentally scarred - no doubt - by what we have just witnessed, let us now try out a different implementation of the `Client` class, and compare the effort required to test it with that involved in the previous example. This time we shall make our `Client` more object-oriented.

Listing 10.7. The Client class - object-oriented version

```
public class Client {

    private final List<IFund> funds;

    ....

    public BigDecimal getValueOfAllFunds() {
        BigDecimal value = BigDecimal.ZERO;
        for (IFund f : funds) {
            value = value.add(f.getValue()); ❶
        }
        return value;
    }
}
```

❶   This time all calculation of fund value is encapsulated within a getValue() method of the IFund type. All the client does is add up the results.

Writing a test for such a class is straightforward - we need only two stubs for this (one per each fund that the client has, and we have decided in advance that for the first test, the client will have two funds)

Listing 10.8. Test of the object-oriented Client class

```
public class ClientTest {

    private final static BigDecimal VALUE_A = new BigDecimal(9);
    private final static BigDecimal VALUE_B =  new BigDecimal(2);

    public void totalValueShouldBeEqualToSumOfAllFundsValues() {
        Client client = new Client();
        IFund fundA = mock(IFund.class);
        IFund fundB = mock(IFund.class);

        when(fundA.getValue()).thenReturn(VALUE_A);
        when(fundB.getValue()).thenReturn(VALUE_B);

        client.addFund(fundA);
        client.addFund(fundB);

        assertEquals(client.getValueOfAllFunds(), VALUE_A.add(VALUE_B));
    }
}
```

Wow, this differs substantially from what we were seeing before. The test is concise and does not contain any information on the internalities of funds. Pursuing this object-oriented approach further, we would have to write tests for each and every class (e.g. we need a test for implementation of the `IFund` interface, and also for the `IRegister` interface), but all of them would be very, very simple indeed. Each of these tests would also depend only on the SUT. No information about other classes would be used within the test code. This is very different from what we saw in Listing 10.5.

Coming back to the question we asked when discussing a non-object-oriented version of this test, would it be hard to write tests for 0, 1 and 7 funds? This time the answer is *no*. It would not be.

10.3.4. How To Deal with Procedural Code?

We have just witnessed the (disastrous) impact that procedural code can have on testing. If your code does not adhere to basic rules of object-oriented design, it will be hard to test. Now, let us discuss what is the right way to deal with such code.

As usual, the best thing you can do is to **act before the damage has been done**. Do not let procedural code creep into your codebase! TDD seems to be very good at deterring procedural code. As discussed previously, it is very painful to write tests for such code. If you start out with the tests themselves, you will definitely end up coming up with solutions that are more object-oriented (and less procedural).

The above advice will not be of much use, though, if you have just inherited 100k lines of procedural code. There are techniques that can help you deal with such an unfortunate situation, but the topic goes beyond the scope of this book. Please refer to the excellent work of [feathers2004] for guidance.

10.3.5. Conclusions

As the code examples within this section have demonstrated, **bad code makes it hard to write tests**. Allow me to back up this claim with two quotes, illustrating the most important points connected with what we have just been discussing.

> Consistency. It is only a virtue, if you are not a screwup.
>
> — Wisdom of the Internet ;)

The misery begins with a single, innocent-seeming line such as *"ask object x for the value of y (x.getY())* and make some decisions based on the value of y". If you encounter code which breaches the *"Tell, Don't Ask!"* principle, then do not copy and paste it into your code. What you should do, instead, is clean it, usually by adding methods in places where they ought to be[6]. Then proceed - writing clean, well-designed code.

 Do not copy other sloppy work! Do not become one of the blind led by the blind! An abyss awaits you if you do. (Wow, that has really got you scared, hasn't it?)

Every time a mock returns a mock, a fairy dies.
— Twitter @damianguy *2009 Oct 19*

When writing a test requires you to have a test double which returns another test double, then you know you are about to do something very bad indeed. Such a situation indicates that the code you are working with contravenes *"Law of Demeter"*, which is really most regrettable. Repair the code, and only then get down to testing it. After all…you do not want fairies to die, do you?

10.4. Rewriting Tests when the Code Changes

A change in the requirements occurs. Developers analyze it and implement the required changes. Then tests are run and some of them fail. You can see the disappointment written all over the developers' faces when they sit down to *"fix these *(&(#$ failed tests!"*.

Have you ever witnessed such a scenario? Have you ever had the feeling that your tests are a major nuisance, and that their existence makes the process of introducing changes a good deal longer and harder than it would be without them? Well, I have certainly seen this many times, and have personally become angry at the fact that after having performed some updates of production code I also had to take care of the tests (instead of moving on to another task).

There are two explanations of why this situation is so common. The first relates to the quality of your tests, the second to the code-first approach.

---

[6]If you need more information about this, please read about the "Feature Envy" code smell.

Let us agree on something, before we begin. If you rewrite part of your implementation, then **it is normal that some of your tests will start to fail**. In fact, in the majority of cases this is even desirable: if no tests fail, then it means your tests were not good enough![7] The real problems arise if:

- the change which made the tests fail is really a refactoring - it does not influence the observable external behaviour of the SUT,

- the failed tests do not seem to have anything to do with the functionality that has changed,

- a single change results in many tests failing.

The last of the above highlights the fact of there being some duplication in respect of tests – with the result that multiple tests are verifying the same functionality. This is rather simple to spot and fix. The other two issues are more interesting, and will be discussed below.

10.4.1. Avoid Overspecified Tests

> The most important rule of thumb we follow to keep our tests flexible is: Specify exactly what you want to happen and no more.
>
> — JMock tutorial

What is an overspecified test? There is no consensus about this, and many examples that can be found describe very different features of tests. For the sake of this discussion, let us accept a very simple "definition": **a test is overspecified if it verifies some aspects which are irrelevant to the scenario being tested**.

Now, which parts of the tests are relevant and which are not? How can we distinguish them just by looking at the test code?

Well, good test method names are certainly very helpful in this respect. For example, if we analyze the test in the listing below, we find that it is a little bit overspecified.

---

[7]This is exactly the behaviour that mutation testing takes advantage of; see Section 11.4.

Listing 10.9. Overspecified test - superfluous verification

```
@Test
public void itemsAvailableIfTheyAreInStore() {
    when(store.itemsLeft(ITEM_NAME)).thenReturn(2); ❶

    assertTrue(shop.isAvailable(ITEM_NAME)); ❷

    verify(store).itemsLeft(ITEM_NAME); ❸
}
```

❶   stubbing of a DOC,
❷   asserting on the SUT's functionality,
❸   verifying the DOC's behaviour.

If this test truly sets out to verify that *"items are available if they are in store"* (as the test method name claims), then what is the last verification doing? Does it really help to achieve the goal of the test? Not really. If this cooperation with the store collaborator is really a valuable feature of the SUT (is it?), then maybe it would be more appropriate to have a second test to verify it:

Listing 10.10. Two better-focused tests

```
@Test
public void itemsAvailableIfTheyAreInStore() {
    when(store.itemsLeft(ITEM_NAME)).thenReturn(2);

    assertTrue(shop.isAvailable(ITEM_NAME));
}

@Test
public void shouldCheckStoreForItems() {
    shop.isAvailable(ITEM_NAME);

    verify(store).itemsLeft(ITEM_NAME);
}
```

Each of the tests in Listing 10.10 has only one reason to fail, while the previous version (in Listing 10.9) has two. The tests are no longer overspecified. If we refactor the SUT's implementation, it may turn out that only one fails, thus making it clear which functionality was broken.

This example shows the importance of good naming. It is very hard to decide which part of the `testShop()` method is not relevant to the test's principal goal.

Another test-double based example is the use of **specific parameter values** (`"my item"`, 7 or `new Date(x,y,z)`) when something more generic would suffice (`anyString()`, `anyInt()`, `anyDate()`)[8]. Again, the question we should ask is whether these specific values are really important for the test case in hand. If not, let us use more relaxed values.

Also, you might be tempted to test very defensively, to **verify that some interactions have not happened**. Sometimes this makes sense. For example in Section 5.4.3 we verified whether no messages had been sent to some collaborators. And such a test was fine - it made sure that the unsubscribe feature worked fine. However, do not put such verifications in when they are not necessary. You could guard each and every one of the SUT's collaborators with verifications that none of their methods have been called[9], but do not do so, unless they are important relative to the given scenario. Likewise, checking whether certain calls to collaborators happened in the order requested (using Mockito's `inOrder()` method) will usually just amount to overkill.

We can find numerous examples of overspecified tests outside of the interactions testing domain, as well. A common case is to expect a certain exact form of text, where what is in fact important is only that it should contain several statements. Like with the example discussed above, it is usually possible to divide such tests into two smaller, more focused ones. For example, the first test could check whether a message that has been created contains the user's name and address, while the second one might perform a full text-matching. This is also an example of when test dependencies make sense: there is no point in bothering with an exact message comparison (which is what the second test verifies), if you know that it does not contain any vital information (verified by the first test).

Based on what we have learned so far, we can say that a good rule of thumb for writing decent, focused tests is as follows: **test only the minimally necessary set of features using each test method**.

---

[8]See Section 6.6 for discussion and more examples.
[9]Mockito provides some interesting functions for this - `verifyZeroInteractions()` and `verifyNoMoreInteractions()`.

As is by no means unusual where problems connected with tests are concerned, the real culprit may be the production code. If your test really needs to repeat the petty details of the SUT's implementation (which will certainly lead to it being overspecified), then maybe the problem lies with how the SUT works with its collaborators. Does the SUT respect the *"Tell-Don't-Ask!"* principle?

10.4.2. Are You Really Coding Test-First?

So the change request came. A developer updated the production code, and then also worked on the failed tests which stopped working because of the implemented change. Wait! What? By implementing changes in production code first, we have just reverted to code-first development, with all its issues! The price that we pay is that now we will have to rewrite some tests looking at the code we wrote a few minutes ago. But this is boring: such tests will probably not find any bugs, and they themselves will most probably be very closely linked to the implementation of the production code (as was already discussed in Chapter 4, *Test Driven Development*).

Much better results (and less frustration for developers) can be achieved by trying to mimic the TDD approach, following the order of actions given below:

- requirements change,

- developers analyze which tests should be updated to reflect the new requirements,

- tests are updated (and fail because code does not meet the new requirements),

- developers analyze what changes should be introduced into the production code,

- code is updated and tests pass.

This is somewhat different from the TDD approach as we have observed it so far. If we write a new functionality, then we ensure that each individual test that fails is dealt with at once. However, when the requirements of an existing functionality change, we may find ourselves forced to rewrite several tests at once, and then have to deal with all of them failing.

We may sum things up here by saying that in order to avoid having to fix tests after code changes (which is pretty annoying, let's face it), you should:

- write good tests (i.e. loosely coupled to implementation), minimizing the number of failed tests,

- use test-first in all phases of the development process - both when working on new features and when introducing changes to the existing codebase.

10.4.3. Conclusions

> The mime: Developing the code first and then repeating what the code does with expectations mocks. This makes the code drive the tests rather than the other way around. Usually leads to excessive setup and poorly named tests that are hard to see what they do.
>
> — James Carr

As with many other things related to quality, how you start makes a difference. If you start with production code, then your tests will (inevitably, as experience proves) contain too many implementation details, and thus become fragile. They will start to fail every time you touch the production code. But you can also start from the other end: writing tests first or, rather, designing your production code using tests. Do that and your tests will not really be testing classes, so much as the functionalities embedded within them, and as such will have more chances of staying green when classes change.

Of course, it would be naive to expect that your tests can survive any changes to production code. We already know that many of our tests focus on interactions of objects (and to do so, use knowledge about the internal implementation of those objects), so such false hopes should be abandoned. The question remains, how many tests will be undermined by a single change in your production code, and how easy will it be to update them so they meet the altered requirements.

Probably the most important lesson we should remember is that **we should write tests which verify the expected outcome of systems behaviour, and not the behaviour itself**. If possible, let us verify that the system works properly by analyzing returned values. Only when this is not possible should we resort to interactions testing. As Gerard Meszaros puts it (see [meszaros2007]): *"use the front door"*.

The focus should be on the goal of the test. There is usually a single feature that is tested by each test. We should put aside anything that is not really essential to its verification. For example, by using stubs (whose behaviour is not verified) instead of mocks (which are verified) whenever possible. Another example is the use of more argument matchers - both in stubbing and verification (see Section 6.6).

And finally, now for some very obvious advice: your tests should be run very frequently. If not, then one day you will learn that 50% of them need to be rewritten. And then there will be nothing you can do - except wail in despair!

10.5. Things Too Simple To Break

> Yep, you should be unit testing every breakable line of code.
>
> — Bob Gregory

> It's necessary to be very good at testing to decide correctly when you don't need it, and then very good at programming to get away with it.
>
> — Twitter @RonJeffries *2012 Jan 31*

After reading about the benefits of developer tests, you should be tempted to test **everything**. Very good, this is the right attitude. If you code **test-first**, then you get high code coverage "for free". Everything is tested as a result of writing methods to satisfy a failed test. But if you follow the **code-first** approach, then you might quickly start questioning the idea of testing everything. In the case of some code parts, writing unit tests seems superfluous. This section is devoted to exactly these sorts of doubt or uncertainty.

 Please note, that only a minority of methods are too simple to be considered *"unbreakable"*. Most of the code you write calls for decent tests!

Let us take the example of simple getter/setter methods, as shown in Listing 10.11.

Listing 10.11. Getters/Setters - too simple to break

```java
public class User {
    private String name;

    public String getName() {
        return name;
    }

    public void setName(String name) {
        this.name = name;
    }
}
```

Yes, you definitely **can** write a test for this code - but please ask yourself: what kind of bugs, current or future, do you expect to catch by having such a test?

In my opinion there is no sense to writing tests for such code after the code has already been written. There are two reasons for this, which are as follows:

• there is no logic there worth testing,

• the code has probably been generated by the IDE (which then eliminates the threat of a silly copy&paste error).

However, if the getter and setter methods are to be changed, entailing that some complexity will be added (even of the simplest sort), then a test should be created. For example, if the `setName()` method evolves and takes care of validation, along the lines shown in Listing 10.12, then it surely should be tested.

Listing 10.12. Getters/Setters with validation - not so simple anymore

```
public void setName(String name) {
    if (name == null || name.isEmpty()) {
        throw new IllegalArgumentException();
    }
    this.name = name;
}
```

Many people argue that because of the possible future evolution of code (which is hard to predict when the first version is actually being written), you should write a test even for such trivial cases as the first version of the `setName()` method (the one without validation). I tend to disagree, and I would encourage you to refrain from writing such tests. On the other hand, once things get complicated it is crucial to write them. Then there is no excuse, and tests have to be written.

> It is true that adding tests for even these simple methods guards against the possibility that someone refactors and makes the methods "not-so-simple" anymore. In that case, though, the refactorer needs to be aware that the method is now complex enough to break, and should write tests for it - and preferably before the refactoring.
>
> — J.B. Raisenberg *JUnit FAQ*

However, none of this matters if you write code **test-first**. In that case, every method will be preceded with a case of a test failing. The complexity does not matter. If it exists, there must be a test for it. It does not necessarily mean that your test code will be full of trivial getter/ setter tests. On the contrary, when your design is being guided by tests, you might well find yourself writing less getters and setters than you used to. This is one of the benefits of allowing design to be driven by functionality requirements (expressed in the form of tests).

Returning to the **code-first** approach, let us take a look at another example, which shows a piece of code often included in the "too simple to break" category. Listing 10.13 shows a simple delegator - a method whose main task is to tell some other object to do the job.

Listing 10.13. Delegator - too simple to break

```
public class DelegatorExample {

    private Collaborator collaborator;

    public void delegate() {
        collaborator.doSomething();
    }
}
```

True, proper testing of such simple code does require some effort. If you are to use test doubles (which you probably should do), then the test will probably be longer, and even more complicated, than the tested method itself. This will definitely discourage us from writing unit tests - especially in cases where the benefits are not clearly visible. There is no easy answer to the question of whether you should write a test for such a method. It depends on (at least) three factors, namely:

- the type (i.e. specific features) of the `Collaborator` class,

- the complexity of the delegating method,

- the existence of other types of test.

Let us concentrate on these three factors, and run through a few comments that seem relevant to the issue:

- there is usually (if not always) something more involved than simply telling the collaborator to do the job. A delegating method will take some arguments and pass them to the collaborator, often performing some actions before it does so (validation of parameters, creation of some objects based on received parameters, etc.).

- the collaborator's doSomething() method will often return some values being used by the SUT in diverse ways,

- a collaborator's doSomething() method might throw exceptions, which will somehow have to be handled by the SUT,

- other types of test - e.g. integration tests - might cover this functionality. For example, an integration test might check if a class of service layer delegates tasks to a class of dao layer. However, it is rare for integration tests to cover all the possible scenarios (i.e. exceptions thrown by collaborators), so there might still be some gasps to be filled by unit tests.

My point is that the rather simple appearance of such delegating methods may be deceptive. There can be much more to them than meets the eye. By thinking about possible usage scenarios and interactions between the SUT and collaborators, you can reveal this hidden complexity and test it. But, as has already been said, every instance of such code can be considered individually, and there might be cases where writing a test is a waste of time.

10.6. Conclusions

Among the topics discussed in this chapter, there are two fundamental things that I would like you to remember. The first is the *"Test behaviour, not implementation!"* rule: if you stick to this, it will guide you towards high-quality testing (on every level, not only for unit tests). The second can be expressed by two rules that apply to production code, commonly known as the **Law of Demeter** and the **Tell, Don't Ask!** principle. Expect trouble when testing code that does not abide by either of them.

The rest of this chapter has been devoted to problems of logic within test code, the notion of "things that are too simple to break", and to the problem of test maintenance.

10.7. Exercises

10.7.1. A Car is a Sports Car if ...

After three months of analysis a team of business analysts have decided that a car can be marked with the "sports" tag if it satisfies all of the following requirements:

• it is red,

• it was manufactured by Ferrari,

• its engine has more than 6 cylinders.

Based on these detailed requirements a team of top-notch developers have come up with the following implementation of the CarSearch class:

Listing 10.14. CarSearch class implementation

```
public class CarSearch {

    private List<Car> cars = new ArrayList<Car>();

    public void addCar(Car car) {
        cars.add(car);
    }

    public List<Car> findSportCars() {
        List<Car> sportCars = new ArrayList<Car>();
        for (Car car : cars) {
            if (car.getEngine().getNbOfCylinders() > 6
                    && Color.RED.equals(car.getColor())
                    && "Ferrari".equals(car.getManufacturer().getName())) {
                sportCars.add(car);
            }
        }
        return sportCars;
    }
}
```

The Car, Engine and Manufacturer interfaces are presented below:

Listing 10.15. Car interface

```
public interface Car {
    Engine getEngine();
    Color getColor();
    Manufacturer getManufacturer();
}
```

Listing 10.16. Engine interface

```
public interface Engine {
    int getNbOfCylinders();
}
```

Listing 10.17. Manufacturer interface

```
public interface Manufacturer {
    String getName();
}
```

Your task is to write some tests for the `findSportCars()` method of the `CarSearch` class. Basically, what you have to do is pass some cars to the `CarSearch` class (using its `addCar()`) method, and then verify, whether only sports cars are being returned by the `findSportsCars()` method.

Initially, do this for the original implementation of the `CarSearch` class. Then, redesign the `Car` interface, so that the `CarSearch` class does not violate either the "Law of Demeter" or the "Tell, Don't Ask!" principles, and write the tests once again. Compare the amount of work involved in each case

10.7.2. Stack Test

Based on what was discussed in Section 10.1, implement a `Stack`[10] class and a corresponding `StackTest` class. Please follow the TDD approach, so that the tests are written before the implementation. Make sure you think in terms of class responsibilities!

---

[10]See http://en.wikipedia.org/wiki/Stack_%28abstract_data_type%29.

Chapter 11. Test Quality

A job worth doing is worth doing well.

— An old saying

Who watches the watchmen?

— Juvenal

Developers are obsessed with quality, and for good reasons. First of all, quality is proof of excellence in code writing - and we all want to be recognized as splendid coders, don't we? Second, we have all heard about some spectacular catastrophes that occurred because of the poor quality of the software involved. Even if the software you are writing is not intended to put a man on the moon, you still won't want to disappoint your client with bugs. Third, we all know that just like a boomerang, bad code will one day come right back and hit us so hard that we never forget it - one more reason to write the best code possible!

Since we have agreed that developers tests are important (if not crucial), we should also be concerned about their quality. If we cannot guarantee that the tests we have are really, really good, then all we have is a false sense of security.

The topic of test quality has been implicitly present from the very beginning of this book, because we have cared about each test being readable, focused, concise, well-named, etc. Nevertheless, it is now time to investigate this in detail. In this section we shall try to answer two questions: **how to measure test quality** and **how to improve it**.

In the course of our voyage into the realm of test quality, we will discover that in general it is hard to assess the quality of tests, at least when using certain tools. There is no tool that could verify a successful implementation of the "testing behaviour, not methods" rule (see Section 10.1), or that could make sure you "name your tests methods consistently" (see Section 9.3). This is an unhappy conclusion, but we should not give up hope completely. High-quality tests are hard to come by, but not impossible, and if we adhere to the right principles, then maybe achieving them will turn out not to be so very hard after all. Some tools can also help, if used right.

11.1. An Overview

When talking about quality we should always ask *"if"* before we ask *"how"*. Questions like *"would I be better off writing an integration test or a unit test for this?"*, or *"do I really need to cover this scenario – isn't it perhaps already covered by another test?"*, should come before any pondering of the design and implementation of test code. A useless and/ or redundant test of the highest quality is still, well, useless and/or redundant. Do not waste your time writing perfect tests that should not have been written at all!

In the rest of this chapter we shall assume that a positive answer has been given to this first *"if"* question. This is often the case with unit tests which, in general, should be written for every piece of code you create.

Test Smells

When dealing with production code, we use the "code smell"[1] to refer to various statements in code that do not look (smell) right. Such code smells have been gathered, given names and are widely recognized within the community. Also, there are some tools (e.g. PMD[2] or Findbugs[3]) which are capable of discovering common code smells. For test code there is a similar term - "test smell" - which is much less commonly used. Also, there is no generally agreed on list of test code smells similar to that for production code[4]. What all of this adds up to is that the problem of various "bad" things in test code has been recognized, but not widely enough to get "standardized" in the sort of way that has happened with production code.

Let me also mention that many of the so-called code or test smells are nothing more than catchy names for some manifestation of a more general rule. Take, for example, the "overriding stubbing" test smell, which occurs if you first describe the stubbing behaviour of one stub in a `setUp()` method, and then override it in some test methods. This is something to be avoided, as it diminishes readability. The thing is, if you follow a general rule of avoiding "global" objects, you will not write code which emits this bad smell anyway. This is why I am not inclined to ponder every possible existing test smell. I would rather hope that once you are following the best programming practices - both in production code and test code - many test smells will simply never happen in your code. So in this part of the book I will only be describing those bad practices which I meet with most often when working with code.

---

[1]http://en.wikipedia.org/wiki/Code_smell
[2]http://pmd.sourceforge.net/
[3]http://findbugs.sourceforge.net/
[4]At this point I would like to encourage you to read the list of TDD anti-patterns gathered by James Carr - [carr2006]

Refactoring

When talking about code smells, we can not pass over the subject of **refactoring**. We have already introduced the term and given some examples of refactoring in action, when describing the TDD rhythm. In this chapter we will discuss some refactorings of test code. As with production code refactoring, refactorings of test code help to achieve higher quality of both types: internal and external. Internal, because well-refactored tests are easier to understand and maintain, and external, because by refactoring we are making it more probable that our tests actually test something valuable.

 At this point a cautious reader will pause in their reading – feeling that something is not quite right here. True! Previously, I defined refactoring as moving through code *"over a safety net of tests"*, whereas now I am using this term to describe an activity performed in the absence of tests (since we do not have tests for tests, right?). Yes, right! It is actually a misuse of the term "refactoring" to apply it to the activity of changing test code. However, the problem is that it is so commonly used this way that I dare not give it any other name.

Code Quality Influences Tests Quality

Another point worth remembering is that there is a **strong relation between the quality of your production code and test code**. Having good, clean, maintainable tests is definitely possible. The first step is to write cleaner, better designed and truly loosely-coupled production code. If the production code is messy, then there is a considerable likelihood that your tests will also be. If your production code is fine, then your tests have a chance of being good, too. The second step is to start treating your test code with the same respect as your production code. This means your test code should obey the same rules (KISS, SRP) that you apply to production code: i.e. it should avoid things you do not use in your code (e.g. extensive use of reflection, deep class hierarchies, etc.), and you should care about its quality (e.g. by having it analyzed statically, and put through a code review process).

Always Observe a Failing Test

Before we discuss ways of measuring and improving the quality of tests, let me remind you of one very important piece of advice, which has a lot to do with this subject. It may sound like a joke, but in fact observing a failing test is one way to check its quality: if it fails, then this proves that it really does verify some behaviour. Of course, this is not enough to mean that the test is valuable, but provided that you have not written the test blindfolded, it does mean something. So, make sure never to omit the **RED** phase of TDD, and **always witness a failing test by actually seeing it fail**.

 Obviously, this advice chiefly makes sense for TDD followers. But sometimes it could also be reasonable to break the production code intentionally to make sure your tests actually test something.

11.2. Static Analysis Tools

indxterm:[static analysis tools]Now that we have some basic knowledge regarding tests quality, let us look for the ways to measure it. Our first approach will be to use tools which perform a static code analysis in order to find some deficiencies. Are they helpful for test code? Let us take a look at this.

You will surely use static code analyzers (e.g. PMD or Findbugs) to verify your production code. The aim of these tools is to discover various anti-patterns, and point out possible bugs. They are quite smart when it comes to reporting various code smells. Currently, it is normal engineering practice to have them as a part of a team's Definition of Done[5]. Such tools are often integrated with IDEs, and/or are a part of the continuous integration process. A natural next step would be to also use them to verify your test code and reveal its dodgy parts.

And you should use them – after all, why not? It will not cost you much, that is for sure. Simply include them in your build process and - voila! - your test code is verified. But…, but the reality is different. In fact, you should not expect too much when performing static analysis on your test code. The main reason for this is, that **your test code is dead simple**, right? There are rarely any nested `try-catch` statements, opened streams, reused variables, deep inheritance hierarchies, multiple returns from methods, violations of `hashCode()`/`equals()` contracts, or other things that static code analyzers are so good at dealing with. In fact your tests are this simple: you just set up objects, execute methods and assert. Not much work for such tools.

To give a complete picture I should mention that both PMD and Findbugs offer some rules (checks) designed especially to discover issues within JUnit testing. However, their

---

[5]See http://www.scrumalliance.org/articles/105-what-is-definition-of-done-dod and other net resources for more information on Defintion of Done.

usefulness is rather limited, because only basic checks are provided. For example, they can verify whether[6]:

- proper assertions have been used, e.g. `assertTrue(someBoolean)` instead of `assertEquals(someBoolean, true)`, and `assertNull(someVariable)` instead of `assertTrue(someVariable == null)`,

- a test method has at least one assertion,

- two double values are compared with a certain level of precision (and not with exact equality).

 The bad news is that at the time of writing there are no equivalents of the above rules for TestNG tests. The good news is that they are not really useful anyway, so no one should despair. :)

Another form of static analysis is calculation of various code metrics, such as number of lines per class or per method, and the famous cyclomatic complexity[7]. They will generally tell you whether your code is too complex or not. Obviously, test classes and methods should stick to the same (or even stricter) rules than your production code, so verifying this seems like a good idea. But because you have no logic in your tests (as discussed in Section 10.2), the complexity of your test methods should be very low by default. Thus, such analysis will rarely reveal any problems in your test code.

To conclude, static analysis tools do not help much when it comes to tests code. No tool or metric will tell you **if you have written good tests**. Use them, listen to what they say, but do not expect too much. If you write your tests following the basic rules given in this section, then there is not much they can do for you.

11.3. Code Coverage

> If you can not measure it, you can not improve it.
>
> — William Thomson 1st Baron Kelvin

Having been seriously disappointed by what static code analysis tools have to offer with regard to finding test code smells (see Section 11.2), let us turn towards another group of

---

[6]Please consult Findbugs and PMD documentation for more information on this subject.

[7]http://en.wikipedia.org/wiki/Cyclomatic_complexity

tools, which are commonly used to assess test quality. Are they any better at finding test smells, and weaknesses of any kind, in your test code?

This section is devoted to a group of popular tools which utilize the code coverage technique[8], and can provide a good deal of interesting information regarding your tests. We will discuss both their capabilities and limits. What we are really interested in is whether they can be used to measure, and hopefully improve, test quality. For the time being, we shall leave the technical issues relating to running them and concentrate solely on the usefulness of code coverage tools in the field of test quality measurement.

Code coverage measures which parts of your code were executed: i.e. which parts of the production code were executed during tests. They work by augmenting production code with additional statements, which do not change the semantics of the original code. The purpose of these additional instructions is to record information about executed fragments (lines, methods, statements) of code and to present it, later, as numerical data in coverage reports.

 Code coverage tools also measure some other metrics, - e.g. cyclomatic complexity[9]. However, these do not really relate to test quality, so we shall not be discussing them in this section.

11.3.1. Line and Branch Coverage

"Code coverage" is a broad term which denotes a number of types of coverage measurement, sometimes very different from one another. Wikipedia[10] describes them all in details. However, many of them are rather theoretical, and no tool supports them (mainly because their practical use is limited).

In this section I will present two types of code coverage measure provided by a popular Cobertura[11] tool: **line** and **branch** coverage:

- **Line** coverage is a very simple metric. All it says is whether a particular line (or rather statement) of code has been exercised or not. If a line was *"touched"* during test

---

[8]See http://en.wikipedia.org/wiki/Code_coverage
[9]See   http://en.wikipedia.org/wiki/Software_metric,   and   especially   http://en.wikipedia.org/wiki/Cyclomatic_complexity, for more information on this topic.
[10]See http://en.wikipedia.org/wiki/Code_coverage
[11]http://cobertura.sourceforge.net/

execution, then it counts as covered. Simple, yet misleading - as will be discussed further. This kind of coverage is also known as **statement coverage**.

- **Branch** coverage focuses on decision points in production code, such as `if` or `while` statements with logical `&&` or `||` operators. This is a much stronger measure than line coverage. In practice, to satisfy branch coverage, you must write tests such that every logical expression in your code gets to be evaluated to `true` and to `false`.

The difference between the two is very significant. While getting 100% line coverage is a pretty straightforward affair, much more effort must be made to obtain such a value for branch coverage. The following snippet of code illustrates this[12].

Listing 11.1. A simple function to measure coverage

```
public boolean bar(boolean a, boolean b) {
    boolean result = false;
    if (a && b) {
        result = true;
    }
    return result;
}
```

Table 11.1 shows calls to `foo()` methods, which should be issued from the test code, in order to obtain 100% line and branch coverage respectively.

Table 11.1. Tests required to obtain 100% coverage

line coverage	branch coverage
foo(true, true)	foo(true, false) foo(true, true) foo(false,false)

Now that we understand the types of code coverage provided by Cobertura, let us take a look at the results of its work.

---

[12]The code used to illustrate line and branch coverage is based on Wikipedia example: http://en.wikipedia.org/wiki/Code_coverage

11.3.2. Code Coverage Reports

After the tests have been run, code coverage tools generate a report on coverage metrics. This is possible thanks to the additional information previously added to the production code.

As we shall soon see, coverage reports can be used to gain an overall impression regarding code coverage, but also to scrutinize selected classes. They act as a spyglass and a microscope in one. We shall start with the view from 10,000 feet (i.e. project coverage), then move down to package level, and finally reach ground level with classes.

Figure 11.1. Code coverage - packages overview

Package	# Classes	Line Coverage		Branch Coverage	
All Packages	8	45%	27/60	28%	8/28
com.practicalunittesting.first	2	81%	13/16	50%	4/8
com.practicalunittesting.fourth	2	0%	0/12	0%	0/4
com.practicalunittesting.second	2	43%	7/16	25%	2/8
com.practicalunittesting.third	2	43%	7/16	25%	2/8

Figure 11.1 presents an overview of some project coverage. For each package the following statistics are given:

- the percentage of **line coverage**, along with the total number of lines and number of lines covered,

- the percentage of **branch coverage**, along with the total number of branches and, for purposes of comparison, the number of branches covered.

As you might guess, a red color is used for those parts of the code not executed (not *"covered"*) during the tests. So - the more green, the better? Well, yes and no - we will get to this soon.

Figure 11.2. Code coverage - single package

Package	# Classes	Line Coverage		Branch Coverage	
com.practicalunittesting.first	2	81%	13/16	50%	4/8

Classes in this Package	Line Coverage		Branch Coverage	
Account	75%	6/8	50%	2/4
Money	87%	7/8	50%	2/4

The report shown in Figure 11.2 gives an overview of code coverage for the whole package, and for individual classes of the package. As with the previous report, it gives information on line and branch coverage. Figure 11.3 provides an example.

Figure 11.3. Single class coverage

Classes in this File	Line Coverage		Branch Coverage	
Money	86%	13/15	50%	4/8

```
1     package com.practicalunittesting.first;
2
3     public class Money {
4         private final int amount;
5         private final String currency;
6
7  5     public Money(int amount, String currency) {
8  5         this.amount = amount;
9  5         this.currency = currency;
10 5     }
11         public boolean equals(Object anObject) {
12 1         if (anObject instanceof Money) {
13 1             Money money= (Money)anObject;
14 1             return getCurrency().equals(money.getCurrency())
15                     && getAmount() == money.getAmount();
16         }
17 0         return false;
18     }
19
20         public Money add(Money m) {
21 1         checkCurrencies(m);
22 1         return new Money(getAmount() + m.getAmount(), getCurrency());
23     }
24
25         private void checkCurrencies(Money m) {
26 1         if (!m.getCurrency().equals(currency)) {
27 0             throw new IllegalArgumentException(
28                     "Currencies do not match: "
29                     + currency + ", " + m.getCurrency());
```

Figure 11.3 presents code for our old friend - the Money class. This report shows precisely which parts of the Money class are covered by tests. The green color denotes parts that have been tested, the red those not executed during the tests. The first column of numbers is the line of code, while the second gives some additional information, about the number of times each line was "touched" during the testing. For example, in the case of line 12 (the if statement) the number on a red background says **1**. This means that this if statement has only been executed once. We may guess that the current tests contain only one case, which makes this if evaluate to true. If we were to add another test which evaluated this Boolean expression to false, then the number **1** on a red background would change to **2** on a green background. Also, the coverage of line 17 would change from 0 to 1 (and from red to green).

11.3.3. The Devil is in the Details

Let us take a closer look at this last example of detailed code coverage of the Money class. Listing 11.2 shows tests which have been executed to obtain the following quite high level of coverage: 86% line coverage and 50% branch coverage.

Listing 11.2. Tests of the Money class

```
@Test
public class MoneyTest {

    public void constructorShouldSetAmountAndCurrency() {
        Money money = new Money(10, "USD");

        assertEquals(money.getAmount(), 10);
        assertEquals(money.getCurrency(), "USD");
    }

    public void shouldBeAbleToAddMoney() {
        assertEquals(new Money(3, "USD").add(new Money(4, "USD")),
                new Money(7, "USD"));
    }
}
```

The tests shown in Listing 11.2 are not the best we have seen so far in terms of how they are written, but this is not the point. The thing is, they are highly incomplete, given the requirements that the Money class is supposed to fulfill. We have already discussed the notion that each feature should be tested with more than one test case (i.e. with many values - see Section 6.1). However, it seems that one can obtain quite high coverage by testing just some features with a single test case.

 This is an interesting observation. Interesting, or maybe rather ominous, considering the number of people who feel entitled to an opinion regarding the quality of tests based on code coverage measurements.

What we could do, to achieve even higher coverage, would be to add some more tests. Listing 11.3 shows such an attempt. This test was created only in order to make the branch code coverage higher. If we measure the branch coverage now, we will learn that it has gone up from 50% to 75%.

Listing 11.3. Additional test method of the Money class

```
public void differentMoneyShouldNotBeEqual() {
    assertNotEquals(new Money(7, "CHF"), new Money(7, "USD"));
    assertNotEquals(new Money(8, "USD"), new Money(7, "USD"));
}
```

Please note that there are many important features of the Money class that we are still not verifying. For example, it would be nice to make sure that objects of the Money class are immutable, but if you think about such a test, it would not make the code coverage any higher. We would also like to make sure the addition really works, by verifying it with some more examples. But no, we have not done anything like this, and yet… voila! - we already have 86% line coverage and 75% branch coverage.

This simple example reveals a very important weakness of code coverage measures. **Code coverage tools do not measure whether tests cover requirements!** They only measure what parts of the production code were executed when running the tests.

11.3.4. How Much Code Coverage is Good Enough?

> You should, at least once in your lifetime, get 100% coverage – just so you know how it tastes. Then you can decide whether it is worth the effort.
> — Jaroslav Tulach *Geecon 2011 Talk (paraphrased)*

> I can get 100% code coverage and test nothing because I have no asserts. Stop making coverage a goal, it's only a way!
> — Twitter @unclebobmartin *2011 Apr 8*

Since code coverage exists, there must also be a question we can ask about what is the good/appropriate/required amount of code coverage. The question appears in many forms, usually as a *"should I aim at 100% coverage"*? Like many other dilemmas, this one has also received some quite contradictory answers. Let us have a look at this.

From the examples presented so far, we should already understand that high code coverage, even 100% code coverage, does not mean the tests are of high quality. You can write tests of no value at all (e.g. tests without assertions), whose only goal is to prop up the coverage metrics. In fact, this often happens when management demands that developers obtain certain, usually very high, values of code coverage. If the team cannot fulfill these requirements (for example because of lack of skills), the coverage metrics will be meaningless. Their only value will be in keeping management happy. Nice in the short term, but not very useful in the long run.

The use of red and green colors makes coverage reports resemble those of tests results. On the one hand, this is convenient, because the *"green-is-good"* and *"red-is-bad"* associations are probably well entrenched in developers' minds. On the other hand, a red color used in a test result, and the same red color in a coverage report, do not mean the same thing. Yet it makes developers follow a *"no red policy"* and focus on eliminating anything that shows up as red. This means they might try to get 100% coverage even though, as we have already noted, this might not be the most important thing needing to be done.

This raises another issue. High coverage measures, together with the misguided assumption that *"tests ensure that it works"*, might lead you to a (false) feeling of security. However, in the light of what was discussed previously, you should not feel secure, even if your code coverage does reach the 100% mark. *"Our code is working fine because we have 100% code coverage"* is a **fallacy**.

Also, with regard to what was said earlier in connection with *"things too simple to break"* (see Section 10.5), there are some parts of the code which do not deserve to be tested. This makes 100% code coverage a goal not worth chasing, as it makes developers write tests which are not really worth the effort. A grotesque example might be writing a test for a private constructor in a static class, which is there for the sole purpose of never being called...

So, what is the answer to the question which opened this section? How much coverage is desirable, and how much should be considered inadequate? A popular answer to this has been given by [savoia2007]. Basically, it suggests the following[13]:

- If you begin your adventure with testing, you should not worry about code coverage. Concentrate on writing good tests and honing your testing skills. If you spend too much

---

[13]I would encourage you to read the original version of the article.

time thinking about coverage, you will get depressed (because it is unlikely that you will be able to achieve high values at this point).

- If you are experienced, then you know that there are no simple answers, and you are able to handle this truth and keep on working. No threshold of required code coverage can be taken as given, because the desired level depends on many factors that only you, the author of the code, can possibly understand.

What I, myself, would add, is that no matter what level of experience you have, you should focus on testing all of the important requirements of your classes, and only then check code coverage.

11.3.5. Conclusion

> Code coverage tells you what you definitely haven't tested, not what you have.
>
> — Mark Simpson *StackOverflow discussion 2009*

In this section we have seen the two faces of code coverage. The first face is friendly and helpful. It allows you to get a good understanding of the parts of the code which are not covered by tests and thus find the gaps in your safety net. However, there is also another face to code coverage. This one makes you worry about seeing the color red on coverage reports and waste time writing tests for lines that are not worth it. It also makes you feel secure, and makes you believe that your code works as required (when neither of these are in fact justified).

The point is, that you should choose what is good in code coverage and ignore the rest. You **should use it to**:

- Learn what you definitely have not tested.

- Make sure you do not lose some tests during huge redesigns of your test code (which happens rarely).

- Have a broader picture of gaps in your safety net of tests.

  - This is especially useful if you want to see the time trend of coverage and compare it with other things that happened within the team (trainings, new people joining the team, technology change, etc.)

- It is also good for seeing if there are some parts of the code which are typically being undertested. For example, team members might not have the skills needed for testing expected exceptions, thus leaving such code untested.

But **be wary, and always remember that**:

- **Code coverage does not translate directly into quality**. There is no simple relation here. Period.

- "Covered" does not mean it is really "tested".

- Even 100% code coverage does not mean your tests cover all **business requirements**. They only signify that every statement in your production code gets executed during tests. This is not the same.

- It is completely useless in cases of **multithreaded testing**. Take, for example, code presented in Section 6.7, which is meant to be thread-safe. Imagine you run only a single test case against such code, using only one thread. This is obviously a nonsensical test, because it does not evaluate the most important feature of this code – no matter that you were able to achieve 100% code coverage thanks to such a useless test.

- Never write a test just to push up code coverage. Each test should aim at covering some important functionality of your code

TDD is probably the best way of achieving high "functional" code coverage. By designing your code with tests, you not only make code coverage reports look nice, but also the coverage values become meaningful. This is because they now reflect the amount of functionalities covered by tests.

Code coverage is often used to check the quality of tests, which is not a good idea. As we have learned in this section, coverage measures are not credible indicators of test quality. Code coverage might help by showing you deficiencies in your safety net of tests, but not much more than this. In addition to code coverage, you should use other techniques (i.e. visual inspection - see Section 11.5) to supplement its indications.

11.4. Mutation Testing

> High quality software can not be done without high quality testing.
> Mutation testing measures how "good" our tests are by inserting faults into
> the program under test. Each fault generates a new program, a mutant, that
> is slightly different from the original. The idea is that the tests are adequate
> if they detect all mutants.
> — Mattias Bybro *A Mutation Testing Tool For Java Programs (2003)*

As discussed in the previous section, code coverage is a weak indicator of test quality. Let us now take a look at another approach, called mutation testing, which promises to furnish us with more detailed information regarding the quality of tests.

 Mutation testing, although it has been under investigation for decades, is still in its infancy. I discuss this topic here because I believe it has great potential, which is waiting to be discovered. Recent progress in mutation testing tools (i.e. the PIT mutation testing tool[14]) leads me to believe that this great and exciting idea will finally get the attention it deserves. By reading this section you might just get ahead of your times by learning about a new star that is about to outshine the existing solutions, or …waste your time on something that will never be used in real life.

Suppose you have some classes and a suite of tests. Now imagine that you introduce a change into one of your classes, for example by reverting (negating) one of the if conditional expressions. In doing this you have created a so-called **mutant** of the original code. What should happen now, if you run all your tests once again? Provided that the suite of tests contains a test that examines this class thoroughly, then this test should fail. If no test fails, this means your test suite is not good enough[15]. And that is precisely the concept of mutation testing.

11.4.1. How does it Work?

Mutation testing tools create a plethora of "mutants": that is, slightly changed versions of the original production code. Then, they run tests against each mutant. The quality of the

---

[14]http://pitest.org

[15]In fact, if all tests still pass, it can also mean that the "mutant" program is equivalent in behaviour to the original program.

tests is assessed by the number of mutants killed by the tests[16]. The tools differ mainly in the following respects:

- how the mutants are created (they can be brought to life by modifying source code or bytecode),

- the set of available mutators,

- performance (e.g. detecting equivalent mutations, so the tests are not run twice etc.).

Mutants are created by applying various **mutation operators** - i.e. simple syntactic or semantic transformation rules - to the production code. The most basic mutation operators introduce changes to the various language operators - mathematical (e.g. +, -, *, /), relational (e.g. =, !=, <, >) or logical (e.g. &, |, !). An example of a mutation would be to switch the sign < to > within some logical condition. These simple mutators mimic typical sources of errors - typos or instances of the wrong logical operators being used. Likewise, by changing some values in the code, it is easy to simulate off-by-one errors. Other possible mutations are, for example, removing method calls (possible with void methods), changing returned values, changing constant values, etc. Some tools have also experimented with more Java-specific mutators, for example relating to Java collections.

11.4.2. Working with PIT

PIT Mutation Testing is a very fresh Java mutation testing tool, which has brought new life to the rather stagnant area of mutation testing tools. It works at the bytecode level, which means it creates mutants without touching the source code. After PIT's execution has finished, it provides detailed information on created and killed mutants. It also creates an HTML report showing **line coverage** and a **mutation coverage** report. We will concentrate on the latter, as line coverage has already been discussed in Section 11.3.

We will use a very simple example to demonstrate PIT in action and confront it with code coverage tools. Listing 11.4 shows our "production code", which will be mutated by PIT[17].

---

[16]Okay, I admit it: this heuristic sounds like it was taken from the game series Fallout: *"the more dead mutants, the better"* :).

[17]The idea of this code is taken from the StackOverflow discussion about code coverage pitfalls - http://stackoverflow.com/questions/695811/pitfalls-of-code-coverage.

Listing 11.4. Method with two if statements

```java
public class TwoIfs {

    public int twoIfs(int a, int b) {
        if (a > 0) {
            return 1;
        } else {
            System.out.println();
        }
        if (b > 0) {
            return 3;
        } else {
            return 4;
        }
    }
}
```

Let us say that we also have a test class which (supposedly) verifies the correctness of the twoIfs() method:

Listing 11.5. Tests for the twoIfs method

```java
public class TwoIfsTest {

    @Test
    public void testTwoIfs() {
        TwoIfs twoIfs = new TwoIfs();

        assertEquals(twoIfs.twoIfs(1, -1), 1);
        assertEquals(twoIfs.twoIfs(-1, 1), 3);
        assertEquals(twoIfs.twoIfs(-1, -1), 4);
    }
}
```

What is really interesting is that this simple test is good enough to satisfy the code coverage tool - it achieves 100% in respect of both line and branch coverage! Figure 11.4 shows this:

Figure 11.4. 100% code coverage - isn't that great?

Classes in this File	Line Coverage		Branch Coverage	
TwoIfs	100%	7/7	100%	4/4

```
 1      package com.practicalunittesting;
 2
 3 1    public class TwoIfs {
 4
 5          public int twoIfs(int a, int b) {
 6 3            if (a > 0) {
 7 1                return 1;
 8            } else {
 9 2                System.out.println();
10            }
11 2            if (b > 0) {
12 1                return 3;
13            } else {
14 1                return 4;
15            }
16        }
17    }
```

When we execute a PIT analysis, it will create mutants of the production code from Listing 11.4 by reverting the inequality operators and fiddling with comparison values. Then it will run all tests (in our case only the one test shown in Listing 11.5) against each mutant and check if they failed.

The outcome report shows the code that was mutated together with some information about applied mutations. Just like with code coverage reports, the red background denotes "bad" lines of code, which means that some mutations performed on these lines went unnoticed when testing. Below the source code there is a list of applied mutations. From this list we can learn that, for example, one mutant survived the change of conditional boundary in line 6. The "greater than" symbol was changed to "greater or equal" and the tests still passed. The report informs us that such and such a mutant SURVIVED, which means it was not detected by our tests.

Figure 11.5. Mutation testing - PIT report

```
5       public int twoIfs(int a, int b) {
6   2      if (a > 0) {
7   1          return 1;
8          } else {
9   1          System.out.println();
10         }
11  2      if (b > 0) {
12  1          return 3;
13         } else {
14  1          return 4;
15  } } }
```

Mutations

6	changed conditional boundary : SURVIVED negated conditional : KILLED -> com.practicalunittesting.TwoIfsTest.
7	replaced return of integer sized value with (x == 0 ? 1 : 0) : KILLED
9	removed call to java/io/PrintStream::println : SURVIVED
11	changed conditional boundary : SURVIVED negated conditional : KILLED -> com.practicalunittesting.TwoIfsTest.
12	replaced return of integer sized value with (x == 0 ? 1 : 0) : KILLED
14	replaced return of integer sized value with (x == 0 ? 1 : 0) : KILLED

This simple example shows the difference between code coverage and mutation testing: in short, it is much simpler to satisfy coverage tools, whereas **mutation testing tools can detect more holes** within your tests.

11.4.3. Conclusions

Mutation testing has been around since the late 1970s but is rarely used outside academia. Executing a huge number of mutants and finding equivalent mutants has been too expensive for practical use.

— Mattias Bybro *A Mutation Testing Tool For Java Programs (2003)*

Mutation testing looks interesting, but I have never once heard tell of it being used successfully in a commercial project. There could be many reasons why this idea has never made it into developers' toolboxes, but I think the main one is that **for a very long time there were no mutation testing tools that were production-ready**. Existing tools were lagging behind relative to the progress of Java language (e.g. not supporting Java 5 annotations), and/or were not up to the industry standards and developers' expectations in terms of reliability and ease of use. Because of this, code coverage, which has had decent tools for years, is today a standard part of every development process, while mutation testing is nowhere to be found. As for today, developers in general not only know nothing about such tools, but are even unaware of the very concept of mutation testing!

This situation is likely to change with the rise of the PIT framework, which offers much higher usability and reliability than any other mutation testing tool so far. But it will surely take time for the whole ecosystem of affiliated tools to catch up with what code coverage already has to offer in respect of build tools and IDE plugins, integration with CI servers, and so on[18]

Mutation testing tools have already made significant progress in terms of how they perform with regard to mutant creation (currently available tools work on the bytecode level to avoid recompilation, while earlier tools worked by changing the source code). The real performance issue relates to the fact that mutation testing tools work by executing tests many times over. Even if each execution takes only seconds, this can add up to a huge number, taking into consideration the number of created mutants. This excludes mutation testing tools from the normal TDD fast iteration cycles[19].

To conclude, there is a chance that mutation testing tools will improve our ability to measure the quality of test code, but it is still too early to consider them "the next big thing" in our toolboxes.

11.5. Code Reviews

> People exchange work products to review, with the expectation that as authors, they will produce errors, and as reviewers, they will find errors. Everyone ends up learning from their own mistakes and other people's mistakes.
>
> — Johanna Rothman

---

[18]The situation here changes rapidly - for example, a plugin for Sonar is already available: http://docs.codehaus.org/display/SONAR/Pitest.

[19]As far as I know, this issue is being treated very seriously by mutation testing tools authors, and a lot of improvements have already been made. For example, these tools can select a tiny subset of the potentially "strongest" mutants and only execute tests against them, thus significantly reducing the testing time.

We have already discussed the usefulness of three kinds of tool for measuring and improving test quality: static code analyzers fall far short of our expectations, while both code coverage (see Section 11.3) and mutation testing (Section 11.4) have their uses, and it makes sense to have them in your toolbox. Yet they do not cover the full spectrum of test quality issues. In order to gain really insightful feedback on the quality of our code we need to have another developer analyze it. The process of working with others' code in order to make it better is known as **code review**.

A lot has been written already about code reviews, and it is not my goal to discuss their place and role in the software development process. Let me conclude with a short statement to the effect that **code reviews are a must**, because they help discover bugs, thus improving internal and external code quality, and because they spread knowledge of the code among different team members and help us improve by learning from each other.

All of this is also true for code reviews performed on test code. In the absence of tools which could help us with validating the correctness, and assessing the quality, of our test code, code reviews are the only option for delivering test code of the highest quality. In this section we will discuss various aspects of performing code reviews of test code, and how they differ from reviews of production code.

Before we begin, two important things to remember:

• First of all, if your team performs code reviews (no matter if they are performed by some senior developer, or by your peers), it should also include test code. This code is as important as production code, and your prospects for a hassle-free future as a developer depend on its quality.

• Secondly, issues discovered during reviews of test code can signify two things: that the **tests are weak** in themselves, or that the **production code is of low quality**. Looking into test code often reveals various weaknesses of the production code. This is yet another benefit of having your test code reviewed!

 When reading this section you might have a certain feeling of déjà vu. This is because many of the issues mentioned here simply invert good practices described elsewhere in the various chapters of this book.

11.5.1. A Three-Minute Test Code Review

Code reviews take time. In an ideal world, we would have this time, but in reality things are different. Let us now see what can be done to perform a very quick test code review, so that next time when you have only three minutes and are hesitating about whether to do it at all, you will have a short checklist of things which could be validated, even in such a short time.

Size Heuristics

Some idea of test code quality might be gained by looking at the following features of the test code:

- the number of imported classes,

- the number of test doubles used,

- the length of set-up methods,

- the length of test methods,

- the length of test class.

It is not possible to come up with exact numbers here - which should trigger a red light in your head. However, common sense is usually enough to distinguish right from wrong. For example, three test doubles in a test class are probably fine, but if there are eight of them, then an alarm bell should ring. And what about four, five, six or seven test doubles? Where is the exact border? As usual, *"it depends"*, and you need some more time to decide whether or not things are fine. The same holds true for the number of imports (and the variety of imported classes).

As for the length of the test methods and classes, here, again, common sense should be sufficient.

 Once again, please remember that finding weaknesses in any of the above might be a symptom of bad production code, which is only reflected by the test code.

Violations of reasonable size values for test code usually indicate that the class being tested has too much responsibility.

But do They Run?

Unit tests should run in a matter of seconds, so three minutes will give you enough time to run all of them.

- Is there a build script which allows anyone to execute them, or do they need some manual setup (e.g. running your IDE)? If the latter, then this is something to really worry about.

- How much times does it take for tests to finish? If it is more than 20 seconds (again, this is not a value you should take too literally), then these are probably not unit tests but integration tests.

- Are they really run - do they really get picked out by your build script?

Check Code Coverage

As we noted in Section 11.3, code coverage can inform us about areas of code that are being undertested. Three minutes should be enough time to run the build script and have a look at the code coverage report. What you are looking to find, in such a short period of time, are white areas of untested code. There is no time to ponder over each line, but it is definitely possible to see that some package has 20% code coverage, while the rest is close to 80%[20].

…and if there is no build script which would allow you to generate a code coverage report? Well, then you have one more issue to report to your colleagues.

Conclusions

Three minutes will not allow you to perform a real test code review, but it is enough to uncover some major issues with the test code. If this is all you can have at the moment, then fair enough - it is still much better than nothing.

---

[20]Please, do not take these values literally! They are only meant to be illustrative. See Section 11.3 for more information on desired code coverage levels.

11.5.2. Things to Look For

Now let us assume that we are under significantly less time pressure, and so have time to really look into the test code. Here is the list of things we should be looking for.

Basically, you should pay attention to the same code features as when code reviewing production code. Are the methods short and focused? Has the code been written at the right level of abstraction? Are there any global variables and magic numbers? And so on... In the subsections below, I will be trying to focus on test-related checks.

 Some of the hints below are written from the point of view of a technical team leader, responsible for ensuring the quality of all code. For example, analyzing trends in code coverage reports is probably not something you will be doing on a daily basis. Use common sense to create your own checklist of the issues to look for when code reviewing test code.

Easy to Understand

A good unit test is easy to understand. But its readability can be spoilt by many small issues, which you should look out for.

A good test method has a content-revealing name, which gives information on the particular scenario implemented within it (see Section 9.3). Similarly, variables used in tests should be easy to understand: for example, can you tell which variable is an SUT and which are collaborators? Also, variables used within test code should inform you precisely about what their role is: are they here only to satisfy the API of the method being tested, or are they crucial to triggering some behaviour of the SUT or its collaborators? (see Section 11.6.3).

Are the test methods short and focused? They should test a particular feature of the SUT (see Section 10.1), and nothing more. Look for anything that goes beyond just the simplest actions (arrange/act/assert).

Can you find any `for` loops in the test methods, or instances of reflection being used to set up a test fixture? Both have some legitimate use, but usually cover up deficiencies in production code. Any violation of KISS should attract your attention.

Look for dependencies between tests (see Section 7.2) - they make test code much harder to understand. In the case of unit tests they have very limited use, so their presence in test code should arouse your suspicions. Moreover, global variables, reused between many test methods, should be treated as a code smell.

Look for calls to some external APIs. Readability issues are often there, especially if called methods take many parameters. If you can not understand such code at a glance, then there is probably some room for improvement there (see Section 11.6.2).

Are test classes inheriting from some parent class? How many levels of inheritance are there? Inheritance kills readability.

A common issue is the mixing up of different styles within the codebase. Some developers value the arrange/act/assert pattern, some are more in favor of the BDD approach, some like to instantiate test doubles within test methods, while others prefer to rely on set-up methods for this, and so on. A good unit testing suite will be consistent in this respect, and while code reviewing you should also take a look at this. However, this is not something to be fixed easily, as it takes time for the team members to converge and agree on a common style, shared by all developers.

Another thing which impacts negatively on readability is making use of custom solutions instead of depending on what your testing framework offers. If you find any non-standard approaches to setting up test fixtures (something different from the use of `@BeforeXYZ` annotations, see Section 9.7) or running test methods with different parameters (e.g. running tests in for loops instead of using data providers - see Section 3.6), then by all means kick up a fuss about it.

Similarly, you should take a look at the structure of the test classes. Does each particular part of the test class (e.g. data providers, private utility methods, set-up method, etc.) always appear in the same order? If not, this might be something to fix.

The existence of duplicated code fragments might indicate that the "refactor" phase of the TDD cycle (see Section 4.2) is not being treated seriously. On the other hand, if the duplicated code helps to make the tests more readable, I would leave it alone. This is somewhat different from the situation with production code, where repeated code is almost always a code smell (see Section 11.6.6).

Look at assertions. If a test fails, will you know exactly why? Are the right assertions being used? Are assertion messages clear? (see Section 8.4)

If there is any logic involved (e.g. iteration over the collection returned by the SUT to find out if it contains certain values), then shouldn't it perhaps be encapsulated within a custom matcher class? (See Section 6.5.)

Test doubles are a common source of readability problems. Are the right ones being used? Are the expectations concerning executed methods clear? Is it clear what is verified and what is only stubbed? It also common for maintainability issues to arise here. Look for overspecified tests (see Section 10.4.1). Are matchers used properly (see Section 6.6)?

The creation of objects (see Section 9.8) can also be a weak point of tests. It is common to see a lot of copy&paste code in the test fixture setup parts of test classes, or to find many obscure private methods calling one another to set domain objects in certain states. Definitely something to have a look at.

Documented

Well-written unit tests usually do not need documentation (see Section 9.4). However, it sometimes transpires that you come across things which you wish had been documented, but are not. For example, the selection of test cases might not be obvious (e.g. *"why is this method validated against Dubai and Sydney timezones?"*). Probably there is some business explanation for this, which should be added as a comment (sometimes a link to bug tracker issue is all that is required). If it is not there, then you cannot determine whether the test cases are covering all the important scenarios.

Are All the Important Scenarios Verified?

The most important question to be answered is whether all the important test cases are covered by tests. Often you will find only single executions of tested methods, which is definitely not enough to verify their correctness (see Section 6.1). This is a sign of "happy path" testing, and definitely something to fight against.
Another source of undertested code results from concurrency. If your code is intended to be accessed concurrently, then this is exactly how it should be tested (see Section 6.7). If not, then even 100% code coverage is nothing to be proud of.

We have already discussed one area of code coverage usefulness for test code reviews (that is, its ability to uncover areas not touched by tests at all). However, more can be learned from studying the coverage report, even if the whole idea of measuring test code quality by looking at code coverage is flawed (see the discussion in Section 11.3).

Study the coverage reports to find answers to the following questions (all of them can uncover potential issues):

- Can you see a pattern of untested code across multiple classes? I often find that there are no tests for exceptions thrown. Usually this happens when real collaborators are used instead of test doubles, which makes it hard to simulate some possible paths of code execution.

- If you happen to have historical data on executed tests (your continuous integration server should provide such reports), then see how the number of tests and code coverage measurements change. Ideally the number of tests should grow, and code coverage should at least fluctuate around the same values. If you see some different behaviour, you need to inspect it further.

Additionally, you could apply mutation testing verification (see Section 11.4) to find weak spots in your tests.

Run Them

Some of the issues relating to running tests during code reviews have already been discussed. However, it is now time to have a closer look at them.

 Remember, always execute the tests which are under code review.

Take a look at the build script. See if there are any conditions under which tests are not run (e.g. Maven profiles). Make sure the tests are not skipped.

See how fast the tests run. If you find it unacceptably long, or notice some pauses during the execution of the tests, then look further, and answer the following questions:

- Are these unit tests, or rather integration tests? Typically, setting up an application context or database connection takes time.

- Are the setup methods used properly? Although this happens rarely with unit tests, do look to see whether some objects might, for example, be created before the class rather than just before each method (see Section 9.7).

- Are there any deliberate `Thread.sleep()` calls? (See the next section for some discussion).

Also, look at the messages printed during the execution of the tests (usually on the console). If you cannot keep up with them, it means you have a Loudmouth issue (see Section 8.5).

Make sure the tests are repeatable. Usually they are, but in cases of multithreading tests (see Section 6.7), or tests with random values (see Section 7.1), this might not be the case.

Date Testing

Experience tells me that the testing of time-dependent business logic is rarely done correctly (see Section 6.8). Common issues you should look for are the following:

- Look for any `Thread.sleep()` code constructs which make unit tests run longer than is really required.

- A common mistake is to test only the current date, which means the bug will be discovered exactly on the day the code fails in production. In general you need to make sure all test cases are covered.

11.5.3. Conclusions

Of the many approaches to ensuring the quality of your test code, code reviews are to be recommended the most strongly. They help to find bugs, help your team to converge with respect to how they all go about coding, and serve to disseminate knowledge amongst team members about parts of the software being developed. Moreover, by examining the test code, a lot can be discovered about production code. Frankly, what more could one ask for? The only downside is that to perform a thorough examination of test code, a lot of time is required.

I strongly recommend making test code reviews a part of your team's working routine. Code reviews should belong to your Definition of Done, and they should embrace test code in the same manner that they embrace production code.

11.6. Refactor Your Tests

> God grant me serenity to accept the code I cannot change, courage to change
> the code I can, and wisdom to know the difference.
>
> — Erik Naggum

Now that we know in what ways we can measure test quality, it is time to actually fix
the deficiencies uncovered by code coverage (see Section 11.3), mutation testing (see
Section 11.4) and code reviews (see Section 11.5). In this section we discuss the process
of **refactoring**, which is a common way of altering code. We have already discussed
a refactoring in Chapter 4, *Test Driven Development*, as one of the phases of the TDD
rhythm. In this section we shall discuss the refactorings that are common when working
with tests. Some of them are identical to the ones we perform on production code, but some
are specific to test code.

Numerous examples of making improvements to test code by introducing changes of
various sorts have been given already in other parts of this book – or, indeed, are easily
deducible from what has been discussed earlier. For example, we already know about
the advantages of using `assertEquals()` over `assertTrue()` for comparing objects, and
we know what the advantages of matchers are (see Section 6.5): both can be the source
of multiple refactorings, which should be used to improve the readability of assertions.
Similarly, making use of data providers (instead of `for` loops), or having specialized
`setUp()` methods, can also serve as a refactoring hints. This section supplements what has
already been discussed with new examples and approaches that have yet to be examined.

Before we see some code, let us think about the reasons for test code refactorings. The
first and most significant one is that the **test code is very important** and should be
cleaned so that it is easy to understand and maintain. Refactoring helps you achieve this.
By introducing various, sometimes minor, changes to test code, you can make your tests
convey better exactly what you are trying to test. If a well-written test fails, it is also easier
to find out why.

There is also a question about **how** to refactor test code. The situation is different from that
with production code, because we do not have tests for our tests. However, we can deal
with this issue by following these simple pieces of advice:

• You should perform refactorings in small steps, and rerun tests often along the way.

- Additional tools - code coverage and mutation testing - may help to find out if your safety net of tests is not getting loosened up.

Some people say that before starting to refactor tests, you should first change the SUT's implementation, so the test fails[21]. After refactoring tests and rerunning them, you should still see them failing - which is a sign that the assertions are still working. Now, when you revert the changes in production code, the tests should pass again. I have to admit, I have never used the last technique during any serious refactoring. Moving in small steps worked well enough for me.

Another thing we should discuss is **when** to refactor a particular test. An obvious moment for this is the refactoring phase of the TDD rhythm, but this is not the only one. In fact, I would encourage you to do it every time you do not feel comfortable when browsing the test code. It does not matter if you have written that code yourself or not. Remember the Boy Scout Rule (*"Leave the campground cleaner than you found it!"*) and dare to make the small changes which, added together, still make a big difference!

Before we see some examples, let me inform you that all of them involve real code. Some names of methods and classes have been changed to "protect the innocent". :)

The examples are only big enough to demonstrate what is to be done, and how the code changes after refactoring. Each of the refactorings shown addresses some real issues within the test code. Some of them might not seem very dangerous when looking at ten lines of test code examples, but their importance will grow along with the size of your test codebase. Likewise, the benefits of refactorings are much more clearly visible when they are introduced for real-sized test classes. Please bear this in mind when contemplating the examples in this section.

11.6.1. Use Meaningful Names - Everywhere

We have already discussed the importance of good naming. We have discussed various patterns for test class names and test method names, and pondered over the naming schema for test doubles (see Section 9.3). Throughout the book I have been encouraging you to rename things if you do not feel comfortable with the existing names. Good, meaningful names are invaluable!

---

[21]Please note that this approach is exactly the opposite of what you do when refactoring production code, which should be performed **only if all tests are green**.

This section presents another facet of the same issue. It shows how the simple refactoring of renaming variables can make it easier to understand the logic of test code.

Imagine a test of a class from a security module, which is supposed to allow or deny access to users based on their permissions. First the test registered users (identified by string id) and assigned them some permissions. Then it verified that users had only those permissions that had been assigned to them. Listing 11.6 shows a small part of this test.

Listing 11.6. User_1, user_2, user_3 - who are you?

```
@DataProvider
public static Object[][] userHasPermissions() {
    return new Object[][]{
        {"user_1", Permission.READ},
        {"user_1", Permission.WRITE},
        {"user_1", Permission.REMOVE},
        {"user_2", Permission.WRITE},
        {"user_2", Permission.READ},
        {"user_3", Permission.READ}
    };
}

@Test(dataProvider = "userHasPermissions")
public void shouldReturnTrueIfUserHasPermission(
        String username, Permission permission) {
    assertTrue(sut.hasPermission(username, permission));
}
```

The problem here is that this test is not obvious. For someone who looks at the test for the first time, it is not obvious whether user_2 should or should not have been granted the READ permission. Who the heck is user_2? Well, this must be checked by analyzing the data of previously registered uscrs (probably in a setUp() method somewhere).

A simple change can achieve wonders. Look at the updated version shown in Listing 11.7.

Listing 11.7. Admin, logged on user, guest - I know who you are!

```
@DataProvider
public static Object[][] usersPermissions() {
    return new Object[][]{
        {ADMIN, Permission.READ},
        {ADMIN, Permission.WRITE},
        {ADMIN, Permission.REMOVE},
        {LOGGED, Permission.WRITE},
        {LOGGED, Permission.READ},
        {GUEST, Permission.READ}
    };
}

@Test(dataProvider = "usersPermissions")
public void shouldReturnTrueIfUserHasPermission(
        String username, Permission permission) {
    assertTrue(sut.hasPermission(username, permission));
}
```

Now this is clear! Admin should have all possible permissions. A "normal" logged on user should be able to read and write, but not to remove things. A guest user can normally only see what others have uploaded, but cannot change the content himself or herself. There is no need to consult any documentation: **the code speaks for itself**.

11.6.2. Make It Understandable at a Glance

The readability of tests can be improved in lots of ways. Take a look at the following snippet of test code, which creates an object of the MockServer class:

Listing 11.8. Not easy to understand what type of server is created

```
server = new MockServer(responseMap, true,
                new URL(SERVER_ROOT).getPort(), false);
```

What properties does a server variable have? What kind of server is created? If you do not remember the API of MockServer, then you need to ask your IDE for help, so it explains the meaning of true and false flags being passed to the MockServer constructor. Would it be possible to change this code so it is easier to understand? Yes, by introducing some values whose names tell a story:

Listing 11.9. Self-explanatory values passed to the MockServer constructor

```
private static final boolean NO_SSL = false;
private static final boolean RESPONSE_IS_A_FILE = true;

server = new MockServer(responseMap, RESPONSE_IS_A_FILE,
                    new URL(SERVER_ROOT).getPort(), NO_SSL);
```

Now this makes more sense - this server responds with a file, and does not use SSL.

Another way in which this code could be made more readable is by using the Test Data Builder pattern (see Section 9.8.2).

11.6.3. Make Irrelevant Data Clearly Visible

> If I can change a value without changing the result of the behavior I want
> to check, then I call that **irrelevant data** for this test.
>
> — J. B. Raisenberg

A very frequently performed refactoring consists of changing variable names, and also their values, so that both of these properly reflect their purpose. This is something we have already done in some places when discussing other unit testing issues, but now it is time to take a closer look at this.

This section opens with a quote from J. B. Rainsberger – one that defines a heuristic for recognizing a certain type of (unimportant) test value which should be distinguished clearly from important ones. The following snippet of code illustrates this:

Listing 11.10. Not clear what is important

```
@Test
public void kidsNotAllowed() {
    Person kid = new Person("Johnny", "Mnemonic");

    kid.setAge(12);

    assertFalse(kid.isAdult(), kid + " is a kid!");
}
```

There is nothing wrong with this test method, except that it is not clear whether firstname and lastname are of any importance to the logic being tested. This can be fixed by giving them values which make them convey the message explicitly: *"we are not important, you should not care about us"*. The code below illustrates how this can be achieved:

Listing 11.11. Irrelevant data clearly visible

```
@Test
public void kidsNotAllowed() {
    Person kid = new Person("ANY_NAME", "ANY_SURNAME");

    kid.setAge(12);

    assertFalse(kid.isAdult(), kid + " is a kid!");
}
```

 I usually use an ANY_ prefix, and capital letters only - but this is just one possible instance of how one might do this. Find something which looks good for you.

Apart from reading the test code more easily, another advantage is that if the test fails, the error message will also clearly show what is important:

Listing 11.12. Error message shows what is irrelevant

```
java.lang.AssertionError:
    Person{firstname='ANY_NAME', lastname='ANY_SURNAME', age=12} is a kid!
```

In the event of a value like this being used repeatedly in multiple test methods, I would suggest extracting it as a constant (as you should always do), as well as naming it appropriately:

Listing 11.13. Irrelevant data expressed by both variable names and values

```
private static final String ANY_NAME = "ANY_NAME";
private static final String ANY_SURNAME = "ANY_SURNAME";

@Test
public void kidsNotAllowed() {
    Person kid = new Person(ANY_NAME, ANY_SURNAME);

    kid.setAge(12);

    assertFalse(kid.isAdult(), kid + " is a kid!");
}
```

This renaming of constants is especially important for values other than `String`, so you can have variables like: `ANY_VALID_POST_CODE`, `ANY_NUMBER`, `ANY_DATE`, etc.

In fact, there is no need to wait for the refactoring phase to make irrelevant data clearly visible. When writing a test you should be clear in your mind about which data is important for the scenario you are covering with that test. This is probably the best time to introduce names of variables and values along the lines discussed in this section.

11.6.4. Do not Test Many Things at Once

The tests we have written so far have been pretty focused: they have verified only one thing. However, it often happens that this is not the case. An example of a test which verifies more than a decent test should is presented below.

Listing 11.14. Testing two scenarios at once

```
public class PhoneSearchTest {

    @DataProvider
    public Object[][] getData() {
        return new Object[][] {
                { "48", true }, { "+48", true }, { "++48", true },
                { "+48503", true }, { "+4", false }, { "++4", false },
                { "", false }, { null, false }, { "  ", false }
        };
    }

    @Test(dataProvider = "getData")
    public void testQueryVerification(String prefix, boolean expected) {
        PhoneSearch ps = new PhoneSearch(prefix);

        assertEquals(ps.isValid(), expected);
    }
}
```

The problems with this test are the following:

- When it fails, it will not be instantly clear which feature is not working. Is the PhoneSearch class able to recognize valid prefixes? Is it able to reject invalid prefixes? Which one of these two works, and which does not?

- The name of the test method (testQueryVerification()) is too generic. What exactly is being tested? Likewise, the name of the data provider (getData()) does not reveal its intent clearly enough.

- The test is more complicated than it should be: it uses a boolean flag parameter to decide whether the assertion should pass or fail. This amounts to introducing a form of logic into the test code - something which, as we discussed in Section 10.2, is very bad indeed! That design decision forces us to make use of the assertEquals() assertion method, which is also the most generic one of all.

You can see the refactored version of this test in the next two listings:

Listing 11.15. Refactored test - testing valid prefixes

```
@DataProvider
public Object[][] validPrefixes() {
    return new Object[][] {
            { "48" }, { "48123" },
            { "+48" }, { "++48" }, { "+48503" }};
    }


@Test(dataProvider = "validPrefixes")
public void shouldRecognizeValidPrefixes(String validPrefix) {
    PhoneSearch ps = new PhoneSearch(validPrefix);

    assertTrue(ps.isValid());
}
```

Listing 11.16. Refactored test - testing invalid prefixes

```
@DataProvider
public Object[][] invalidPrefixes() {
    return new Object[][] {
            { "+4" }, { "++4" },
            { "" }, { null }, { "  " } };
}


@Test(dataProvider = "invalidPrefixes")
public void shouldRejectInvalidPrefixes(String invalidPrefix) {
    PhoneSearch ps = new PhoneSearch(invalidPrefix);

    assertFalse(ps.isValid());
}
```

This version of the test differs in the following respects:

- There are two test methods now - one verifies whether the SUT accepts valid prefixes, the other whether the SUT rejects invalid prefixes.

- The `boolean` flag has been removed.

- `assertEquals()` has been replaced with more intention-revealing assertions - `assertTrue()` and `assertFalse()`.

- Each test method has its own data provider.

- The names of all methods, including data providers, have been updated so they are more intention-revealing.

Even if the test has grown in length, it seems to be of higher quality now. When looking at the test code it is easier to deduce *"what are the prefixes that* `PhoneSearch` *accepts?"*, so the documentation aspect has also been improved. Likewise, if this test fails, you will know which part of the SUT's code needs to be fixed.

11.6.5. Change Order of Methods

In order to improve the readability of tests, I often rearange the order of methods so they are consistent across many tests. This is a simple refactoring, which introduces no risk of breaking anything. The gain is that it is much easier to browse test code, because you always know where to expect certain things. In my example, all test classes have the following structure:

- private fields,

- data providers,

- set-up methods,

- test methods,

- private methods.

I rarely deviate from this pattern. Only occasionally do I move a data provider method next to the test method which uses it (but especially if only one test method uses this data provider).

You can usually impose the structure you want while writing the tests. There is no need to wait for the refactoring phase to do this.

11.6.6. Do not Go Too Far

> The goal of refactoring unit tests is slightly different from refactoring mainline code. For the latter, your goal is to modularize the codebase and eliminate tightly coupled relationships. For unit tests, those goals are secondary to creating simple, human-readable tests.
>
> — Keith D Gregory

You might have noticed that so far we have not discussed some very popular refactorings that we use quite often when working with production code. For example, we have not even mentioned **Extract Method**[22] refactoring, which seems to be the most popular (and probably the most powerful) of all. There is a good reason for this, which we shall now discuss.

In general, code redundancy is a bad thing. In the course of the book so far, we have on several occasions discussed the importance of the DRY principle (and not without good reason). However, things are not so black-and-white when it comes to test code. As was discussed previously, test code should be as simple as possible. It should be readable, and free of any logic, so it does not contain any bugs, and can serve as a living documentation of the production code. Because of these expectations, some refactorings well-suited to production code ought to be considered less useful for test code.

Sometimes it is very easy (and thus tempting!) to make the test code more concise by grouping things within a `private` utility helper method. If there are one or two methods like this in a test class, it is not so bad. However, I have witnessed a lot of really unreadable test code, which required me to jump through many tangled `private` methods to understand any one single test method. This is unacceptable. What is still more horrific is the use of template methods and abstract test classes, which, in conjunction with such utility methods, can make test classes completely unreadable.

In production code, you can almost always bet on DRY and win. In the case of test code, you need to strike a balance between the DRY principle and the expressiveness of tests.

I have to admit that many people see it differently. I have read many blog posts which promote excessive use of `private` helper methods, and test class hierarchies. My point of view is different, and I would encourage you to follow the advice given above. However, as usual, any real knowledge will only come with experience, so do not be afraid to experiment a little bit with different approaches and find out what works for you.

11.7. Conclusions

In this chapter we have worked hard to determine precisely **how to measure and improve test quality**. As developers, we love tools which can do something for us, and that is why we started out with a discussion of various tools - static code analyzers (see Section 11.2),

---

[22]See http://martinfowler.com/refactoring/catalog/extractMethod.html

code coverage (see Section 11.3) and mutation testing (see Section 11.4). We discovered what, exactly, they are good at when it comes to helping us achieve high-quality tests, but also realized how very inadequate they are.

Then we turned towards code reviews (see Section 11.5), and found these to be a great way of uncovering the weak spots in our test code. Alas, code reviews take time, and what is more, not all developers perform them well enough. Some developers lack knowledge about what to look for, some do not treat test code with enough respect to bother analyzing it, and some are not allowed to "waste" their precious time on such unproductive activities (no comment...). Finally, we discussed various refactorings (see Section 11.6) that could be implemented so that our tests will be more readable and more easily maintained.

Several times in this chapter I have sought to highlight the various issues relating to achieving high-quality tests. The picture I have tried to create is one in which having really good tests is definitely possible, but is also something that calls for full commitment on your part. The tools can assist you with this task, but they play only a secondary role.

In conclusion, here is a list of "action points" which should help you achieve the goal of high-quality tests:

- Treat test quality as the number-one issue from the very outset.

- Take the refactoring phase of TDD very seriously.

- Test code should undergo a code review in the same way that production code does. You need someone other than yourself to take a critical look at your tests.

- *"Do not live with broken windows"*[23] - bad things tend to get copied, and soon you will have much more to clean than you can handle. Never delay fixing them.

- Think hard about the test cases required (see Section 6.1) and follow the TDD approach in order to cover all important functionalities with tests. This is much more important than trying to satisfy requirements with respect to the measuring of code coverage!

- Use code coverage to uncover untested areas.

- Adhere to the various forms of programming best practice - e.g. the SRP principle and short focused methods. These apply to test code as well.

---

[23]See http://www.artima.com/intv/fixitP.html for a good explanation of this statement.

- Be consistent about the naming and structure of your tests.

11.8. Exercises

"Quality is free" they say[24], but one has to work really hard to achieve it. The single exercise in this section is intended to help you appreciate this simple fact.

11.8.1. Clean this Mess

The listing below presents a naive implementation of the `Fridge` class. It allows one to put food into the fridge, take it out, and inspect it to see whether something is in there.

Listing 11.17. Fridge implementation

```
public class Fridge {

    private Collection<String> food = new HashSet<String>();

    public boolean put(String item) {
        return food.add(item);
    }

    public boolean contains(String item) {
        return food.contains(item);
    }

    public void take(String item) throws NoSuchItemException {
        boolean result = food.remove(item);
        if (!result) {
            throw new NoSuchItemException(item + " not found in the fridge");
        }
    }
}
```

The next two listings show test code of the `Fridge` class, which - after everything we have explored up to now, and taking a mere glance at the code - we can say is a complete mess! It works, which means it tests some features of the SUT, but it could have been much better written. I hope to never see anything like this again in the rest of my life. Anyway, your task for now is to **clean this mess**! Use the knowledge of high-quality testing you have gained from this chapter, but also refer to the examples given previously, in order to rewrite this test! For example, you should probably take care of:

---

[24]See http://www.wppl.org/wphistory/PhilipCrosby/QualityIsFreeIfYouUnderstandIt.pdf

- the proper naming of test classes, methods and variables,

- the use of parametrized tests,

- duplicated code,

- and many more issues that are hidden there.

Make sure you do not loose any test case by redesigning this test class!

The two test methods of the FoodTesting class are shown below:

Listing 11.18. testFridge() method

```
public void testFridge() {
    Fridge fridge = new Fridge();

    fridge.put("cheese");
    assertEquals(fridge.contains("cheese"), true);
    assertEquals(fridge.put("cheese"), false);
    assertEquals(fridge.contains("cheese"), true);

    assertEquals(fridge.contains("ham"), false);

    fridge.put("ham");
    assertEquals(fridge.contains("cheese"), true);
    assertEquals(fridge.contains("ham"), true);

    try {
        fridge.take("sausage");
        fail("There was no sausage in the fridge!");
    }
    catch(NoSuchItemException e) {
        // ok
    }
}
```

Listing 11.19. testPutTake() method

```
public void testPutTake() {
    Fridge fridge = new Fridge();
    List<String> food = new ArrayList<String>();
    food.add("yogurt");
    food.add("milk");
    food.add("eggs");
    for (String item : food) {
        fridge.put(item);
        assertEquals(fridge.contains(item), true);
        fridge.take(item);
        assertEquals(fridge.contains(item), false);
    }

    for (String item : food) {
        try {
            fridge.take(item);
            fail("there was no " + item + " in the fridge");
        }
        catch(NoSuchItemException e) {
            assertEquals(e.getMessage().contains(item), true);
        }
    }
}
```

Appendix A. Automated Tests

> […] if it's common enough to be worth automating, I automate it. If not, I just slog through it.
>
> — Bobby Tables *stackexchange.com (2010)*

For many years automated tests have been recognized as a great way to make your software robust and bug-free. The idea is so pervasive that there are many tools (build tools, IDEs), and even languages, that facilitate the process of executing such tests. Nevertheless, I have seen enough under-tested projects to be sure that the issue has yet to be taken on board as widely as it should be.

A.1. Wasting Your Time by not Writing Tests

Even if you don't write tests, you surely perform some other operations to verify that your code works properly. In order to make sure that the code does what you expect it to do, and to find bugs, you can:

- have debugging sessions (with the help of your great IDE),

- add lots of log messages so you can later browse log files,

- click through the user interface of your application,

- preform frequent code reviews.

All of the above techniques have their legitimate uses. Visual inspection is useful. A debugger and logs can sometimes save your life. Clicking through GUI will help you get to know how it feels to be your user. Code reviews will allow you to find various weaknesses in your code. But if these techniques are the only ways in which you verify the proper functioning of your code, then **you are doing it wrongly**.

The main problem is that all these actions are very time-consuming. Even if your experience allows you to use a debugger very effectively, or you have strong Linux shell skills, making finding stuff in amongst tons of logs a trivial matter, it still takes some time.

Clicking GUI cannot really be accelerated – you must wait for the application to fetch the data, for the browser to render it, and for your brain to locate the right place to click. A decent code review cannot be done in just a couple of minutes. Moreover, time required for testing multiplies, if you are to test your application against many software versions or environments (e.g. multiple web browsers, databases or operating systems).

The time factor is crucial: there is, quite simply, no time to repeat the process. You will have to check once that it works and voila! – finished. After you go back to this code (to add/update functionality) you will want to skip the already tested part, because it simply hurts too much to even think of browsing the logs all over again!

 Remember, your time and skills are too precious to be wasted on simple, repeatable tasks that can be done more effectively by machines. What you should concentrate on is teaching the machines to do those tasks!

The second issue is that you are trusting your senses, your judgment and your honesty here. This brings with it a few problems:

- you may overlook something (e.g. omit a line of log files, forget to check everything that should be checked, etc.),

- you may misconstrue or forget criteria of verification, accepting failed tests as passed,

- you may fall victim to the *"it is not a bug, it is a feature"* fallacy when testing, and persuade yourself that it really works fine,

- you may deceive yourself into thinking it works, even if it doesn't.

Yes, I know, you do not make mistakes, so you cannot possibly miss a single log line, and of course you are 100% honest with yourself… Well, but if you do not ever make mistakes, how come the bug you are looking for happened in the first place? And about honesty: I can only speak for myself, but it does happen, sometimes, that I only see what I wanted to see, and ignore anything that speaks against how I would wish things to be. Has it really never happened to you? No? Are you sure?

What makes it even more painful is that clicking GUI again and again, or browsing log files for the n-th time, is so boring! Your mind will scream *"get me out of here, I want to do some coding!"*, and it will likely tell you *"everything works fine"*, just so you move on to some more interesting tasks.

In short, verification methods that are not automated suffer from the following disadvantages:

- they are time-consuming and, as such, the first things to be abandoned when a deadline nears,

- verification criteria might not be clear, and the outcome of the verification process can be distorted by human error,

- they are boring, so people do them without due care and attention, or avoid doing them at all,

- they can be hard to repeat exactly (e.g. it is easy to omit some steps during the configuration or execution phases of the test),

- it may be hard to deduce from log files where the source of a bug is, and sometimes lengthy investigation is required to find it,

- they are not included in the build process, and are only run long after the new features or changes were actually introduced into the software, making the feedback they give less valuable (i.e. it costs much more to repair damaged parts not discovered right after they have been damaged – see Figure 1.5),

- people might easily disdain what they see (e.g. *"this exception has nothing to do with the functionality being tested; it was always there, and it is harmless"*), it is quite easy to just sweep issues under the rug (…no one else has noticed this exception in the logs, have they?).

In my experience, the majority of errors occur when code gets changed, not when it is written for the first time. When you implement a new functionality the list of requirements is usually clear. You simply implement them one by one, making sure that everything works fine. This is simple. More problems emerge when you are asked to introduce some changes. Ooops, the original list of requirements is long gone, the people who wrote the original code are not around anymore, and your manager assumes that *"adding this small piece of functionality shouldn't take long, should it?"* And then, if you don't have a safety net of tests, you are in trouble. While adding or changing new functionality you are likely to break something that used to work fine. Such mistakes result in so-called **regression bugs**. When tests are automated it makes it harder for them to creep in.

A.1.1. And what about Human Testers?

Are human testers still required? Is there a place for them in the development cycle? The short answer to this question is: "it depends". It depends on the type of application you are working on – on the technology and the testability of your software.

It is outside the scope of this book to discuss this (fascinating) topic. However, since I am putting a lot of effort into trying to persuade you to automate your tests (which will, in effect, diminish the role and responsibility of human testers), I have to tackle this subject, if only very briefly.

Looking at the current tendencies in the field of development, I see a major change happening in the way development teams are being organized, especially with respect to the role of testers. A new role – of "developer in tests" – has been created, and its name stresses the importance of developers' tests as a vital part of every development. Code and tests are being developed in parallel, and every piece of code committed to the SCM[1] is tested (on different levels – from unit tests to end-to-end tests). Automation, and continuous integration, is our daily bread right now. What is more, some teams have achieved an even higher level of confidence in their automated tests, which allows them to continuously deploy automatically tested software right up to the production stage.

There is still a place for human testers. However, the situation is changing before our very own eyes, and the role and place of testers is being redefined. It is expected that you – a developer, I suppose – will also have some testing skills.

A.1.2. One More Benefit: A Documentation that is Always Up-To-Date

> [...] ordinary narrative documentation is more susceptible to drifting from the implementation of the program and will thus become outdated (e.g., design changes, feature creep, relaxed practices in keeping documents up-to-date).
>
> — Wikipedia on Unit Testing

---

[1]SCM, Source Code Management, relates to all kind of software tools which allows one to track file versions. Commonly used tools in software development are Subversion, CVS or Git. For more information see http://en.wikipedia.org/wiki/Source_Code_Management.

Documentation lies. It is rarely up-to-date, and reading it often leaves many questions unanswered. It makes no difference whether it is a separate document or Javadocs comments. In general, writing useful documentation and maintaining it throughout the lifetime of a project is a very hard task. A task that we repeatedly fail to perform successfully.

I consider tests to be part of documentation. Not the whole of the documentation, but a vital part of it. Tests will not tell you about the business purpose of an element, neither will they reveal why some code fragment looks the way it does. They have to be accompanied by other documentation that fills in these gaps. But they will leave no room for doubt about how your code should be used, and what happens when you execute method x with parameters a and b. And if you run them frequently, then you are guaranteed that the code really behaves in the way they describe. This is very different from "traditional documentation". The documentation written in the form of tests is always up-to-date.

A.2. When and Where Should Tests Run?

Running tests is not about making anyone happy: not you, not your manager, not even some book authors. It is all about getting **rapid feedback about your work**. In particular, it tells you whether your code adheres to the specified requirements (which you have written in the form of tests).

Because rapid feedback is so valuable, an obvious answer to the "when" question is: "as often as possible". This advice can be implemented right away for unit tests, which are ultra-fast by their very nature. But for other types of test you should adjust their execution frequency so they do not slow development down. If your integration tests run for 10 minutes, then it would probably be better if they were not run every time a few new lines of code were added. But why not, say, run them thrice a day – e.g. when you go for dinner, or for coffee? Well, that probably makes sense.

The answer to the "where" question is more complicated, because two factors are in play. The most important thing is to make sure that your application works on the production environment. It is really nice to know that it works on your local box, but customers rarely care about this. What they need, and what you should deliver, is an application that runs on the production environment. So ideally your end-to-end tests should be run right there.

It also means that your unit tests and integration tests should be run outside developers' boxes to avoid the "it worked on my machine" syndrome. The first thing you can do in connection with this is set up a continuous integration server (CI).

All in all, then, to shorten the feedback time you should run every possible test on the developer's machine, but in order to know the quality of your application from the customer's point of view you should run them on a production-like environment[2].

The solution is rather obvious. Your tests will be run more than once, so you can:

- find bugs as soon as possible,

- eliminate the threat of having code that only works on the developer's box.

You will also need to maintain more than one test execution environment.

If I were to give some pieces of general advice, they would be the following:

- Keep your unit tests separated from other types of test,

- Run unit tests frequently (i.e. before every commit) on developers' machines,

- Your CI server should run unit tests on every commit, or by frequent polling for SCM changes (e.g. every minute),

- Run integration and/or end-to-end tests on developers' machines after a bigger chunk of functionality is finished (or run them at least once a day if this is not the case),

- Integration tests should be run regularly on the CI server – at least once a day (i.e. nightly),

- End-to-end tests should be run regularly, e.g. once a day, and every time a bigger chunk of functionality is finished[3].

---

[2]By 'production-like environment' I mean an environment that is as close as possible in every respect to a real production environment. Ideally this should be the production environment itself, but that is rarely available for testing.
[3]End-to-end tests vary a great deal, depending on the application you are writing, so it is hard to generalize about them.

Developers' machines are the first line of defense. The CI is a testing workhorse. The production environment is where the value of your application is proved (or debunked). Utilize all of them for testing, to make sure your software works as required

If you are attracted by the idea of running tests all the time, then take a look at Infinitest[4] and JUnitMax[5] Eclipse plugins. Both bring "continuous integration to your IDE" by running tests repeatedly in the background as you code.

---

[4]http://improvingworks.com/products/infinitest
[5]http://junitmax.com/

Appendix B. Running Unit Tests

There are many ways to run tests written with TestNG, as the majority of tools support it out-of-the-box. This section describes how to run TestNG tests using the most popular IDEs and build tools: Eclipse, IntelliJ IDEA, Gradle and Maven.

 The tools presented in this section are capable of much more than simply executing tests. Please consult their documentation to find out more.

As far as Gradle and Maven are concerned, I will assume that your project has a layout compatible with what was discussed in Section 3.1. The main requirement is that your production code resides in `src/main/java` and test classes in `src/test/java`. Both Gradle and Maven treat this layout as the default. If you use a different directory structure then you will need to inform your build tool about it. Please refer to the appropriate documentation about how to do it.

One could ask why it is that we need to bother with build tools, if our powerful IDEs are capable of running tests. The thing is, the tests we write will be executed on the machines of other developers (who may be using different IDEs), and even on the IDE-free environment of a CI server. Having a build script capable of running tests is the first step in helping to overcome the *"it works on my machine"* syndrome.

 This appendix concentrates on running tests on your local machine. However, bear in mind that every team should have a separate machine (a **continuous integration server**) dedicated to the building (compiling, testing, packaging, etc.) of the code it is developing. Continuous integration is well beyond the scope of this book, but there is plenty of information available on the Internet if you need it.

B.1. Running Tests with Eclipse

To run TestNG tests with Eclipse, you will need to install the TestNG Eclipsc plugin. It is currently maintained by Cédric Beust, author of TestNG, and is updated frequently. The plugin is stable, but some minor issues have arisen with new versions of Eclipse and/or TestNG. They get solved very quickly by Cédric (provided that users are kind enough to furnish the necessary detail in their descriptions of such problems on the mailing list).

The installation process is no different from any other Eclipse plugin. A detailed description is available at the TestNG website. It describes both the installation procedure and how to use it - including creating TestNG test classes, running tests, viewing results and applying Quick Fixes relating to TestNG tests.

After installing the TestNG Eclipse plugin, your IDE should recognize TestNG test classes and facilitate running them.

If you prefer to use a mouse, then right-click on the selected test class (e.g. `MoneyTest`) and choose Run As / TestNG Test. To run more tests right-click on, for example, `src/test/java` directory (or any package inside it which includes some tests), in project tree view, and choose the same option as previously: Run As / TestNG Test. Likewise, to run a single test method, right-click it and choose Run As / TestNG Test.

Figure B.1. Running a single test with Eclipse

Figure B.2. Running multiple tests with Eclipse

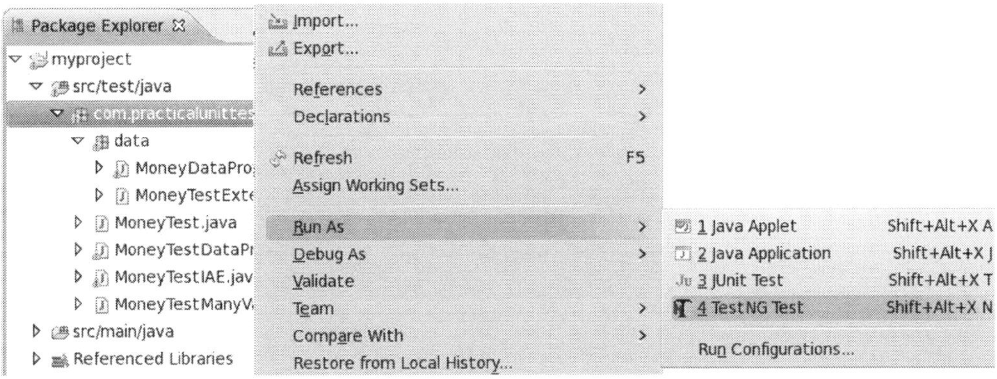

If you prefer typing, then first make sure you have the correct test class in focus (i.e. that it is open in the editor and the cursor is there, or that it is highlighted in Package Explorer). To run all tests from this selected class, place the cursor somewhere outside any test method and press **SHIFT+ALT+X** followed by **N**. If you want to run a particular test method, place the cursor on this method, and use the same combination: **SHIFT+ALT+X** followed by **N**.

In order to rerun the same test (or tests), press **F11**.

B.1.1. Debugging Tests with Eclipse

Just like with running tests, you can run a debug session in more than just one way:

- by right-clicking on a test class, tests package or test method, and selecting the Debug As / TestNG Test option,

- or by typing **SHIFT+ALT+D** followed by **N**.

In both cases a Debug perspective will open. To rerun the same debugging session press **F11**.

B.2. Running Tests with IntelliJ IDEA

IntelliJ IDEA comes bundled with a TestNG-J plugin, which makes it recognize TestNG tests. There are many ways to execute TestNG tests while working with this IDE.

If you prefer using the mouse, then right-click on the selected test class (e.g. `MoneyTest`) and choose Run "MoneyTest". To run more tests, right-click on, for example, `src/test/java` directory (or any package inside it which includes some tests), in project tree view, and choose the appropriate Run ... option. Likewise, to run a single test method, right-click it and choose Run "MoneyTest".

Figure B.3. Running a single test with IntelliJ IDEA

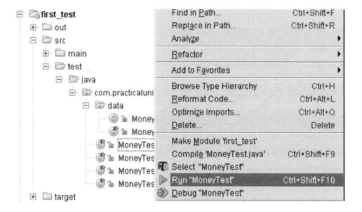

Figure B.4. Running multiple tests with IntelliJ IDEA

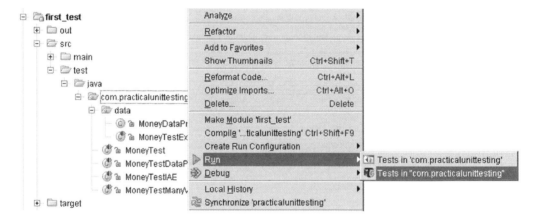

If you prefer typing, then first ensure that you have got the right test class in focus (that it is open in the editor and the cursor is there). To run all tests from this selected class, place the cursor somewhere outside any test method and press **CTRL+SHIFT+F10**. If you want to run a particular test method, then place the cursor on this method, and use the same combination: **CTRL+SHIFT+F10**.

In order to rerun the same test (or tests) press **SHIFT + F10**.

B.2.1. Debugging Tests with IntelliJ IDEA

As with running tests, you can run a debug session in more than just one way:

- by right-clicking on a test class, tests package or test method and selecting the Debug ... option,

- or by using the **ALT+SHIFT+F9** keys.

To rerun the same debugging session press **SHIFT+F10**.

B.3. Running Tests with Gradle

In this section we will discuss running TestNG tests with Gradle. Gradle is a very powerful and complex build tool. Please refer to its documentation to learn about its various features.

To run TestNG tests with Gradle, you must inform it that it is supposed to look for TestNG tests and provide TestNG dependency for the `testCompile` scope (so the TestNG JAR is available in the classpath, to execute tests). The Listing B.1 listing shows a minimal build file - called `build.gradle` - that can be used to execute tests. It should be placed in the root of your application.

Listing B.1. Basic Gradle build script

```
apply plugin: 'java' ❶

repositories {
    mavenCentral() ❷
}

dependencies {
    testCompile 'org.testng:testng:6.4' ❸
}

test {
    useTestNG() ❹
}
```

❶   Tells Gradle to prepare for the compilation of Java classes.

❷   Defines the repository used to download dependencies (in this case it is the central repository of Maven, which contains TestNG JAR files).

❸   Defines libraries used for the compilation (and execution) of tests (in this case `testng-6.4.jar`).

❹   Instructs Gradle to look for TestNG test classes to run tests.

As you can see, Gradle uses a convention-over-configuration approach, so if you stick to the default values (by keeping code in `src/main/java` and tests in `src/test/java`, as we have done), then you will not need to specify them. That way build scripts are very concise.

To run the tests you will have to execute `gradle test` from the command line. You will see something similar to the following output:

Listing B.2. Output of "gradle test" command

```
>gradle test
:first_test:compileJava
:first_test:processResources
:first_test:classes
:first_test:compileTestJava
:first_test:processTestResources
:first_test:testClasses
:first_test:test

BUILD SUCCESSFUL
```

The last printed line assures us that all tests have passed successfully. You can make Gradle print much more information - also regarding executed tests - by using `-i` switch, or by writing your own listener (see Section 8.3.2).

In the event of failed tests, Gradle will print error messages. Please refer to Section 8.2 for more information on the reports which could be used to investigate the failed tests.

The `gradle test` command will execute all tests in your project - which, by the way, is advisable. To run a single test use the `gradle -Dtest.single=MoneyTest` test syntax.

B.3.1. Using TestNG Listeners and Reporters with Gradle

You can instruct TestNG to use some listeners and/or reporters by passing the fully qualified name of their classes within the `test` configuration part of the build script:

Listing B.3. Using a custom TestNG listener and reporter with Gradle

```
test {
    useTestNG()
    options {
        listeners << 'com.practicalunittesting.DotTestListener',  ❶
        listeners << 'fully.qualified.path.to.ExcelReporter'  ❷
    }
}
```

❶❷ Both listeners and reporters are registered identically. (Note the comma after the first line!)

 At the time of writing the book a bug in Gradle prevents it from properly printing some information to the System.out which may influence the work of your custom TestNG listeners. It should be fixed in version 1.0, so it is very probable that it works fine now, when you read these words. Anyway, if you plan to write custom listeners and run them with Gradle, please see http://issues.gradle.org/browse/GRADLE-2058 to learn about the current situation.

B.3.2. Adding JARs to Gradle's Tests Classpath

In the event of your tests requiring some additional libraries, you will need to add them to the testCompile scope together with the relevant TestNG dependency, for example:

Listing B.4. Gradle - adding libraries required by test classes

```
dependencies {
    testCompile 'org.testng:testng:6.4'
    testCompile 'org.hamcrest:hamcrest-all:1.1'
    testCompile 'com.practicalunittesting.listeners:1.0'
}
```

The configuration shown above would result in having TestNG, Hamcrest and some custom listeners available on the test classpath.

B.4. Running Tests with Maven

To use Maven for running your tests you should at least read the documentation for the Maven Surefire Plugin[1], and in particular its section devoted to running TestNG tests with Maven. In addition, read the documentation for the Maven Surefire Report Plugin[2] and the Maven Site Plugin[3]. Both can be used to generate nice HTML test reports. If you plan to use Maven for running more than unit tests you should take a look at the Maven Failsafe Plugin[4]. In any case, make sure you have an understanding of basic concepts of Maven - for example, its lifecycle. If you try using Maven without such knowledge, you will very quickly become frustrated.

This section provides basic information about running tests with Maven. There is much more to know about Maven (which is quite a complex tool, with all sorts of quirks of its own), but what is presented here should be enough to enable you to execute your unit tests with Maven.

As with Gradle, Maven will be happy with the default layout of your project. You need only inform Maven that it should use the TestNG dependency in the scope test (which makes Maven add TestNG JAR to the classpath during test execution).

---

[1]http://maven.apache.org/plugins/maven-surefire-plugin/
[2]http://maven.apache.org/plugins/maven-surefire-report-plugin/
[3]http://maven.apache.org/plugins/maven-site-plugin/
[4]http://maven.apache.org/plugins/maven-failsafe-plugin/

Listing B.5. Basic Maven build script

```xml
<?xml version="1.0" encoding="UTF-8"?>
<project xmlns="http://maven.apache.org/POM/4.0.0"
    xmlns:xsi="http://www.w3.org/2001/XMLSchema-instance"
    xsi:schemaLocation="http://maven.apache.org/POM/4.0.0
        http://maven.apache.org/maven-v4_0_0.xsd">
  <modelVersion>4.0.0</modelVersion>
  <groupId>com.practicalunittesting</groupId>
  <artifactId>first-test</artifactId>
  <packaging>jar</packaging>
  <version>1.0-SNAPSHOT</version>
  <dependencies>
    <dependency>
      <groupId>org.testng</groupId>
      <artifactId>testng</artifactId>
      <version>6.4</version>
      <scope>test</scope>
    </dependency>
  </dependencies>
</project>
```

Now execute `mvn test` from the command line. Maven will automatically recognize TestNG test classes located in `src/test/java` and run them. You will see something similar to the following output (some lines omitted):

Listing B.6. Output of "mvn test" command

```
[INFO] ------------------------------------------------------------------
[INFO] Building first-test 1.0-SNAPSHOT
[INFO] ------------------------------------------------------------------
[INFO]
-------------------------------------------------------
T E S T S
-------------------------------------------------------
Running TestSuite
Tests run: 1, Failures: 0, Errors: 0, Skipped: 0, Time elapsed: 0.295 sec

Results :

Tests run: 1, Failures: 0, Errors: 0, Skipped: 0

[INFO] ------------------------------------------------------------------
[INFO] BUILD SUCCESS
[INFO] ------------------------------------------------------------------
```

The last printed line assures us that all tests have passed successfully.

In the event of failed tests, Maven will print error messages to the console. Test results are kept in the `target/surefire-reports` directory in text, and XML format. If you prefer something more readable, Maven makes it simple to generate an HTML report as well. As was mentioned previously, you could use the Maven Surefire Report Plugin or the Maven Site Plugin to achieve this.

B.4.1. Using TestNG Listeners and Reporters with Maven

As with Gradle, you can write your own listeners and reporters (see Section 8.3) and make Maven use them. You can use the same listeners as we did for Gradle (see Listing 8.7 for an example). The only difference is how you inform Maven that it is to use them. An example of the Maven Surefire Plugin configuration is presented in Listing B.7.

Listing B.7. Using a custom TestNG listener with Maven

```
<plugin>
    <groupId>org.apache.maven.plugins</groupId>
    <artifactId>maven-surefire-plugin</artifactId>
    <version>2.12</version>
    <configuration>
        <properties>
            <property>
                <name>listener</name>
                <value>com.practicalunittesting.DotTestListener</value>
            <property>
            <property>
                <name>reporter</name>
                <value>com.practicalunittesting.ExcelReporter</value>
            </property>
        </properties>
    </configuration>
</plugin>
```

B.4.2. Adding JARs to Maven's Tests Classpath

To add other libraries to the test classpath (so that, for example, you can use Hamcrest in your test code), you will need to specify them in the same way that we specified the TestNG dependency. For example:

Listing B.8. Maven - adding libraries required by tests classes

```
<dependencies>
    <dependency>
        <groupId>org.testng</groupId>
        <artifactId>testng</artifactId>
        <version>6.4</version>
        <scope>test</scope> ❶
    </dependency>
    <dependency>
        <groupId>org.hamcrest</groupId>
        <artifactId>hamcrest-all</artifactId>
        <version>1.1</version>
        <scope>test</scope> ❷
    </dependency>
    <dependency>
        <groupId>com.practicalunittesting</groupId>
        <artifactId>listeners</artifactId>
        <version>1.0</version>
        <scope>test</scope> ❸
    </dependency>
</dependencies>
```

❶❷❸ Make sure you use the `test` scope so Maven adds them to the test classpath.

Appendix C. Test Spy vs. Mock

As we mentioned in Section 5.2, test spies and mocks have a great deal in common. Their purpose is identical: they are there to verify the correctness of calls from the SUT to its DOCs (so-called "indirect outputs"). However, there are some subtle differences between the two, which are definitely worth discussing. As you will soon learn, some of the differences between the two are clear, and some are still being discussed by the community.

 (DISCLAIMER) It is really hard to compare such theoretical entities as the mock and the test spy without comparing their specific implementations - like the ones provided by EasyMock and Mockito. I have put a lot of effort into making sure that this section abstracts out from specific and particular solutions, but I think that it (inevitably) reflects the current state of mocking and test-spying frameworks.

C.1. Different Flow - and Who Asserts?

Let us compare two snippets of test code. The first one, shown in Listing C.1, has been written with a test spy (using the Mockito framework). The second snippet, shown in Listing C.2, has been written with a mock (using the EasyMock framework).

Before looking at both tests, let us remind ourselves that a typical test without test doubles (like the ones discussed in Section 3.9) consists of three parts: : first it **arranges** things (i.e. sets up the SUT and DOCs), then it **acts** (i.e. calls the SUT's methods), and finally it **asserts** (i.e. verifies returned values).

Listing C.1. Sample test spy test

```
// arrange
SomeClass sut = ...; ❶
ClientDAO testSpyClientDAO = mock(ClientDAO.class);
sut.setClientDAO(testSpyClientDAO);

// act
sut.deleteClient(req, resp);

// assert
verify(testSpyClientDAO).deleteClient("1234"); ❷
```

❶   The SUT gets created (it does not matter how).
❷   Assertions are done explicitly by test method.

In the case of the test spy the three phases are clear. However, in Listing C.2 we can see that this is not the case with the mock. The assertion phase happens in two places within the code - when the expectations are set, and when the framework is asked to actually verify whether they have been met.

Listing C.2. Sample mock test

```
// arrange
SomeClass sut = ...; ❶
ClientDAO mockClientDAO = createMock(ClientDAO.class); ❷
sut.setClientDAO(mockClientDAO);

// assert - part I
expect(mockClientDAO.deleteClient("1234")); ❸
replay(mockClientDAO); ❹

// act
sut.deleteClient(req, resp);

// assert - part II
verify(mockClientDAO); ❺
```

❶   The SUT gets created (it does not matter how).
❷   Creation of mock, but this time using the static `createMock()` method of EasyMock.
❸❺   No assertions are done directly by the test method. Instead, some expectations are expressed regarding the mock's behaviour. Real assertions are done within the mock object after the test method has called the `verify()` method.

❹   Informing the mock that the expectation part is over, and that now the real execution begins.

As the Listing C.1 and Listing C.2 show, there is a difference when it comes to the ordering of actions in the tests. Tests based on test spies follow the "arrange, act, assert" pattern. However, tests based on mock objects reverse the order by first stating our expectations, and then exercising the code. This feature of mock-based tests may come across as unintuitive, and is one of the main reasons for switching to a test-spy approach.

C.2. Stop with the First Error

The difference in the order of actions described in the previous section has some impact on the way tests fail. The difference is as follows:

- mock-based tests fail during the execution of methods, as soon as any of them do not match expectations,

- test-spy-based tests fail during the verification phase, after all methods have been executed.

This has some impact on the ability of mocks and test spies to provide a good, descriptive error message. It seems that test spies are able to provide more detailed information in assertion messages than mocks (based on precisely the kind of information about method calls which would never arise, and thus would not be available, in the case of quickly failing mocks). On the other hand, mocks fail immediately where some runtime information is available. If our test spy is not recording this information, it will not be available when it fails.

C.3. Stubbing

Some authors differ in their opinions as to whether test spies also have stubbing capabilities. However, the majority, including Gerard Meszaros, the father of test doubles taxonomy, answer this question in the affirmative. Mockito also provides stubbing capabilities for its test spies.

C.4. Forgiveness

There is a general idea that test spies are more "forgiving" than mocks. This means that test spies let us specify which interactions are to be verified, and turn a blind eye to the rest. In fact, this is one of the notable features of the Mockito test-spying framework. Its author, Szczepan Faber, promotes such an approach as a way of testing only what should be tested at some given point in time, without paying attention to interactions that are beyond the scope of that particular test[1]. The motivation behind such behaviour is to avoid overspecified tests, which are a big problem to maintain (see Chapter 10, *Maintainable Tests*). However, the idea is disputed within the community, and some people would rather vote for stricter verification of the SUT's actions.

Without getting involved in the details of this debate, let us say that in general mock frameworks are stricter than Mockito. However, some of them – e.g. EasyMock - support both styles of testing. By default, its mocks are "strict" (which means they fail tests if any unexpected interaction occurs), but also allow one to use so-called "nice" mocks, which verify only selected interactions - exactly the way the test spies of Mockito do.

To conclude, "forgiveness" is not supported by test spies exclusively, even though they do seem more inclined towards it than mock objects.

 There is some unclarity about how the terms "nice" and "strict" are to be understood when used to characterize mocks. By "strict" mocks, [meszaros2007] has in mind mocks which will fail if the received method calls are in a different order than the expected one. Mocks which are "nice" or "lenient" will accept a different order, and only pay attention to the methods and values of parameters. But based on my observations I would say that most other people follow a different definition of the meaning of the terms "nice" and "strict" when used here - exactly like that given previously in this section.

C.5. Different Threads or Containers

If the SUT is running inside a different "environment" than the test code which invokes it (e.g. some kind of container, or a different thread), then it may happen that this environment will eat up all the exceptions and messages reported by a mock in the runtime. In the case

---

[1]Please refer to http://monkeyisland.pl/2008/07/12/should-i-worry-about-the-unexpected/.

of a test spy, which acts like a callback object, all errors will be reported after the execution has finished, from within the same environment (e.g. thread) which the test code uses. That way no information gets lost.

C.6. Conclusions

Historically, we all used mocks. They were mentioned in the title of the famous "Mock Roles, Not Object" paper ([freeman2004]), which brought mocks to the masses, and for a long time no distinctions between test doubles were made at all - we just called all of them "mocks". Today, things are different, because we have learned from experience that there are, indeed, differences between test doubles. They also exist between mocks and test spies - even though both can be used (almost) interchangeably.

There are some reasons why I would consider it preferable to use test spies rather than mocks. Of these, the two most important are that they allow me to keep to the **arrange/act/assert** pattern, and that they promote the writing of focused tests, which are only interested in selected aspects of the code I intend to test.

Appendix D. Where Should I Go Now?

> So where does the Newborn go from here? The net is vast and infinite.
> — Motoko/2501 *Ghost in the Shell (2005)*

There is so much we have discussed in this book! So much, and still not enough. Every topic we have covered opens on to new subjects still to be discovered. Each thing we have learned steers us towards other things that we do not yet know about. The question *"Where should I go now, after I have learned so much about unit tests?"* does not have just one valid answer. Instead, there are thousands of them, depending on your requirements and likings. Below, you will find some hints concerning what topics to tackle next. The majority of them are strongly focused on developers' tests (I hope you will follow this path!), but some are of a more general nature and aim at making you a better developer in a broader sense.

- It is essential that you build up your knowledge of testing tools.

  - Scan the documentation of TestNG and Mockito, searching for things that this book does not cover (you will find some, for sure). Read the announcements of new versions, so you are up-to-date with the newer features they offer.

- Master the tools you use (IDE, build tools, command line), with regard to writing and executing tests.

- Take some time to learn other testing tools, especially if learning new languages. While it is still possible to use TestNG and Mockito with other JVM languages (e.g. Groovy or Scala), it might be beneficial to learn tools which have been designed using features offered by these languages. After reading this book you should have a very good understanding of unit tests in general, so you will be able to grab any new tool and use it properly.

- Start coding TDD if you have not yet done so. If possible, try to team up with some more advanced peers for pair programming. Also, there are some plugins for IDEs which aim at making it more fun to write tests - see if they help you.

- Mastering TDD and writing higher-level tests should lead you towards BDD ([north2006]). Very good, this is the right direction.

- This book has demonstrated in detail how to write unit tests; however, there is a mountain of things to learn when writing and testing whole applications. Reading [freeman2009] seems like the best possible way to dive into the world of testable software. Also, you should start writing integration and end-to-end tests. Which books you should read, and which tools you should look at, depends very much on the set of technologies you use, so it is hard to recommend anything here.

- If you happen to work a lot with legacy code then grab a copy of [feathers2004].

- Unit tests are really helpful, provided that you have a process for running them automatically. This brings us to the topic of build tools and continuous integration servers. If your team does not use them yet, then do make it happen. If your team is already there, then make continuous delivery your goal.

- Share your knowledge and experience (or lack thereof) with others. You can do it in various ways:

  - Take part in some community events, especially **code retreat** meetings[1]. This is a **GREAT** way of honing your skills (and involves a lot of unit testing!). Other ideas - like doing **code kata**[2] - are also worth trying.

  - Share your code using sites like the GitHUB social coding platform (http://github.com).

  - Ask for guidance/help/comments using sites like RefactorMyCode.com (http://refactormycode.com/) or StackOverflow (http://stackoverflow.com).

  - Involve yourself in some open-source project to collaborate with others on some cool features.

---

[1]See http://coderetreat.org/
[2]See http://en.wikipedia.org/wiki/Kata_%28programming%29

Bibliography

You cannot open a book without learning something.

— Confucius

Books

[beust2007] Cédric Beust, Hani Suleiman, "Next Generation Java Testing: TestNG and Advanced Concepts", Addison-Wesley Professional, 2007

[feathers2004] Michael Feathers. "Working Effectively With Legacy Code", Prentice Hall, 2004

[fowler1999] Martin Fowler, Kent Beck, John Brant, William Opdyke, Don Roberts, "Refactoring: Improving the Design of Existing Code", Addison-Wesley Professional, 1999

[freeman2009] Steve Freeman, Nat Pryce. "Growing Object-Oriented Software, Guided by Tests (Beck Signature)", Addison Wesley, 2009

[gof1994] The "Gang of Four": Erich Gamma, Richard Helm, Ralph Johnson, John Vlissides, "Design Patterns: Elements of Reusable Object-Oriented Software", Addison-Wesley, 1994

[goetz2006] Brian Goetz, Tim Peierls, Joshua Bloch, Joseph Bowbeer, David Holmes, Doug Lea, "Java Concurrency in Practice", Addison-Wesley Professional, 2006.

[martin2008] Robert C. Martin. "Clean Code: A Handbook of Agile Software Craftsmanship", Prentice Hall, 2008

[meszaros2007] Gerard Meszaros, "xUnit Test Patterns, Refactoring Test Code", Addison Wesley, 2007

Documentation

[testngJavadocs] TestNG javadocs, http://testng.org/javadocs/

[testngDocumentation] TestNG documentation, http://testng.org/doc/documentation-main.html

[mockitoJavadocs] Mockito javadocs, http://docs.mockito.googlecode.com/hg/latest/index.html

[mockitoDocumentation] Mockito documentation, http://docs.mockito.googlecode.com/hg/latest/org/mockito/Mockito.html

[unitilsJavadocs] Unitils javadocs, http://www.unitils.org/apidocs/index.html

[unitilsDocumentation] Unitils documentation, http://www.unitils.org/

[hamcrestDocumentation] Hamcrest documentation, http://code.google.com/p/hamcrest/

[festJavadocs] FEST Fluent Assertions javadocs, http://fest.easytesting.org/assert/apidocs/index.html

[festDoocumentation] FEST Fluent Assertions documentation, http://fest.codehaus.org/Fluent+Assertions+Module

Articles

[beck2008] Kent Beck, Just Ship, Baby, http://www.threeriversinstitute.org/JustShip.html

[bybro2003] Mattias Bybro, "A Mutation Testing Tool For Java Programs"

[carr2006] James Carr, TDD Anti-Patterns, http://blog.james-carr.org/2006/11/03/tdd-anti-patterns/

[faber2008] Szczepan Faber, "Should I worry about the unexpected?", http://monkeyisland.pl/2008/07/12/should-i-worry-about-the-unexpected/

[fowler2007] Martin Fowler, "Mocks Aren't Stubs", http://martinfowler.com/articles/mocksArentStubs.html

[freeman2004] Steve Freeman, Nat Pryce, Tim Mackinnon, Joe Walnes. "Mock Roles Not Object", http://www.jmock.org/oopsla2004.pdf

[north2006] Dan North, Introducing BDD, http://dannorth.net/introducing-bdd/

[ma2005] Yu-seung Ma and Jeff Offutt and Yong Rae Kwon, "MuJava : An automated class mutation system."

[savoia2007] Alberto Savoia, How Much Unit Test Coverage Do You Need? - The Testivus Answer, http://www.artima.com/weblogs/viewpost.jsp?thread=204677

Glossary

API	Application Programming Interface
ATDD	Acceptance Test Driven Development
BDD	Behaviour Driven Development
CEO	Chief Executive Officer
CI	Continuous Integration
CPU	Central Processing Unit
CSS	Cascading Style Sheets
CSV	Comma Separated Values
CVS	Concurrent Versions System
DAO	Data Access Object
DI	Dependency Injection
DOC	Depended On Component
DRY	Don't Repeat Yourself
DSL	Domain Specific Language
DTO	Data Transfer Object
FAQ	Frequently Asked Questions
GUI	Graphical User Interface
HTML	HyperText Markup Language
HTTP	HyperText Transfer Protocol

IDE	Integrated Development Environment
JAR	Java ARchive
JDBC	Java DataBase Connectivity
JDK	Java Development Kit
JNDI	Java Naming and Directory Interface
JUG	Java User Group
JVM	Java Virtual Machine
KISS	Keep It Simple Stupid
LDAP	Lightweight Directory Access Protocol
LOC	Line Of Code
OO	Object-Oriented
ORM	Object-Relational Mapping
OSGi	Open Services Gateway initiative
PDF	Portable Document Format
PIM	Personal Information Manager
PM	Project Manager
POJO	Plain Old Java Object
QA	Quality Assurance
SCM	Source Code Management
SQL	Structured Query Language
SRP	Single Responsibility Principle

SSL	Secure Socket Layer
SUT	System Under Test
TDD	Test Driven Development
UI	User Interface
XML	EXtensible Markup Language
XP	EXtreme Programming
YAGNI	You Ain't Gonna Need It

Index

Y

Thank You!

Thank you for buying and reading this book! I really hope you have enjoyed it and taken a lot from it.

In case of questions, comments, or mistakes spotted, please feel free to contact me by posting to practicalunittesting@googlegroups.com.

Remember to visit http://practicalunittesting.com for source code and some additional materials.

Best Regards,
Tomek Kaczanowski